Empire in Transition

LIBRARY PRESS@UF

AN IMPRINT OF UF PRESS AND
GEORGE A. SMATHERS LIBRARIES

Empire in Transition

The Portuguese World in the Time of Camões

EDITED BY ALFRED HOWER
AND RICHARD A. PRETO-RODAS

LibraryPress@UF
GAINESVILLE, FLORIDA

The Florida and the Caribbean
Open Books Series

In 2016, the University Press of Florida, in collaboration with the George A. Smathers Libraries of the University of Florida, received a grant from the National Endowment for the Humanities and the Andrew W. Mellon Foundation, under the Humanities Open Books program, to republish books related to Florida and the Caribbean and to make them freely available through an open access platform. The resulting list of books is the Florida and the Caribbean Open Books Series published by the LibraryPress@UF in collaboration with the University of Florida Press, an imprint of the University Press of Florida. A panel of distinguished scholars has selected the series titles from the UPF list, identified as essential reading for scholars and students.

The series is composed of titles that showcase a long, distinguished history of publishing works of Latin American and Caribbean scholarship that connect through generations and places. The breadth and depth of the list demonstrates Florida's commitment to transnational history and regional studies. Selected reprints include Daniel Brinton's *A Guide-Book of Florida and the South* (1869), Cornelis Goslinga's *The Dutch in the Caribbean and on the Wild Coast, 1580–1680* (1971), and Nelson Blake's *Land into Water—Water into Land* (1980). Also of note are titles from the Bicentennial Floridiana Facsimile Series. The series, published in 1976 in commemoration of America's bicentenary, comprises twenty-five books regarded as "classics," out-of-print works that needed to be in more libraries and readers' bookcases, including Sidney Lanier's *Florida: Its Scenery, Climate, and History* (1876) and Silvia Sunshine's *Petals Plucked from Sunny Climes* (1880).

Today's readers will benefit from having free and open access to these works, as they provide unique perspectives on the historical scholarship on Florida and the Caribbean and serve as a foundation upon which today's researchers can build.

Visit LibraryPress@UF and the Florida and the Caribbean Open Books Series at http://ufdc.ufl.edu/librarypress.

Florida and the Caribbean Open Books Series Project Members

This book is reissued as part of the Humanities Open Books program, funded by a grant from the National Endowment for the Humanities and the Andrew W. Mellon Foundation.

Contents

Preface

THE EIGHTEEN papers in this volume—fourteen in English and four in Portuguese—represent a selection of those presented at the international multidisciplinary conference on the subject "The Portuguese World in the Time of Camões: Sixteenth-Century Portugal, Brazil, Portuguese Africa, and Portuguese Asia," held at the University of Florida September 29–October 1, 1980. Commemorating the four-hundredth anniversary of the death of the great Portuguese poet Luís de Camões, it was the thirtieth annual conference sponsored by the University of Florida's Center for Latin American Studies, and it marked the beginning of the fiftieth year of Latin American studies as an organized program at the university.

Additional support for the conference was provided by the Calouste Gulbenkian Foundation in Lisbon, the Portuguese and Brazilian embassies in Washington, the American Portuguese Society in New York, and the University of Florida's Center for African Studies, College of Liberal Arts and Sciences, Department of History, Department of Romance Languages and Literatures, and Brazilian-Portuguese Club.

Fifty-one persons, representing twenty-eight academic institutions in Portugal, Brazil, Canada, the Netherlands, and the United States, participated in the conference as speakers, chairpersons, or commentators. The conference was organized and directed by Alfred Hower, professor of Portuguese, with the assistance of a committee composed of R. Hunt Davis, Jr., director of the Center for African Studies; David A. Denslow, associate professor of economics; Elsbeth Gordon, director of Grinter Galleries; Nancy Macaulay of Micanopy, Florida; Lyle N. McAlister, distinguished service professor of history; Terry L. McCoy, associate director of the Center for Latin American

Studies; Gláucio Ary Dillon Soares, professor of sociology and Latin American Studies; Charles Wagley, graduate research professor of anthropology; and Rubén García, assistant professor of Portuguese, who served as secretary. The conference was opened by Robert Q. Marston, president of the University of Florida, and Helen I. Safa, director of the Center for Latin American Studies.

Professors Davis, Denslow, McAlister, Soares, Wagley, and García also served as chairpersons or commentators at the various conference sessions, as did the following members of the University of Florida faculty: Charles F. Sidman, dean of the College of Liberal Arts and Sciences; Neil W. Macaulay, Jr., professor of history; Maxine Margolis, associate professor of anthropology; Marianne Schmink, assistant professor of Latin American studies; René Lemarchand, professor of political science; Harry W. Paul, professor of history; Sidney R. Homan, associate professor of English; Andrew M. Gordon, associate professor of English; and Charles H. Wood, associate professor of sociology.

The following scholars from other universities also contributed their valuable services as chairpersons or commentators: Fred Clark, University of North Carolina; Douglas Wheeler, University of New Hampshire; John B. Jensen, Florida International University; Jane Malinoff Kamide, University of Iowa, now at the Universidade de Londrina, Paraná, Brazil; Ernest Rehder, Florida State University; Gerald M. Moser, Pennsylvania State University, emeritus; Cleon Capsas, University of South Florida; and Richard A. Preto-Rodas, University of Illinois, now at the University of South Florida.

The following papers contributed strongly to the conference but for various reasons could not be included in the present volume: "Ciência e Humanismo no Século XVI Português—A Propósito da Dicotomia Althusseriana de J. Barradas de Carvalho," by Onésimo T. Almeida (Brown University); "The Case of an Italian *Dom Sebastião*," by Vicente Almazán (Wayne State University); "The Anecdote / Memoir Tradition in Sixteenth-Century Portugal," by Christopher C. Lund (Rutgers University); "The Social and Regional Impact of the Coimbra Inquisition in the Sixteenth Century," by José do Nascimento Raposo (McMaster University); "Os Portugueses na América do Norte do Século XVI" by Victor Pereira da Rosa (University of Ottawa); "Men under Stress: An Interdisciplinary Approach to the Social and Psychological Aspects of the Carreira da Índia," by A.J.R. Russell-Wood (Johns Hopkins University); "O Tema do Desconcerto na Lírica de Camões," by Marie Sovereign (Pompano Beach, Florida); "A Study of

Military Leadership: The 'Sargento-Mor' in Colonial Brazil," by David Tengwall (Anne Arundel Community College, Arnold, Maryland).

In addition to the papers and the discussions that followed, the conference program included a number of events designed to acquaint the university and city community with various aspects of Portuguese and Brazilian culture: a concert of Renaissance music of Portugal provided by the Calouste Gulbenkian Foundation and performed by the University's Renaissance Ensemble under the direction of Professor John S. Kitts; an exhibition of "Colonial and Modern Brazilian Architecture" with photographs by Roy C. Craven, director of the University Gallery, arranged by Elsbeth Gordon; a documentary film on Manueline art and architecture, "Visions of Stone," produced by John Mackenzie, Jr., and provided through the courtesy of the American Portuguese Society; a bilingual reading of his own poetry by the distinguished Portuguese poet Alberto de Lacerda; an exhibit by the University Libraries of works by and about Camões and other materials pertinent to the subject of the conference; special radio programs featuring Brazilian and Portuguese classical music presented on the university's FM station; and a buffet dinner organized by Nancy Macaulay, which included Brazilian and Portuguese food furnished by the respective embassies and the Portuguese Wine Information Bureau in New York (courtesy of Mr. José F. Antas, director).

The papers in this volume appear substantially as submitted by the authors, with minor editorial revisions; because of an unavoidable delay in publication, several have been updated where necessary. They are presented in the language in which they were written with the exception of the one by José Honório Rodrigues, which has been translated from Portuguese into English with the author's approval and aid.

Special thanks for their contributions to the conference are hereby extended to José Blanco, trustee of the Calouste Gulbenkian Foundation; Luís Amorim de Sousa, press counselor and cultural affairs officer of the Portuguese Embassy; Luís Felipe de Seixas Corrêa, cultural affairs officer of the Brazilian Embassy; William Henderson, secretary of the American Portuguese Society; Ivan A. Schulman, former director of the University's Center for Latin American Studies, now of Wayne State University; Professors Charles Wagley, Lyle N. McAlister, Neil W. Macaulay, and Rubén García for their helpful counsel; Helen I. Safa and Terry L. McCoy, director and associate director, respectively, of the Center for Latin American Studies for their constant support; and all those who participated in the confer-

ence. The generous contribution of the Calouste Gulbenkian Foundation in Lisbon toward publication of this book is deeply appreciated.

Finally, the editors wish to dedicate their efforts in the organization of the conference and production of this book to their parents:

To Manuel and Beatrice Preto-Rodas
and in memory of Louis and Bertha Hower

A.H.

Introduction

THERE IS little doubt that the High Renaissance ushered in a period of bright expectations for Portugal. With a maritime route firmly established to the Far East, trading centers dotting the entire African coast, and a vast new world beyond the western horizon, sixteenth-century Portuguese understandably saw themselves as the spiritual heirs of Imperial Rome. Closer to home, Portuguese students and scholars actively participated in the rebirth of classical lore and the development of a humanistic outlook in such important academic centers as Paris, Salamanca, and Bologna. By the middle of the sixteenth century, repatriated Portuguese scholars like the Gouveias, their numbers swollen with foreigners directly hired by the Crown, were busily promoting the cause of humanistic research at the University of Coimbra's newly established Arts College. Throughout the kingdom, urban life was flourishing and there prevailed an air of lively curiosity.[1] Perhaps the best example of such promise is provided by Damião de Gois whose healthy patriotism was enhanced by a generous spirit of toleration for other cultures, from Lapland to Ethiopia.[2]

Within a scant generation, however, bright expectations had been dashed and the survival of national autonomy itself was in jeopardy. By the end of the sixteenth century the nature and character of the Renaissance in Portugal, including its intellectual foundations and global reach, had undergone a profound shift. The Arts College at Coimbra was no more, and former luminaries like Damião de Gois were at least isolated or, at worst, persecuted for their independence of thought. The combination of missionary zeal and chivalric adventure that once sparked the expansion to the Far East had been sundered by bureaucratic incompetence and petty rivalry. For the progressively younger defenders of Lusitanian interests, only greed remained as a motive. Inherited privilege and an appearance of religious orthodoxy gradually displaced valor and intelligence as conditions for social advancement.

Certainly the most eloquent expression of this crucial period in Portugal's history is found in the works of Luís de Camões. Imbued with humanistic values, endowed with a genius equal to the erudition of his time, and inspired by dreams of imperial grandeur, Camões was no less aware of the shortcomings of empire and the heavy demands it imposed on the limited resources of his people. The tensions of sixteenth-century Portugal that countered idealism with cynicism, hope with suspicion, and splendor with squalor appear everywhere in his poetry and letters. To be sure, positive factors tend to outweigh a negative point of view just as they did elsewhere in Portuguese society, at least until mid-century, but a cautionary note can be heard in his works just as the same note leaves an echo throughout even the most promising years of the sixteenth century. The very same André de Resende who provided Camões with the term *Lusíadas* to designate his countrymen, a term redolent of classical antiquity and heroic stature, had also upbraided the Portuguese for their sloth and provincial backwardness in his *Oratio por Rostris* (1534).[3] Similarly, independence of thought and respect for reason, which mark the writings of Damião de Gois or Sá de Miranda, both conspicuous contributors to the humanism that characterized Camões's outlook, coexist with the establishment of the Inquisition and an increasing insistence on the ideological conformity demanded by Counter-Reformation Catholicism.

The reader of these proceedings will have ample opportunity to appreciate the cultural polarities of the sixteenth-century Portuguese world. Thus, the grandeur usually associated with the seat of empire is hardly evident in the jaundiced view of an Italian visitor to Portugal as reported by Professor António H. Oliveira Marques, and the role of a competent monarch is obviously more ideal than real as can be seen in Professor Fothergill-Payne's essay on good kingship. On the other hand, an unusually independent thinker can be found well beyond the High Renaissance despite the vicissitudes of religious persecution and exile, as is apparent in the paper concerning Uriel-Gabriel da Costa.

Renaissance curiosity and humanistic tolerance combine with emulation of classical literary standards to produce the epic characteristics of Pero Vaz de Caminha's *Carta*, which is analyzed by Professor Stern. The ethnocentric side of the sixteenth-century coin, however, is suggested by Professor Sturm's analysis of Manuel da Nóbrega's revealing query concerning Brazilian natives: "Estes têm alma como nós?" Camões's own prestige as a literary model and an example of the classical norms so dear to Renaissance writers is central to an understanding of the stirrings of a new literature in the exotic setting of Pernambuco, as we read in Professor Garcia's study concerning Bento Teixeira's *Prosopopéia*. But the very survival of Portuguese as the language of Brazil hung in the balance until well into the eighteenth century, as Professor Honório Rodrigues demonstrates.

The tension between panegyric and misgiving that underlies Camões's epic poem appears in a new light after one reads the papers of Professors Moser and Winius, which deal with the Portuguese presence in Asia. Whatever else may be said of Lusitanian mismanagement and noble intentions gone awry, no one can fault Camões's contemporaries with being naïvely unaware of a deteriorating situation. That the very concept of a civilizing mission is a debatable one is suggested by Professor Miller's paper on Angola. Here one finds not an inchoate world subsequently developed by the Portuguese but rather a sophisticated society fully formed when initially encountered by Lusitanian navigators in search of their route to the East.

In Camões's own works one finds the coexistence of incongruities in the poet's reverence for traditional standards and official ideology coupled with a hearty respect for the rough and tumble of harsh reality that tends to mock such standards and ideology. Not surpisingly, therefore, his public from the sixteenth century to our time has reflected a variety of interpretations and critical perspectives. Professor Melczer's paper underlines the poet's abiding significance for European readers of varying persuasions throughout modern history. Indeed, only a truly universal appeal could explain Camões' curious survival in American towns and villages in the nineteenth century as recorded in Professor Andrews's investigations. Yet, our poet was decidedly a child of his epoch, nurtured in the classics, as Professors Livermore and Concepción point out, and loyal to his country's vision and sense of cultural mission, as depicted in the essays of both Professors Silva Dias.

Patriotism and religious allegiance, however, need not imply an unquestioning acceptance of prevailing social values. In Camões one detects the ironic temper of Cervantes, another Iberian genius who similarly transcends his historical context.[4] Both adhere to conventional norms even while they find such norms inadequate and seem to suggest that anachronisms may often continue to provide questionable direction in a new age. Certainly it is a mark of Camões's genius that he succeeds in promulgating the glories of his people while nonetheless striking a dubious note with respect to national aspirations. The resulting irony explains both the venerable sage of Restelo and

Gil Vicente's parody of the Indian campaign, as we see in Professor Tomlins's paper. That such irony is a constant in Portuguese letters is pointed out by Professor Lacerda in his provocative essay linking *Os Lusíadas* with Eça de Queirós's monumental nineteenth-century novel, *Os Maias*.

In these papers the reader will find that sincere expressions of high national principles hardly rule out mean-spirited policies and ineptitude. In Camões, as in several other Portuguese and Spanish writers from the Renaissance to the present, one finds an uneasy alliance between the need for dreaming and inspiration and the no less imperious need to maintain a critical point of view. In allowing for both fancy and sober objectivity, a priori ideals, and factual reality, Portugal's national genius presages the birth of a peculiarly modern temper, one which seems ever to be in transition.[5] That such a temper found a place in sixteenth-century Portugal is hardly coincidental.

Richard A. Preto-Rodas

Notes

1. See Luís de Matos, "L'Humanisme portugais et ses relations avec l'Europe," *Bulletin des études portugaises* 26 (1965): 45–65.

2. See Elizabeth Feist Hirsch, *Damião de Gois: The Life and Thought of a Portuguese Humanist, 1502-1574* (The Hague, 1967).

3. See Odette Sauvage, *L'Itinéraire Erasmien de André de Resende (1500– 1573)* (Paris, 1971). An annotated version of *Oratio pro Rostris* is found on pp. 99–137.

4. Whence the observation "Donde acaban [*Los Lusíadas*] empieza *Don Quijote*." See Ramiro de Maetzu, *Don Quijote, Don Juan, y la Celestina* (Buenos Aires, 1963), p. 46, and António José Saraiva, "Os *Lusíadas*, O *Quixote*, e O Problema da Ideologia Oca" in *Vértice* 21 (1961): 391–404.

5. See Jorge de Sena, "Maneirismo e Barroquismo na Poesia Portuguesa dos Séculos XVI e XVII," *Luso-Brazilian Review* 2 (1965): 29–53. In his perceptive analyses of the sixteenth century in general and of Camões in particular, the late Professor Sena demonstrates the modernity of this period (in comparison with nineteenth-century Romanticism, for example): "já que esses homens [i.e., seiscentistas] sabiam criticar-se a si mesmos." See his *Uma Canção de Camões* (Lisbon: Portugália Editora, 1966), p. 317.

I

The Portuguese in Europe

A View of Portugal in the Time
of Camões

A. H. de Oliveira Marques

SEVERAL YEARS ago, when looking for unpublished materials on Portugal, I found in a library in Germany a very interesting manuscript. Its title was "Ritratto et Riverso del Regno di Portogallo" (Portrait and Reverse of the Kingdom of Portugal), and its probable date was the late sixteenth century, although the actual handwriting pointed to a seventeenth-century copy.[1]

I have not yet had the time to do extensive research on its author, who probably went to Portugal as a member of one of the many delegations and missions from several Italian states which visited that country throughout the sixteenth century. I have not found him in the lists of voyages to Portugal by foreigners, published by several well-known historians and bibliographers. For several reasons, however, I believe he may have been a clergyman: he says not a word of criticism of the clergy, he praises the Inquisition, he hates the Jews, he virtually ignores women. Apparently he visited Portugal after the death of King Sebastian in 1578 but before the conquest of the country by Philip II of Spain in 1580. In one of his references he mentions "the Portuguese king who was very good and very holy"—an appropriate description of old King Henry, uncle and successor of Sebastian, who was a cardinal and, moreover, head of the Inquisition. This reference means that the author knew Portugal in 1579 or 1580, around the time of Camões's death.

He wrote in plain Italian, Tuscan, with some terms nowadays considered obsolete or local, and I have wondered whether a linguistic analysis could give us some evidence of his regional background in Italy. He divided his text into two parts, redacted as if they were reports to somebody higher in the social hierarchy and written by

3

different persons. In the first part or the *Portrait* itself, he tries to give a factual, positive description of Portugal and the country's good aspects. But in the second part, the *Reverse*, he proceeds to turn over this picture and look at its other side, which depicts the bad qualities and the ugly aspects of the Portuguese and their country. He devotes a little more time to this *Reverse*—twenty manuscript pages in a total of thirty-seven—which is, in fact, a terrible libel against Portugal and its people, whom he evidently despises beyond all measure.

It will be helpful at this point to recall briefly the geographical aspects and the physical extension of the Portuguese empire at the time the manuscript was written.[2] Built up from 1415 onward, the Portuguese empire in 1580 was practically intact, having reached the peak of its extension and prosperity. Only in Morocco had the Portuguese decided to abandon several towns and fortresses that were more costly than productive. Yet Ceuta, Arzila, and Mazagan and Tangiers remained Portuguese.

Along the African and the Asian coasts, up to present Indonesia, Portugal owned a long chain of fortresses and trading centers, generally having very little surrounding territory. This was a deliberate policy, for Portugal did not have the demographic or military resources to master vast areas. Hers was a commercial, maritime empire rather than a territorial one. The author of our manuscript, however, seems unable to understand this. Faithful to the traditional idea of "empire"—which meant land possessed by a lord—he refers to the Portuguese empire with disdain: "all they have is by the seashore with no penetration inland" and, consequently, "easy to lose." This is why, he adds, the sovereign of Portugal titles himself only as "king of the trade and navigation with those countries." He was partly correct. The official titles of all Portuguese monarchs since Manuel I (early sixteenth century) were "King of Portugal and Algarves, both here and yonder in Africa, Lord of Guinea, Lord of the conquest, navigation, and commerce of Ethiopia, Arabia, Persia, and India."

The only real "empire" the Portuguese had was Brazil. Our manuscript correctly calls it a "province" divided into captaincies, some belonging to private lords and two of them to the Crown. The capital was Bahia, and Brazil's main products were correctly listed as sugar, cotton, leather, amber, and brazilwood.

From Asia and Africa the Portuguese imported spices, drugs, textiles, cotton, indigo, gold, china, precious stones, etc. "It is unbelievable," our text says, "the amount of spices they bring, for the ships are loaded with pepper without using any sacks, in the way corn is loaded in Sicily. The transparent porcelains all come from there, and so do rubies, diamonds, pearls, and all the other precious stones. All the merchandise that arrives in Alexandria, Egypt, from the same countries by another way is not a millesimal part of what arrives here, and from where all the world is supplied"—a correct statement, confirmed by every source.

Yet the government was not rich. Everything was spent, and spent quickly, for maintaining fortresses and garrisons was expensive. Sending the annual convoys of ships to India and Brazil was still more expensive. Salaries of civil servants, pensions, and subsidies to nobles and clients (Camões, let us not forget, was one of the many who received a yearly pension, called *tença*), charitable works, gifts, embassies, dowries, luxury, building activities, and so on completely depleted the royal treasury. From time to time the government ran into debt and had to pawn and mortgage the future by looking to the next year's revenues. Foreign and national creditors were many. Our manuscript, however, gives us some more detailed causes for the state's debts such as bad administration and stealing: "All rob the king," it says, "even if they don't wish to." "All live from the king, all receive income from the king's income." Salaries were so low that even an honest servant was compelled to defraud the administration. This double tradition of Portuguese administration, involving a great number of poorly paid civil and military servants has continued almost until the present. In this matter, then, one can trust our manuscript with respect to its account of the sixteenth century.

The capital and main city of Portugal was Lisbon. One of the largest cities in Europe, Lisbon had several rich and beautiful churches and monasteries, besides some attractive and comfortable dwellings. Its most famous monuments were, as they still are, the monastery of Jerónimos and the tower of Belém, both built by Manuel I in the early sixteenth century. In spite of its pleasant climate and good air, Lisbon was not a very beautiful town. Its streets were neither broad nor straight nor clean, and its houses were not very impressive for their architecture. Such was the opinion of a late Renaissance man, sensitive to new concepts in city building and city planning and used to them in his native country. It was only after the 1755 earthquake that a part of Lisbon was built according to a well-determined plan and with some regularity in the size and external aspect of the houses. Moreover, our author complains of the lack of sewers or canals that could take waste to the river and deplores the practice of discarding garbage into the streets. The smell was terrible, despite the extensive use of musk, amber, and benzoin.

Traveling in those days was not easy. Although some of the rivers were partly navigable, boats offered little comfort and one had to travel together with beasts and merchandise. Most Portuguese preferred to travel by land. The roads must not have been extremely bad, because our author, so often critical, neglects to mention their quality. Instead he sharply criticizes the lack of conveyances. There was no organized system of transport for passengers. If one had no horses of one's own, one had to ride on the same mules that carried bales of goods, bags, and all kinds of burdens, sitting with both legs to the same side. There were no carts, coaches, horses, or servants available, as there were in Italy.

The lodging system was also very inconvenient. Hostels were located too far apart. Often one had to stay the night in small cottages called "vendas" (those who know Portugal are certainly familiar with many places named "Venda" of something). In such "vendas" there was practically nothing besides a place to stay and a stable for the horses. With luck one could perhaps find some bread and wine. Moreover, peddlers had priority over foreigners or any other travelers. So if one arrived at the same time as a peddler or shortly after, one might well eat nothing. Hostels were few and poor. Even in Lisbon there were only two, and for a long time there had been none. As our critic pointed out, travelers were forced to stay at some dirty and stinking houses where only errand boys and slaves went.

Several pages are devoted to the subjects of justice and administration, which are fairly correct with regard to structures and general organization. At the local level there were judges (*juízes ordinários* and *juízes de fora*). At a second level there was the *Relação do Cível*. At a third and last level there was the *Tribunal da Suplicação*. Other courts existed for special matters: finance courts, overseas courts, religious and ecclesiastical courts, etc. The city of Lisbon had a system of justice of its own. All this is well known by historians. The accurate and extensive description of such matters in the manuscript points to the possibility that its author had a juridical background.

More interesting, however, are the author's comments on how justice was actually administered. Here his prejudice against the Portuguese once again surfaces as he points out that competent and impartial persons, good citizens, were not accepted as justice officials. Only petty lawyers, for the most part of low birth and totally unknown, were accepted, and their decisions were more unjust than just. There were too many laws, he argues, all of them rather vague in their purpose, and every new monarch would enact some more. There were even laws on food, on dressing, on punishment of slaves, on morals, etc. All these comments are accurate: Portugal could present a large corpus of legislation by the late sixteenth century. It was actually a remarkable achievement for a small country located so far from the major centers of civilization. Laws regulating food, dressing, etc., did exist at that time—but not only in metropolitan Portugal. From the fourteenth century on, regulations had been enacted in the attempt to prevent excesses in luxury and in spending, particularly involving dressing and nourishment. These were the so-called Pragmatics, and they continued well into the eighteenth century. However, in spite of their number and restrictions, they were mostly ignored by the populace.

Lawsuits and law records were numerous, our author continues, all full of delays, appeals, ambiguous sentences, false testimonies, etc. If one had some money to collect from the government, one could be sure of never receiving it (perhaps not too different anywhere in the world even today). The main purpose of justice officials, he says, was not to hasten and make quick justice but rather to accumulate records and so make themselves feel important and solicited. Thus, a judge in criminal causes liked to have his prisons filled with people while a judge in civil causes liked to be surrounded by widows and orphans begging for mercy. "I believe," he adds, "that if they could dispatch all the people in one day they would not do it, because they would not feel like masters and lords anymore." The same happened with the king's treasurers, who forced creditors to wait for years and obliged them to implore for their payments day after day. "Poor you," he concludes, "if you have any problem which involves justice. Some law will certainly be found that punishes you for a crime you never thought of."

We find in this manuscript some interesting remarks on culture and cultural life. Unlike the situation in Italy, all Portuguese legislation was written in Portuguese instead of in Latin, thus enabling many people to have direct access to the legislative texts and to the procedure of justice. Such texts had an unusual value, given the lack of special materials to teach reading and writing. While many other countries used texts of well-known prayers for this purpose, in Portugal very often the child was given the transcript of a suit at law, and this text served as primer. What a scandal, cries our Italian author, not a psalm, not the Sunday prayer, not even Our Lady's office! (His observation is confirmed by other sources.)

The University of Coimbra reorganized by John III in 1537 deserves no praise, he continues. No one who has really learnt something has ever studied there—again a gross exaggeration but not without some basis. The best Portuguese scholars of the time had studied abroad. In the mid-sixteenth century, laws were passed that tried to force students to stay in the country. Coimbra had indeed little prestige, if compared with Salamanca or Paris or Oxford. Many professors actually were foreigners. There was another university at Évora, in the south of Portugal, founded by the Jesuits in 1559, but our author does not even mention it.

The population of Portugal, according to him, could be classified in three main groups, which he calls the natives, the New-Christians, and the slaves. The "natives" were the Portuguese proper. Our man does not like them: "They are unpolished, lazy, silly, and proud," he says. They believe they know everything about the world and that they are the best of all. Yet as Portugal is located very far from the center of the civilized world, they know in fact very little and are thoroughly unacquainted with other peoples except for Indians and Negroes, he says with contempt. For the Portuguese, he goes on, all foreigners can be summed up in three groups: Flemish, if they are tall and blond; Castilians, if they are dark-complexioned; and Bretons, if they are not well dressed. A satirical and exaggerated comment, but one that gives a fairly good idea of the main countries Portugal traded with in the late sixteenth century: northern Europe, especially Flanders, France, and Spain, besides, of course, Africa, Asia, and America. From an ecumenical standpoint, no other country, not even Spain, had such a worldwide system of human and commercial relations. From a European's point of view, however, one can understand our author. The "natives" were further divided into three social classes: the nobles, the middle class, and the plebeians.

In the Portrait, the number and titles of the upper nobility are appraised quite precisely and correctly: two dukes, one marquess, ten counts. The wealthiest and most powerful of all was the Duke of Bragança, who at the time was John I, married to Lady Catherine. The duke was one of the most important candidates for the throne, in competition with Philip II of Spain. The feudal jurisdiction of the upper nobility was very limited, our author remarks, because the king had to confirm every seignorial sentence. This is a correct statement. As to the customs and ways of life of the Portuguese nobles, the manuscript is very severe. They were excessively proud, formal, jealous, daring, and mercantile. Some stories are told about these bad qualities, some actually very funny. One example will suffice.

A Portuguese nobleman traveling in the country stopped at a hostel where the only food available was sausages (*chouriços*). He was starving, but he did not want to eat them for he considered them a plebeian kind of nourishment. Some young Spanish noblemen who were staying at the place decided to make a fool of him. They would teach him, they said, the correct way of eating sausages without losing nobility. He had only to close his eyes and ask someone to introduce the sausages into his mouth. Well said, the Portuguese thought, and he asked one of the young Spaniards to do him that favor. He closed his eyes, opened his mouth wide, but what he ate was not sausages at all, but something else which he kept spitting out for days after.

A historically established feature of the sixteenth-century Portuguese nobility was their participation in trade throughout the empire. Despite the fact that they loathed the words "merchant" and "trade," they were pure traders whose activities prevented the natural development of a Portuguese bourgeoisie as existed in England or in Holland. The king himself was a notorious trader, and the royal palace in Lisbon was built over the main trading depot where all the pepper and the other merchandise arrived and was sold. He rewarded many of his noble servitors by granting them permission to travel to India and China, where they might conduct their business as they pleased. With one or two voyages they often came back rich. And of course as soon as they were back in Portugal, they forgot all about commerce and profit and proceeded to malign traders and their despicable activities. Our Italian author clearly shows his resentment against them, as is to be expected from a native of a country which had lost a great part of its former trade with the East to the Portuguese.

If one tries to ascertain the traits of the Portuguese nobles in the sixteenth century, one may possibly agree with our writer. Pride did certainly exist. It persisted well into the eighteenth century. In a paper presented to the Historical Congress in Bucharest, Professor Russell-Wood pointed out how great was the pride of being a Portuguese in those days, especially among members of the nobility. Formality, also a typical Portuguese characteristic until the present, as well as jealousy and boldness, are correctly observed.

Our manuscript is much less revealing concerning the middle class and the plebeians. Of the middle class, it says only that those people were unbearable because they wanted to copy the nobles in all their worst features. With respect to the common folk, its observations are even thinner. They are, it says, the most disgraceful and lowest rabble that exists in the world. They have no sense of honor, love, or charity. They are all thieves, but even as thieves they are stupid and plain. One wonders how different were the lowest strata of society in sixteenth-century Europe, even in more cultivated countries like Italy or Flanders.

New-Christians was the name given to the Jews who had been

forced to become Christians in Spain and Portugal in the late fifteenth and early sixteenth centuries. Our author, probably a clergyman, hates and despises them. He says that the worst live in Portugal because there they find more tolerance for their pseudo-Christian way of life. In this area he is correct. The Portuguese New-Christians virtually bought their freedom from the government and were able to live tolerably unmolested for almost fifty years. Only in the 1540s was the Inquisition introduced in Portugal in an active way. But even so, money could play its role for a long time in lessening the persecutions of New-Christians. Such a fact was for our author a clear definition of their wicked and vicious character. He bitterly complains of the wedding alliances they had been able to forge with "Old-Christians." And he goes on to accuse them of cheating, dissimulating, lying, and violating oaths. He remarks: "I saw many of them reprehending others who were angrily blaspheming or saying bad words, and in this reprehension they preached a sermon with all the commandments of Our Holy Mother the Church. Yet a few days later, I saw that they themselves were arrested by the Inquisition and punished for not believing in God and for other sins!"

On the slaves our author agrees with many other contemporary witnesses in saying that they were very numerous. The famous Belgian humanist Clenardus, who had visited Portugal several decades before, says the same. "The towns look like chessboards, with as many blacks as whites," a vivid image of a racial community so different from what people elsewhere in Europe were used to seeing. As interesting is our author's comment on the various ethnic origins of the slaves: They cannot understand one another, and, he adds, "if they all spoke the same language, they would easily become masters of the realm."

Today historians estimate that the slaves of Lisbon may have accounted for up to 10 percent of the total population of the city. Of some 100,000 inhabitants at that time, 10,000 would thus have been slaves—a large number indeed. They were actually very often seen by any observer, because they passed most of their time outside their masters' houses, doing all kinds of commissions. Moreover, they made themselves easily visible. Very different from the "native" Portuguese, who were sad and gloomy, "the slaves were always merry," our author tells us, "laughing, singing, dancing, and openly getting drunk in every public square."

In addition to social classification of the Portuguese, the manuscript goes on to describe their character and general way of life. The author has few words of praise. The Portuguese, to start with, were hypocrites. Flattery, dissimulation, and eternal boasting commanded every action of their lives. He elaborates by providing examples of such bad qualities. Moreover, they are extremists in all things and unable to follow the middle way. Their selfishness and covetousness appear clearly whenever they contact foreigners, since the only thing they want is to get something from foreign visitors. Shabby in their dress, they prefer black to any color. They are dirty, especially, he says, when they are in mourning, for at such times they never shave or comb their hair or wash themselves, so that they look like bears. They tend to shout instead of speak. Even the women are much less graceful than their Spanish or Italian counterparts.

Some of these observations were probably accurate, but others are exaggerated and show only the superiority of a man coming from the peak of civilization—sixteenth-century Italy—and arriving in a country at the western end of Europe. Unlike other European countries, Portugal was more open to the exotic worlds of Asia, Africa, and America than it was to the sophistications of the Renaissance.

In spite of its many errors and exaggerations, this manuscript is interesting and differs from the usual medieval or sixteenth-century descriptions. It is much more personal and offers a greater number of ideas and suggestions on subjects that were usually ignored and therefore are hardly known to historians for lack of sources: the history of customs, the history of characters and temperaments, and the history of peoples as such. In this manuscript we look into the real persons, not only into monuments or structures. Complemented by some other reliable sources, especially by two sixteenth-century collections of jokes and sayings which have recently been published,[3] the Portrait offers good material for rewriting history. I hope that somebody, in Portugal or elsewhere, may analyze it and draw some conclusions on the thoughts, actions, and ways of life of Camões's fellow-countrymen. And Camões himself? Was he a part of the proud nobility? of the unbearable middle class? of the base plebeians? Of the dissimulating New-Christians? Who was he in fact?

Notes

1. Niedersächsisches. Staatsarchiv, Hanover, st. A P2399.

2. For a discussion of the political history of Portugal in the sixteenth century and its course toward the union with Spain, see A. H. de Oliveira Marques, *History of Portugal*, 2d ed. (New York: Columbia University Press, 1976), pp. 306–13.

3. *Ditos Portugueses Dignos de Memória. História íntima do século XVI*, ed. José H. Saraiva (n.p., Publicações Europa-América, n.d.); Christopher C. Lund, *Anedotas Portuguesas e Memórias Biográficas da Corte Quinhentista* (Coimbra: Livraria Almedina, 1980).

A Prince of Our Disorder: "Good Kingship" in Camões, Couto, and Manuel de Melo

Peter Fothergill-Payne

THE SIXTEENTH and seventeenth centuries in the Iberian Peninsula were a period of immense, fundamental change covered by a veneer of divinely appointed stability. The why and wherefore of change is the stuff of other studies. The question here is how several people who were central to their time faced the question of how to bring about that best of all possible worlds that would result from the universe unfolding "as it should." I propose to address it by examining how Camões, Diogo do Couto, and Francisco Manuel de Melo suggested to their readers that the well-being of the nation might best be forwarded and safeguarded.

Although the United Provinces comprising Spain and Portugal became a fixture on the political scene during this period, the more generally accepted form of government was the hereditary monarchy. Accordingly, discussion of good kingship was the substance of far more writing at that time than was then recognized.

Space does not permit examination of the medieval attitudes to kingship; suffice it to say that generally kingdoms were seen as family property or as fiefs held at divine pleasure. *Mutatis mutandis,* one finds this sort of attitude enshrined in fairy tales where the old king tends to offer his daughter and half the kingdom to the right candidate. To be sure, the real world provides us with a number of examples of astute cold-blooded dynastic expansionism.

For members of royal families and their retainers, the Renaissance understanding of kingship was given immensely more perspective by the arousal of their historical sense and by the sense of mission transmitted by their reading of the classics. Thus, they tended to see themselves as the continuers of the eternal evolution of the divine plan with the added impetus imparted by the Christian Revelation. As Camões put it to Sebastião:

E vós, ó bem nascida segurança,
Da lusitana antiga liberdade. . . .
. . . .
Dada ao mundo por Deus, que todo o mande
Pera do mundo a Deus dar parte grande.

[*Lus.* I, 6][1]

Indeed, the view of the prince as facilitator and prime element in the fulfillment of the divine plan is in that aspect essentially different from the Roman one that Horace sketches out in his letter to Augustus. The Horatian view portrays the monarch (if I may use the neologism) as the center of the machine of state while being a man of superior qualities who, one understands, serves out of a sense of magnanimity rather than divine obligation:

Quum tot sustineas et tanta negotia solus,
Res Italas armis tuteris, moribus ornes,
Legibus emendes; in publica commoda peccem,
Si longo sermone morer tua tempora, Caesar.[2]

But this is not, by a long way, the only attribute that Camões would have his prince possess, and so I propose now to examine what we might irreverently term his "shopping list," starting with a little-remembered but, to me, significant incident hidden in his play *El-Rei Seleuco*. That play, we remember, is in all probability adapted from Plutarch's *Life of Demetrius* (though Hernâni Cidade cites other possibilities) and hinges on the old king ceding his wife to his only son by a previous marriage. But *why* is the question that Camões answers after his own fashion. The physician called in to treat the young man's malady discovers the cause and tells the king that the prince is in love with the physician's own wife, so that no cure is at hand:

Físico:
       Forçado será que muera
       Porque no muera mi honor

To which the king invokes an argument so strong that the king himself will shortly bow before it:

> *Rei:*
>
>> Pois como! A um só herdeiro
>> Deste Reino não dareis
>> Vossa mulher . . .?!

Dynastic continuity, we note, is the lever, not social class or fatherly love. And a little later:

> *Rei:*
>
>> A mulher que eu tivesse
>> Dar-lha-ia. Oxalá
>> Que ele a Rainha quisesse![3]

and follows through by granting his wife to his son when he learns that the cure lies there. I do not think we should be party to the wishy-washy business about how powerful love is with which the page favors us a little later. The important remark is the one involving dynastic necessity, just quoted. But on to the real meat of Camões's work on this subject, namely the *Lusíadas,* which he dedicated, as we know, to King Sebastião. As I have argued elsewhere,[4] it can be read as a continuous exhortation and *exemplum* to that youthful and impetuous prince to fulfill his destiny and accomplish what Camões sees as his country's salvation by taking the poet's advice to become a good king. So let us see if we can crystallize the poet's position as it develops in his epic.

One watchword of the *Lusíadas* that we have tended to lose from sight in our own time is the poet's insistence that every word is true, that is to say, that it is history. In other words, the epic is worthy of study as containing precepts for our present and future conduct (or, better said, for Sebastião's conduct). If we examine the historical vignettes that punctuate the poem within this context, we will see emerge from them both a continuous exemplum of those kings who have in the past led Portugal forward on the path of greatness and also a contra-exemplum of those who by their personal flaws have halted her on that same road.

Clearly I cannot summarize the poem, nor do I need to do so here. One need only recall Vasco da Gama's little history lesson recited to the King of Melinde in which the history of Portugal from earliest times is shown as a contrastive series of "good" and "bad" kings in a country characterized as being the crown on the head of Europe.

From its foundation Portugal is shown as having had two kings who were full of martial prowess and open loyalty commanding a people who, albeit few in number, are never abashed by any task. Of particular interest in this context is the way in which Camões presents the Egas Moniz episode so as to preserve intact the picture of royal loyalty and straight-dealing which introduces the theme of the "grão fidelidade portuguesa" for the vassals who, like Gama (and himself), should be fostered by good kings of Portugal.

In contrast to the first pair of valorous kings we meet

> Sancho segundo, manso e descuidado
> Que tanto em seus descuidos se desmede
> Que de outrem quem mandava era mandado.
> De governar o Reino, que outro pede,
> Por causa dos privados foi privado.

[Lus. III, 91]

Although the poor fellow just didn't make it among the high rollers of vice, he nonetheless was weak enough to let the kingdom get out of hand because

> A rei não obedece, nem consente,
> Que não for mais que todos excelente

[III, 93]

With Dinis things get better, since he looks after the well-being of the kingdom in a pacific way, primarily by founding the University of Coimbra and carrying out a wide-ranging public works program (III, 98). All of which brings us to the celebrated Inês de Castro episode in which Alfonso is shown as derogating from the obligations of good kingship by listening to bad counsel and allowing himself to be pressured by the people "com falsas e ferozes razões" (III, 123–24). With respect to Dinis's grandson, Dom João, one cannot but notice the approval with which the poet tells us how right the Portuguese were to support John, Master of Avis "como de Pedro único herdeiro/Ainda que bastardo, verdadeiro" (*Lus.* IV, 2). The "Velho do Restelo" passage, which closes the canto, also has some remarks that might give the aspiring good king pause, with its warnings clothed in references to the Prometheus legend and its references to the dangers of vainglory and the dangers of abusing the virtues of his subjects and putting the kingdom under considerable strain.

The poet expands his use of history as exemplum in the same vein, even while the scene varies, from Calicut to the Isle of Love. The underlying message remains constant, i.e., besides being the Lord's anointed, a good king must be strong, both physically and morally. He must be devoted wholeheartedly to the national interest even at the cost of personal fame and glory. He must be capable of choosing loyal, disinterested, experienced counsellors and captains. He must be able to distinguish and follow sound, disinterested advice even in the face of popular and court pressure. He must shun "descansos corruptores." He must keep his feet on the ground by subordinating flights of chivalric fancy to finding practical answers to national imperatives. He must do all this, in addition to cultivating a profound sense of inherited divine mission.

In short, as we look down the shopping list expressed in this bald fashion, we can see how Camões was reading history to elicit from it the most persuasive arguments his Renaissance mind could muster to turn Sebastião from the fatal road to Alcácer-Quibir and to remedy the present ills as he saw them. It seemed obvious that the court and royal administration were falling into public disrepute, given the way in which Sebastão, in a fashion not unlike that of the monarchs who were his contemporaries, tended to bestow personal favors on those around him by awarding them state offices and administrative preferment. The ill-advised monarch also used state revenues to defray the costs of their (and his) pleasures and pastimes rather than to further the ends of government. At the same time the poet pointed to a particular aspect of royal neglect, i.e., the unequal burden of taxation (exemption was then seen as a low-cost reward) and the misuse of empire (which is hinted at in the last canto).

It is particularly this last point that is the mainspring of Diogo do Couto's *O soldado prático,* and it is through this work that I propose to expose the next stage of my argument. It is, of course, very different in tone and development from Camões's poem but nonetheless shares with it the stress on factuality and the desire to show (albeit in more down-to-earth tones) the way to better government.

The setting of the book is partly contemporary with the experience of Camões and partly subsequent to it in that Couto held office under Philip II after the union of the two crowns. The conception of the work is probably pre-1580 although its dissemination took place under the new dispensation, which would account for some of the consciously pro-Philip turns and formulae. Attributing alleged misgovernment to Sebastianist times clearly allows Couto a greater degree of freedom of expression, while the formulation of the whole text in the present tense would leave his readers in little doubt that the lessons he draws are still applicable to Philip's administration.

The picture that Couto draws of the evils of his time is, of course, too well known to need more than a brief summary here of those aspects pertinent to my argument. We remember how the *soldado*, in his attempt to clear his discharge papers, is inveigled by the *fidalgo* and the *despachador* freely to recount his distilled experience of many years spent in the Indies. This he proceeds to do over a period of three whole days (which, I suppose, points to an even more easygoing office practice than that which seems to govern modern bureaucracies). The experience allows him to analyze pretty thoroughly how far downhill things have gone and to suggest certain remedies.

All the ills seem to stem from two main sources: the present decayed state of public morality and the unwillingness or inability of the king to take the appropriate remedial steps. What are they? Couto portrays a collapse of the royal administration because over the years individuals at every level from viceroy to simple soldier have seen their self-interest rewarded and their public spirit punished either by their superiors' use of rank to make them conform or by the need to bribe their way through the administrative labyrinth. The situation was compounded by the seeming insistence of the king's ministers at home on appointing to high office in the overseas administration individuals who are neither qualified nor experienced and whose only motivation is self-enrichment. This tendency is evidenced early in the following exchange involving the fidalgo, "que ia entrar em uma das melhores fortalezas da India," and a high-minded cleric:

> Senhor, lembre-vos que ides entrar na mercê que el-Rei vos fez por vossos serviços, e que nela podeis ganhar o Céu, como eu neste hábito, com estas cousas. Contentai-vos com o que é vosso, deixai viver os pobres, e fazei justiça.

> Ao que lhe respondeu o fidalgo:

> —Padre meu, eu hei de fazer o que os outros capitães fizeram; se eles foram ao Inferno, lá lhe(s) hei-de ir ser companheiro; porque eu não vou a minha fortaleza, senão pera vir rico.[5]

The sale of offices, too, he sees as a prelude to disorder, and he makes his point by backing it with an exemplum drawn from Roman history:

> porque nunca o Império Romão começou a declinar senão
> depois que o imperador Cómodo Antonino XIX . . . come-
> çou a vender os magistrades e ofícios públicos . . . que foi o
> primeiro que ensinou este caminho pera se os reinos per-
> derem. (p. 58)

But the main weight of his argument bears down the lack of reliable
communications and apparent lack of interest in affairs so far off (the
second of these is a false perception, incidentally) (p. 67), the unjust
tax system, and the way in which royal appointees are personally
responsible for discrepancies in their books on laying down office
(p. 44). But most of all, for Couto, it is the way in which the king's ministers treat the royal treasury as if they were the monarch's sworn enemies (p. 26).

In a rather half-hearted way through the mouth of the despachador, he suggests that part of the cause lies simply in the fact that kings
are after all human beings like the rest of us:

> Mas os reis da terra não podem tanto: são de carne, e hão-de
> ter seus dias de passatempos; também são sujeitos a paixões
> e enfermidades, pelo que não pode ser estarem todo o
> tempo à pá. . . . o arco, se lhe não afrouxam a corda, facil-
> mente quebra. (p. 22)

To all of which he offers the following solution: the monarch must
nonetheless take his duties more seriously (pp. 22–23) and set things
to rights, since his ultimate responsibility under God still lies with him.
Couto is willing to offer the means, which involve purging the royal
service of any who are not manifestly worthy by character and, more
important, by past service and experience. Those who are worthy are
to be appropriately rewarded to keep them from the temptation of
lining their own pockets (p. 71). Following in the footsteps of D. Dinis,
the judiciary should really be, and should be perceived to be, independent of the monarch. But, most important, to establish a highly organized bureaucracy with better records, double-entry bookkeeping,
and audits is advisable to render unlikely an opportunity for feather-
bedding. Couto accepts that the monarchy is subject to human frailty
and that there is no way in which *that* job can be filled by competitive
examination. It follows that the organization of the state must be
structured to absorb the impact of that unchangeable fact. Such a re-
alization, minor though it may seem to us who, in the past decade,
have come to accept the manifest feet of clay of our most revered lead-

ers as something of a reassurance, is nevertheless a crucial one in Iberian thinking. In public pronouncements thinkers will continue to speak after the manner of Camões, but in private they will start to reflect a view that I propose to describe after studying some of the works of Francisco Manuel de Melo.

D. Francisco Manuel was active as an author through four decades, three of which are of particular interest to us, namely the period 1630–60, which coincides nicely with the Restoration. He was, by common consent, a man of many parts and generally recognized as a superior talent even by his enemies. I should like to address myself to two aspects of his thought, that of the student of strategy and that of the incipient political scientist as evidenced in his *Política Militar, Guerra de Cataluña,* and three of the *Epanáforas de Vária História Portuguesa,* the I*a* (*Política*), II*a* (*Trágica*), and IV*a* (*Bélica*). (The III*a* [*Amorosa*] is generally admitted to be atypical.)[6]

Taking these works in chronological order (which is how they are listed here), we note first how often the terms *político* and *política* appear both in the titles and in the body of the text. Next we are struck by the manner in which events are recounted and possibilities envisaged. Nothing could be closer to the "scenario" approach that we observe in our own day.

The *Política Militar* was D. Francisco Manuel's second published work, his first being a sonnet cycle in Spanish on the subject of Inês de Castro. The work is nothing more or less than a scenario. It is, purportedly, a model discussion, which guides the aspiring commander-in-chief of an expeditionary force through all the eventualities, from appointment to laying down office, of a combined operation on behalf of the Spanish monarch.

A lot of what he says there is, at best, unsurprising, but what does stand out is the following: besides urging his captain-general to be "discreto" in the sense the word had then, he enjoins on him a course of quite blatant *Realpolitik,* which would have done credit to Karl von Clausewitz. He also pinpoints what, to him, are going to be the bugbears of sound political strategy in his time: lack of efficiency and experience in subordinates, lack of sufficient supplies (both cash and matériel), and, above all, lack of reliable, swift communications. In short, he discounts severely the part that Machiavelli accorded to Fortuna, though he retains the Renaissance view of history and makes occasional mention of the divine role in punishing derogation of the obligations of leadership. But, that apart, his advice is a pure exposition of what game strategists call the mini-max approach.

Seven years later, in 1645, we see him publish the account famil-

iarly known as the *Guerra de Cataluña*. Although occasional doubts
have been thrown on its claim to unvarnished accuracy, I cannot help
remarking on its consistency with the *Política* in the way in which he
judges the actions and motives of the leaders on both sides, particularly of the Spanish generals, the Royal Council, and the Count-Duke
of Olivares. His analysis of the causes of events is exemplary, and his
insight, which reveals that it is not the actions and events in themselves
that matter but the way in which they are perceived, is eons ahead of
his time, as is his advice on the attitude to adopt in the face of sedition:
"No es la espuela aguda que domina el caballo desbocado; la dócil
mano del jinete lo templa y acomoda."[7] Indeed, his strong statements
about the necessity of avoiding repressive and punitive action is point-
edly made in his account of the advice offered the king in the Royal
Council by the Conde de Oñate, who counseled moderation, in
marked contrast to the spirited call to arms uttered by his Eminence
Cardinal D. Gaspar de Borja y Velasco.

Melo repeats much of his analysis in his *Epanáforas*, which deals
with events that happened under the Spanish monarchy but that, presumably, given the change of government in the interim, the writer
feels freer to comment on in his critique of kingly failings. These he
lists as follows: lack of vigor both physical and moral, remoteness, the
general confusion of the immense dominion, its lack of a coherent
system of government, the lack of perception of the implications that
events present, the fact that they are seen as "foreign" in almost every
part of their domains. Furthermore, the kings lack "um espírito con-
stante para as expedições militares, e um juízo prudente para os
negócios civis" and compound the fault by choosing as their plenipo-
tentiaries persons as little endowed with the desirable characteristics
as themselves. Now we might be tempted to put Melo's position down
to an attempt to ingratiate himself with the newly enthroned João IV
were it not for the consistent analysis he brings to bear on that prince's
behavior under the previous administration.

In conclusion, all three authors studied here reveal an attitude
that progressively brings the ordering of events and the mechanisms
of government onto a far more human plane, although all three re-
tain the same basic statements on the didactic usefulness of the study
of history. And, more intriguingly, although each in turn might have
stood to gain increasingly by a more flattering exposition of events,
each writer takes a step toward demythifying the rules of political behavior just as belief in absolutism and the Divine Right was peaking in
the Peninsular context. The result, in the final analysis, is a job description that we could use unchanged today if we were to go in search

of a candidate to fill the presidency of a particularly large (and occasionally vulnerable) multinational corporation.

Notes

1. References are to the standard Canto and stanza numbering.

2. Horace, *Epistolae*, II, 1: "Since alone you support the burden of so many great affairs, protecting the Italian state by your arms, gracing it by your moral example, improving it by your laws, I were an offender against the public good were I to waste time and delay you with a long letter."

3. Luís de Camões, *Obras Completas* (Lisbon: Sá da Costa, 1947), 3: 121–22.

4. Peter Fothergill-Payne, "The Discoveries, Divine Destiny or Disaster?" in *Acta* of the colloquium "Camões and His Times" (Toronto: University of Toronto Press, in press).

5. Diogo do Couto, *O soldado prático* (Lisbon: Sá da Costa, 1954), p. 14. All further page references are to this edition.

6. In that it is the only one that does not deal with Melo's own experiences.

7. Francisco Manuel de Melo, *Historia de los Movimientos, Separación y Guerra de Cataluña en Tiempo de Felipe IV* (Madrid: REH, 1912), p. 89.

Uriel-Gabriel da Costa: Heir to the Rationalism of the Portuguese Renaissance

Richard A. Preto-Rodas

*To the memory
of Edward Glaser*

URIEL DA COSTA was born in Porto, probably in 1580, the same year as the annexation of Portugal by Spain and the death of Luís de Camões. Baptized Gabriel, da Costa was a member of a family of prosperous *cristãos novos* whose patriarch, Bento da Costa Brandão, was a devout Catholic. His mother, Branca, however, came from a family that, according to recent research, had long maintained clandestine observance of Jewish customs and traditions.[1] Gabriel himself experienced religious doubts as a young man and, for reasons I shall discuss, decided to embrace his forefathers' religion shortly after the death of his own father in 1608. Even as a minor cleric at the church of Cedofeita, he succeeded in converting most of his family to Judaism. Aware of the terrible dangers inherent in such a move, Gabriel da Costa liquidated his holdings in 1615 and fled into exile with his entire family save a sister who had refused to follow the law of Moses.

Hardly arrived in Amsterdam, the European center of Jewish life for refugees from the Iberian Peninsula, da Costa, now known as Uriel following his circumcision, began to manifest the same independence of spirit and critical perspective regarding official Jewish orthodoxy that had led him to abjure Catholicism.[2] His first tract, a criticism of basic rabbinical precepts, resulted in his excommunication and isolation from the entire community including his family. It seems, however, that his mother, who had taken the name of Sara, refused to abandon her son and became something of a dissenter in her own right. In a subsequent publication Uriel da Costa attempted to refute the doctrine concerning the immortality of the soul. This additional

22

affront to rabbinical authority proved frustrating to the community elders, since they lacked the power to impose additional punishment on the heretic. They did succeed in convincing the civil authorities of the danger that such a view posed for Christian beliefs, and da Costa was accordingly fined and sentenced to a week in prison. But where excommunication and fines failed, isolation and constant harassment succeeded, and the heretic eventually recanted after several years of ostracism.

The former crypto-Jew was now a crypto-agnostic. When Uriel dissuaded two would-be converts to Judaism, he was denounced. At about the same time a nephew reported that his uncle failed to keep a kosher home. Faced with financial ruin and renewed domestic strife, Uriel once again recanted and submitted to a humiliating penitential ritual. With prospects now dashed for a promising match with a wealthy younger woman, the sixty-year-old widower became painfully aware that the future promised little. There were but two options, both intolerable: either to live the life of a hypocrite within the community or to lead a lonely existence as a dissenter in a foreign country. Broken in spirit, the dejected Uriel da Costa composed a brief autobiography recounting his spiritual travails and committed suicide on an April day in 1640. His testament, *Exemplar Vitae Humanae,* has reached us in a Latin version, which may be the original language in which it was written; in view of his tracts in Portuguese, however, it is possible that *Exemplar* represents a translation from a Portuguese original.[3] My own quotes are from the Latin version.

Despite so modest a published corpus, Uriel da Costa holds a secure if secondary place in history for a variety of reasons. Philosophers cite his role as a probable influence on the development of Baruch Spinoza, who was an eight-year-old member of the Amsterdam community when Uriel took his own life.[4] For writers and thinkers of a more romantic bent, Uriel's tragic story suggests the struggle of the intrepid free thinker doing battle against religious intolerance. As such he has inspired one opera, a play, three novels, and a recent highly subjective biography.[5] And there is probably no history of Jewish thought that omits his criticism of Talmudic traditions and the belief in personal immortality.

In what follows I should like to trace the evolution of Uriel da Costa's thought as representative of an attitude reflecting a rationalistic current that flowed throughout the Renaissance period in Spain and, especially, in Portugal. Like other educated Iberian Jews who later dissented from rabbinical authority, Uriel da Costa was deeply influenced by secular humanism, which created a spiritual brotherhood comprising Jew and Gentile, a brotherhood where intellectual kinship provided a stronger bond than the ties of ethnic and religious affiliation.[6] A man of thirty-five by the time he left Portugal, da Costa should be regarded, therefore, as a Portuguese thinker of the late Renaissance with an affinity to certain secularistic tendencies that were fairly prevalent throughout the sixteenth century. And there can be little doubt that in all his work our author embodied the Renaissance humanist's reverence for close textual analysis and intellectual independence.

The naturalistic cast to da Costa's *Weltanschauung* was apparent to his first and most famous opponent, Samuel da Silva, who accused Uriel of being a follower of Epicurus. Although da Costa initially defended himself against the charge, he acknowledged eventually that, in fact, Epicurus was a congenial thinker. Basic to Uriel da Costa's perspective there is an unstated but ever-present assumption that knowledge of the truth should result in well-being and happiness, the *eudaimonia* of the ancient Greeks.[7] Thus, when at Coimbra the young law student experienced "anxietates et angustias" (p. 36) in considering the prospects of an afterlife of damnation, he concluded that such a fearsome belief must be irrational and false. Like Epicurus, whose works he had yet to read, he too felt that reason should free man from irrational fears. As a corollary Uriel, even as Gabriel, rejected the possibility of an afterlife and thus denied the persistence of any experience—good or bad—after physical death.

No longer a Catholic Christian, da Costa was not yet ready to reject all religion. But it is revealing that his decision to adopt Judaism was probably prompted less by his family's background than by his perception that Judaism, at least as portrayed in the Pentateuch, seems to ignore the troublesome matter of personal immortality and an attendant belief in eternal retribution which he had already discarded for philosophical reasons.[8] Our author suggests an additional rational inducement for preferring the Old Testament to the New. He reasoned that the greater the consensus concerning an object of speculation, the more likely its truth. Since all believers, Jewish, Moslem, and Christian, revere the Old Testament but only Christians and some Moslems accept the New, it follows that the former is probably more creditable than the latter. Thus it was that by the age of twenty-five Gabriel-Uriel resolved to base his beliefs on a scrupulous interpretation of the Pentateuch even while admitting to some doubts regarding certain tenets of his new faith ("super aliquibus dubitarem") (p. 38).

When ten years later in Amsterdam he found himself in the real world of Jewish practice and belief, Uriel da Costa was struck by the central role of rabbis in commenting on the scripture and prescribing ritual observance. There is something of the Protestant reformer in his insistence that all the faithful should remain loyal only to the simple faith as set forth in the Pentateuch. He bitterly accused the priestly caste of "Pharisees" of having corrupted the purity of the law. One might also argue that in Uriel's reverence for the primary text above all, coupled with his impatience for commentary and secondary sources, the imprint of Erasmian humanism can be discerned. In his rejection of commentary in general in favor of personal exegesis of the text, da Costa echoes his fellow cristão novo, Juan Luis Vives (and other Iberian Erasmians), who would have the scholar abandon the mediation of all authorities and commentators and "volver a la fuente misma cristalina."[9]

Uriel's own return to "la fuente misma cristalina" resulted in his first tract, *Propostas contra a tradição* (1616), wherein he asserts that the Pentateuch provides no basis for practices such as the obligatory wearing of phylacteries and the details prescribed for the rites surrounding circumcision. For our rationalist only the written text ("a lei escrita") is admissible, and it must be interpreted in light of one's understanding ("o entendimento"). In no case should one allow for the vagaries of traditional commentary ("a lei da boca"). Excommunication simply served to steel his resolve to do battle against "a lei da boca" and the efforts of authority to repress the truth as he understood it in light of "o entendimento." His subsequent tract, *Exame das tradições farisaicas*, is an even more ambitious effort as he sets out to demonstrate that there is not a shred of evidence in the Pentateuch for affirming a belief in the immortality of the soul. Although the work itself and even its date have long been lost, three central chapters escaped oblivion when they were reproduced by Samuel da Silva in a treatise entitled *Tratado da imortalidade da alma* (1623).[10]

Uriel takes up the weapons of the rationalist humanist as he lashes out against what he regards as superstition and fantasy. And while respect for the text is everywhere apparent in his copious references to the Torah, it is equally evident that reason and empirical verification take priority over even the written word. Thus, when a scriptural text suggests the possibility of life after death, as in Elijah's ascension into heaven or the appearance of the dead Samuel before Saul, Uriel da Costa is quick to reject the biblical account as so many "sonhos confusos" or, at the very least, poetic license which "é necessário entender com juízo de homens" (p. 29). To be sure, such accounts are not to be found in the Pentateuch itself, but it is clear that our selective reader has progressed considerably from his earlier days at Coimbra when he accepted Jewish law and the Old Testament as the basis of his beliefs. Throughout the *Exame* there is far less concern with a defense of the purity of the Mosaic law as found in the Pentateuch than there is with demonstrating that man is a rational animal whose reason is but an attribute that does not survive the fate of all animals: "O mesmo dos outros animais . . . seu espírito . . . se extingue e acaba" (p. 20).

It would, however, be misleading to classify Uriel at this point among such Renaissance agnostics as, let us say, António de Gouveia.[11] In his attempt to reconcile reason with his vestigial religious beliefs, our author asserts that none other than God has led him to reject a belief in immortality. Apparently, for Uriel, God himself is an Epicurean insofar as He recognized that only anguish would result from allowing his creature, Uriel, to entertain the prospect of survival after death and consequent punishment. The author accordingly attributes to God his own insight regarding the comfort of extinction: "Que a coisa que mais me afligiu e cansou nesta vida foi entender e imaginar . . . que havia bem e mal eterno para o homem" (p. 34). With but one life to live, suffering and sacrifice for nonexistent future benefits are pointless. Uriel thus goes on to ridicule intentional privations such as fasting and chastity and looks upon asceticism as not only unnecessary but even as a kind of madness ("loucura").

Uriel da Costa is well aware that the clergy of his time, whether Jewish or Christian, based the dogma of an afterlife on the need for sanctions and rewards, which were not apparent in this world. To counter this view, our author is obliged to affirm that all reward and punishment are meted out in this life, although it may seem at times that the wicked escape retribution while the good suffer. Here our dissenter is less the empiricist than he is the rationalist, for he seems to ignore the evidence of experience as he defends a priori his belief in a just God while denying future reward and punishment. At this point in his thinking, Uriel da Costa has little patience with the *topos* according to which the world is inherently unfair and fortune is fundamentally capricious. So it is that he expresses strong disapproval for Luís de Camões's poem, "Ao desconcerto do mundo," which he proceeds to quote in its entirety. The scandalized Uriel da Costa would heartily concur with critics in our own day who discern a distinctly unorthodox and secularistic current in Camões's works,[12] and he angrily accuses the poet of daring to judge God himself with such verses as "Só para mim anda o mundo concertado." To Camões and anyone else who would question the justice of providence our author counsels: "Louco homem . . . abaixe um pouco as asas da sua imprudente presunção com que quer tomar o lugar de Deus e fazer-se com ele juiz na terra" (p. 27).

Subsequent events, however, could only have shaken even our author's trust in a just world, for he found himself the target of ever-increasing pressure from both civil and religious authorities. A second treatise on the mortality of the soul, now lost, was written in response to Samuel da Silva's criticism and seemed to provoke additional controversy and dismay. I think it is important, however, not to exaggerate the impact of da Costa's thesis. The essential mortality of man was hardly a novel concept during the late Renaissance, and here too Uriel owes much to important currents which persisted despite the opposition of religious orthodoxy and a reinvigorated scholasticism. The very substance of his thesis was eloquently stated in Peter Pompanazzi's *De Immortalitate Animae* (1516), whose reverberations continued subsequently wherever Aristotelianism held sway, such as at the Colégio de Artes in the Coimbra of mid-century. And more recently a fellow Iberian, Juan Huarte de San Juan, had studied human intelligence under a cool, analytic light in his *Examen de ingenios para ciencias* (Baeza, 1575). The *Examen* proved to be remarkably popular in Sephardic circles in the Netherlands, where at least five editions were published between 1590 and the middle of the 1600s. Among the Catholic Juan Huarte's conclusions regarding the soul there was an assertion that fundamentally reinforced Uriel's own position: "Solo nuestra fe divina nos hace ciertos y firmes que [el alma] dura para siempre jamás."[13]

We cannot say just when Uriel da Costa abandoned his attempts to provide a rationalistic basis for Judaism. It is clear from the *Exemplar* that by the end of his life he had come to the conclusion that one's only moral guide is reason and that religious sects are but fragmented and partial glimpses of the brotherhood of all men as reasoning creatures. Thus, he regards both Old and New Testaments as "not of God but mere human inventions like all the other religious laws that have ever been in this world" (p. 45). He acknowledges that it was only the prospect of solitude in a foreign country whose language he had never mastered that had induced him to recant and rejoin the community of the Portuguese synagogue. But his compromise with principle and reason was short-lived, and he refers to it as "playing the role of an ape among other apes" ("simiam . . . inter simias agendo," p. 45). The *Exemplar* rises to a crescendo as the author bitterly denounces the ethnocentrism of all people, especially of his own whom he describes as self-styled true believers in the midst of scorned Gentiles, themselves divided by partisan spirit and parochial loyalties.

In his testament's final pages our author aligns himself firmly with such stoics as Marcus Aurelius as he proclaims that only reason should unite all men and only nature ought to be our guide. But he ruefully admits that the ideal falls far short of a harsh reality characterized by the superficial but all too real distinctions of Jew, Christian, and Moslem. One wonders whether he would qualify his earlier severe criticism of Camões's "Ao desconcerto do mundo" as he invokes a similar *topos*, that of life as "an absurd play on the world's stage" ("in hoc mundi vanissimo theatro," p. 68) where he himself played an unstable and absurd role ("quam personam . . . in vanissima et instabilissima vita mea").[14] Philosophically convinced of the unity of the human family but all too aware of his own marginal place as a Portuguese-speaking agnostic in a Dutch city, Uriel da Costa availed himself of yet another page from the manual of Stoic naturalism. One reads in Epictetus, for example: "The door is open. When things are intolerable do as children do. Say: I will play no more . . . and so depart rather than to stay and moan." And so Uriel chose to "play no more."[15] Of him one might say what Camões wrote of another suicide: "Que dando morte breve ao corpo humano/Tenha sua memória larga vida."[16]

One can sum up Uriel da Costa with Jorge de Sena's evaluation of Sá de Miranda: "[foi] o homem solitário e eminentemente social ao mesmo tempo."[17] If da Costa read Sá as he obviously read Camões, he must have sensed a true brother in such works as "Basto" and "Montalvo." Sá de Miranda's shepherds also fiercely defend intellectual independence and devotion to reason as hallmarks of what it means to be fully human. Like Uriel they also recognize that because of their rationalism they are alienated from their fellow men who live in a society wracked by religious intolerance, superstition, and hypocrisy. The dilemma is a poignant one; reason is that common bond that unites all men in a natural community, but most of our fellow men live in mutual isolation because they order their lives not according to reason but in keeping with conflicting beliefs in the various and sundry "idols" described by Francis Bacon. Moreover, in the writings of both Sá de Miranda and Uriel da Costa there is a melancholy awareness that reason also separates them from nature, in all things save one their model and guide. For the aged Sá, "Tudo o mais renova, isto [ser velho] é sem cura!,"[18] a view shared by Uriel when he writes: "A árvore se for cortada tem esperança de tornar . . . a ser renovada . . . mas o homem morre . . . e não se levantará" (p. 16).

The work of Uriel da Costa can be fully appreciated only when viewed within the larger context of the critical-humanistic tradition as exemplified by a Juan Huarte, a Camões, and a Sá de Miranda. One might easily expand such a list to include a Damião de Gois, a Fernão Mendes Pinto, and other figures of the Renaissance in Portugal who contributed to what Jaime Cortesão has described as "o humanismo universalista dos portugueses." [19] Not coincidentally, such Renaissance writers and thinkers all ended their lives, if not in suicide like Uriel, certainly in solitude as they both rejected and were rejected by the tribalized society in which they lived.

Notes

1. For data relevant to his family and to Uriel da Costa's life in Portugal see C. M. de Vasconcelos, "Uriel da Costa—Notas relativas à sua vida e às suas obras," *Revista da Universidade de Coimbra* 7 (1918); A. de Magalhães Basto, "Alguns documentos inéditos sobre Uriel da Costa," *O Instituto* 79 (1930): 442–54 and 80 (1931): 425–563; I. S. Révah, "La religion d'Uriel da Costa, Marrane de Porto (d'après des documents inédits)," *Revue de l'Histoire des Religions* 61 (1962): 45–76.

2. See Uriel da Costa, *Três Escritos*, ed. A. Moreira de Sá (Lisbon: Instituto de Alta Cultura, 1963). This publication contains all of da Costa's extant writings, including his autobiography. Page references in the text are to this volume.

3. Although some assert that the *Exemplar* was originally composed in Latin (see C. M. de Vasconcelos, p. 320), others are just as categorical in claiming Portuguese as the original language: see Sol Bernstein, "Uriel da Costa" in *The Universal Jewish Encyclopedia* (New York: Universal Jewish Encyclopedia, Inc., 1939), 1: 74. The point is moot: see N. Porges, "Gebhardt's Book on Uriel da Costa," *The Jewish Quarterly Review* 19 (1929): 37–74.

4. See Leo Strauss, *Spinoza's Critique of Religion* (New York: Schocken Books, 1965), pp. 37–63; cf. Luis Washington Vita, "Uriel da Costa," *Revista Brasileira de Filosofia* 12 (1962): 355–77.

5. See the bibliography in Moreira de Sá's edition, pp. 6–8; cf. J. Sonne, "Da Costa Studies," *The Jewish Quarterly Review* 22 (1932): 247–93; M. S. Belenkii, *Tragediia Uriella Akosty* (Moscow: Nauka, 1968). The most recent novel based on da Costa's life was published in 1984: Agustina Bessa Luis, *Um Bicho da Terra* (Lisbon: Guimarães Editora).

6. See I. S. Révah, *Spinoza et le Dr. Juan de Prado* (Paris: École Pratique des Hautes Études–Études Juives, 1959), pp. 1–36; C. M. de Vasconcelos, p. 286.

7. Strauss, pp. 38–50; cf. Porges: "His [Uriel's] stand was not based on 'Marrano doubt' but on free-thinking" (p. 66). Regarding the "Moda" of Epicureanism and Stoicism in Iberia at the time, see Humberto Piñera, *El Pensamiento Español de los Siglos XVI y XVII* (New York: Las Americas, 1970), pp. 242–43.

8. See Porges, pp. 65–66.

9. See Piñera, p. 48; cf. Odette Sauvage, *L'Itinéraire Erasmien de André de Resende (1500–1573)* (Paris: Fundação Calouste Gulbenkian, 1971).

10. The *Tratado* has recently been edited and published. See Samuel da Silva, *Tratado da Imortalidade da Alma,* ed. Pinharanda Gomes (Lisbon: Imprensa Nacional, Casa da Moeda, 1982). For a critical review of this edition that qualifies the editor's unflattering view of Uriel da Costa's position in the debate, see Diogo Pires Aurélio, "Portugueses, mas nem tanto" in the *Diário de Notícias, Revista de Livros* for 4 April 1983, pp. v ff.

11. See D. M. Gomes dos Santos, "Buchanan e o ambiente coimbrão no século XVI," *Humanitas* 15 (1963): 261–327.

12. See António José Saraiva, *História de Cultura em Portugal* (Lisbon: Jornal do Foro, 1962), 3: 518–636; for the *topos,* see Ernst Robert Curtius, "The World Upside-Down" in *European Literature and the Latin Middle Ages,* trans. W. R. Trask (New York: Pantheon Books, 1953), pp. 94–98. Belenkii considers Camões a major influence in da Costa's intellectual formation; cf. C. M. de Vasconcelos: "Uriel lia e trelia e sabia (i.e., Camões) de cor," p. 295.

13. See Carlos G. Noreña, *Studies in Spanish Renaissance Thought* (The Hague: M. Nijhoff, 1975), pp. 240–41; cf. J. V. de Pina Martins, *Pico della Mirandola e o Humanismo Italiano nas Origens do Humanismo Português* (Lisbon: Editorial Verbo, 1964).

14. See Curtius, "Theatrical Metaphors," in *European Literature,* pp. 138–44; cf. Frank J. Warnke, "The World as Theatre," in *Versions of Baroque-European Literature in the Seventeenth Century* (London and New Haven: Yale University Press, 1972), pp. 66–89.

15. See *The Stoic and Epicurean Philosophers,* ed. Whitney J. Oates (New York: Random House, 1940), p. 266.

16. See Soneto XCIV in Luís de Camões, *Obras Completas,* ed. Hernâni Cidade (Lisbon: Sá da Costa, 1962), 1: 241.

17. Jorge de Sena, "Reflexões sobre Sá de Miranda ou A Arte de ser Moderno em Portugal," *Da Poesia Portuguesa* (Lisbon: Ática, 1959), pp. 23–30; cf. J. V. de Pina Martins, "Sá de Miranda, Poeta e Inovador," in *Cultura Portuguesa* (Lisbon: Editorial Verbo, 1974), pp. 65–80.

18. Sá de Miranda, "O sol é grande," in *Obras Completas,* ed. M. Rodrigues Lapa (Lisbon: Sá da Costa, 1960), 1: 318; cf. A. Júlio da Costa Pimpão, "O sol é grande," *Biblos* 19 (1938): 263–312.

19. See Jaime Cortesão, *O Humanismo Universalista dos Portugueses* (Lisbon: Portugália Editora, 1965), pp. 119–92; Elizabeth Feist Hirsch, *Damião de Gois: The Life and Thought of a Portuguese Humanist, 1502–1574* (The Hague: M. Nijhoff, 1967); Luís de Matos, "L'Humanisme portugais et ses relations avec l'Europe," *Bulletin des Études Portugaises* 26 (1965): 45–65.

II

The Portuguese in Brazil

The Victory of the Portuguese Language in Colonial Brazil

José Honório Rodrigues

The indigenous languages: Tupi and others

IN HIS LETTER to the king relating what happened when Pedro Ál-vares Cabral landed on the coast of Brazil, Pero Vaz de Caminha made the observation that it had been impossible "for there to be any useful talk or understanding" between the Portuguese and the In-dians. They could not understand each other's language and had to resort to exchanging impressions by gesticulating, as if they were mute. The decision was therefore made not to take any Indians by force since nobody could understand them but instead to leave two exiles behind and have them learn the Indians' language. In another passage Caminha wrote that "an old man waited there, holding a ca-noe paddle in his hand. He kept talking in front of all of us while our captain stood next to him but we didn't understand him and he didn't understand us." And on the day of departure, May 1, after Mass, Caminha wrote that "it seemed to me and to everyone else that the only thing needed for these people to become Christians was for them to understand us."[1]

When Pero de Magalhães Gândavo elaborated his *História da Província de Santa Cruz* (1575), he stated that "one language is used all along the coast; certain words may differ in some places but this does not prevent them [the natives] from understanding each other. This is true as far as the latitude of 27°; beyond that there are heathens of a different kind that we don't know as much about who speak a differ-ent language. The language I refer to, which is the general language

Translated by James C. Trager, University of Florida, and edited by Alfred Hower and Richard A. Preto-Rodas.

spoken along the coast, is very soft and is easy for any nation to learn."[2]

By 1531, before Gândavo wrote his *História,* there were already Portuguese who knew the language of the Indians. In the *Diário de Navegação de Pero Lopes de Sousa,*[3] it is stated that Francisco Chaves and the "Bacharel of Cananéia" and five or six Spaniards approached the Portuguese warship in a brigantine across from Cananéia. "This 'bacharel' [university graduate] had been living here in exile for thirty years, since the first expedition in 1501. He and Francisco Chaves were excellent interpreters in this land." Like Caramuru they learned the language by living with the natives, especially those who spoke Tupi.

Studies in the indigenous language began early, with the Jesuits. Padre João Azpilcueta Navarro (d. 1557) was the first to translate the "Suma da Doutrina Cristã" into the Tupi language. Padre Manuel da Nóbrega, the head of all the Jesuits, stuttered and never did learn Tupi, but he stimulated studies in it. In the first of his *Cartas do Brasil* he wrote to Padre Mestre Simão Rodrigues de Azevedo in 1549 that "we are trying to learn their language, and in this Padre Navarro is the best of all of us. We have decided that when we are more secure and better established we will go and live in their villages and learn their language with them and start to indoctrinate them little by little. I have tried to put into their language the sermons and some of the sayings of Our Lord, but I have not been able to find an interpreter to help me in this, for they are so primitive that they do not even have the necessary words. I hope to translate them to the best of my ability with the help of a man [Diogo Álvares, known as Caramuru], who grew up as a young man in this land."[4]

In another letter, dated August 10, 1549, he wrote to his professor in Coimbra, Dr. Navarro, that Padre João de Azpilcueta Navarro "already knows their language, which apparently greatly resembles Basque, so that he can communicate with them and is the best of all of us." In his letter to Simão Rodrigues in 1550 he states that "some of us are very weak and awkward in the language of this country, but Padre Navarro has Our Lord's special grace in this regard because while traveling through the villages of the Negroes [i.e., the Indians] in just the few days that we have been here he is able to communicate with them and preach in their language."[5]

One of the serious matters for Nóbrega was whether the Indians "will be able to confess through interpreters," and thus it was urgent to learn the language that was most widely spoken on the coast. He repeats again in a letter to King Dom João in 1554 that "in Bahia we cannot communicate with the heathens now because we lack interpreters."[6]

Padre Navarro died young, in 1555, and the extreme need for interpreters who spoke Tupi was seen immediately. Throughout the decade of the 1550s, however, some Portuguese colonists were already learning Tupi and other indigenous languages simply by living with the natives, i.e., without taking formal lessons. They also learned African languages, for Negroes from Guinea had already been introduced into Brazil, as Nóbrega's letters reveal.

Padre Navarro, a Basque, was replaced by the Canary Islander José de Anchieta, who quickly learned the most widespread indigenous language, in which he wrote the *Arte da Gramática da Língua mais usada na Costa do Brasil*[7] and the "Diálogo da Doutrina Cristã." A century later Padre António Vieira would say about this ability of Padre Anchieta: "How widely used was the language of Brazil in this province of ours is well testified by its first *Arte da Gramática,* of which the author and inventor was the great Anchieta and which can rightly be esteemed as one of his miracles."[8]

Anchieta himself, with his sharp hearing, perceived that there were a great number of tribal groups who differed in their speech. Before writing the *Arte* he wrote, from São Vicente in 1554, to his brothers in Coimbra that "as for the language, I am making progress although still very little in comparison with what I would know if I had not been occupied in studying the grammar; nevertheless I have learned almost all of its modes. I haven't put it into an *Arte* yet because there is no one here who can profit from it. The only ones who will profit from it are myself and those who will come from Portugal knowing grammar." But already in 1560 in the College of Bahia, and probably since 1555 in Piratininga, the language of the land was being studied in Anchieta's grammar but in manuscript copies, for, as we have seen, it was not until 1595 that it was printed, in Coimbra. Referring to customs in Brazil in the "Informação do Brasil e de suas Capitanias de 1584," one of the major documents of the early history of Brazil, he wrote that "all the peoples of the coast who speak the same language eat human flesh."[9]

When the visitor Padre Christóvão Gouvêa arrived in Bahia, he was welcomed to the college with three speeches, one in Portuguese, one in the Brazilian language, and the third in Latin. Anchieta states in his "Fragmentos Históricos" that "as the priests did not know the language of the land, the brothers served as interpreters for the doctrines and peregrinations and confessions of the mestizos, wives, and children of the Portuguese, especially in the general confessions, for the purpose of better satisfaction and understanding."[10] The mestizos, the children, and the wives (who were Indians) of the Portuguese needed interpreters because they did not speak Portuguese.

Anchieta was the one who most distinguished himself in mastering the native Brazilian language. Besides himself and Azpilcueta Navarro, only Pero Corrêa and Manuel Chaves, who both lived in São Vicente and were received into the order as brothers, mastered it. The Jesuit priests who came to Brazil had to read Anchieta's *Arte da língua brasílica* immediately.[11] Luís da Grã (1523–1609), who replaced Nóbrega as Provincial and had been the Superior of São Vicente and Rector of the College of Pernambuco, ordered that "every day there should be an hour lesson in the native Brazilian language, which we here call Greek; he is the teacher of the language because he understands it and knows how to explain its rules better than all others, even though they may be very good as interpreters."[12]

Though Anchieta was the first to write the *Arte da Gramática*, Fernão Cardim (1540?–1625) was the first to describe in any orderly way the diversity of nations and languages in Brazil.[13] Cardim wrote that

> in all of this province there are many and various nations with different languages, although there is one principal language that some ten nations of Indians understand. The latter live along the sea coast and in a great stretch of the interior; they all speak one single language, although they may differ in a few words, and it is this language that the Portuguese understand. It is easy and elegant and soft and rich; its difficulty is that it has many forms. The Portuguese who have any communication with the Indians learn it in a short time, and the Brazilian-born children of Portuguese know it better than the Portuguese, males as well as females, especially in the Captaincy of São Vicente. The padres communicate with these ten nations of Indians because they know their language and because these Indians are better disposed and more domesticated; they were and are old friends of the Portuguese and fought against their own relatives and other indigenous nations. There were so many of the latter that it seemed impossible to put an end to them, but the Portuguese have fought them so much that almost all have been killed and the rest have such fear of them that they leave the

coast and flee as far as three or four hundred leagues into the interior.

Cardim then enumerated those who spoke different languages—the Potiguar, the Viatan, the Tupinambá, the Caeté, and many other groups—a total of seventy-six different nations and different languages, peoples who were brave, savage, and unconquered, contrary to the heathen who lived along the seacoast. The only exceptions cited by Cardim were the Tapuia who lived along the São Francisco River and others who lived closer by. Contact with the latter might be fruitful, but "the other Tapuia cannot be converted because they are nomadic and they have many different and difficult languages."[14]

Cardim, in his "Informação da Missão do P. Christóvão Gouvêa às Partes do Brasil, Ano de 83,"[15] referred several times to prayers and speeches made in the native Brazilian language and declared that the Indians regarded a good interpreter so highly they called him a master of speech. "When they want to test one to determine whether he is a great interpreter, many of them gather together to see whether they can tire him out by talking to him in a body all night long and sometimes for two or three days, without getting irritated."[16] The Indian children who attended school to learn to read and write were bilingual, speaking their own language and Portuguese.[17]

Gabriel Soares de Sousa, in his *Tratado Descritivo do Brasil em 1587*, described the lives and customs of the heathen Potiguar, Caeté, Aimoré, Tupinikin, Guaitacá, Papaná, Tamoio, Goianá, and Carijó and distinguished the languages they spoke. He stated that the Caeté spoke the same language as the Tupinambá, which was also spoken by the Potiguar. The Aimoré were wilder than the other savages and after losing their language they made up "a new one that no other nation of heathens understands in this whole state of Brazil."[18]

The Tupinikin, Soares stated, were the lords and possessors of the lands along the seacoast of Brazil. There were many wars and many losses, but in time peace was made and from then on they were very faithful and true to the Portuguese. He explained that even though the Tupinikin were adversaries of the Tupinambá, "there is no greater difference between them in language and customs than there is between the people who live in Lisbon and those who live in Beira." They were regarded as more domesticated than heathen and aided the Portuguese against the Aimoré, the Tapuia, and Tamoio.

The Guaitacá were lords of the coastland that formed part of the Captaincy of Espírito Santo and part of Paraíba do Sul or of São

Tomé. These heathens, Soares pointed out, had a language different from that of the Tupinikin, Papaná, and Tamoio. The Papaná lived along the sea between the Captaincy of Porto Seguro and that of Espírito Santo, from where they were pushed into the interior by their adversaries, the Tupinikin. Their language was understood by the Tupinikin and Guaitacá, although not very well.[19]

The Tamoio occupied the coast from the Cape of São Tomé to Angra dos Reis. "These heathens are tall and robust, they are valiant men and very bellicose and enemies of all other heathens except the Tupinambá to whom they are related. Their languages resemble each other and they have the same customs and religion and lead the same kind of life and are friendly to each other" but are enemies of the Guaitacá.[20]

The Goianá had their lands along the coast from Angra dos Reis to the Cananéia River where they shared a border with the Carijó. They were always at war "with the Tamoio on one bank of the river and with the Carijó on the other and they kill each other cruelly." The language of these people was different from that of their neighbors, but they and the Carijó did understand each other.[21]

The Carijó, enemies of the Goianá, possessed the coastland of the Cananéia River, where they bordered on the territory of the Goianá. They were a domesticated people, rational, and little disposed to bellicosity. They did not eat human flesh nor did they kill whites who came to negotiate with them. They sustained themselves by hunting and fishing and planted manioc and vegetables. Their language was quite different from that of their neighbors.

The most complete description of Indians in Gabriel Soares de Sousa's work concerns the Tupinambá, who populated Bahia and were its first settlers. The Tupinambá were divided into several bands, some of whom were enemies of each other, but all spoke a language that was almost general along the coast of Brazil.[22]

In the *Diálogos das Grandezas do Brasil* (1618) by the New Christian Ambrósio Fernandes Brandão, little can be gathered concerning the language of the Indians. He repeats earlier authors in stating that their language lacks the letters *F, L,* and *R,* a sign that they have neither faith nor law nor royalty (*fé, lei, rei*)[23] and, finally, speaking of the Tapuia, he says that their speech is different "because the other heathens don't understand them, since they have a very complicated language."[24]

Well into the seventeenth century, when ethnic, cultural, and linguistic miscegenation had developed with the attempt toward the

Lusitanization of the Indians and the Indianization of the Portuguese, and also the Africanization of Indians and whites, each becoming assimilated with the others, António Vieira began his activities and his preaching. He spoke of the necessity "for the apostles or their successors in their ministry to abound in the love of God in order to teach in this land, where even greater love of God is necessary than anywhere else. And why? For two reasons: the first, because of the quality of the various peoples; the second, because of the difficulty of the languages." [25]

Continuing his sermon, which he delivered in São Luís, Vieira described the linguistic problems that the Portuguese had to contend with in Brazil. Portugal, he pointed out, sent missionaries to countries such as Japan, China, and Persia, where there was only one language.

> However, the missionaries that Portugal sends to Maranhão, although it does not have the name of empire or kingdom, are truly those whom God reserved for the [most] difficult undertaking, because they come to preach to people of so many, so diverse, and so unknown languages that the only thing known about them is that they are without number. . . . The Amazon River, from the city of Belém upstream, already has been measured to be more than 3000 [leagues], but its origin is still uncharted. For this reason the natives call the region Pará and the Portuguese call it Maranhão, which mean "sea," and "big sea." The name of Babel would be insufficient for it, for at the tower of Babel, as St. Jerome says, there were only seventy-two languages, whereas those spoken along the Amazon are so many and so diverse, that their names and number are unknown. The ones that were known by the year 1639 upon the discovery of Quito, numbered one hundred and fifty. Later many more were discovered, yet only the lesser part of the river and its immense tributaries and the nations which inhabit them has been discovered. So many are the peoples and so mysterious their tongues and of such new and unheard-of intelligence! [26]

Vieira accentuated the difficulties of learning these new languages, preaching that "if it is difficult to hear a language that you do not understand, how much more difficult it must be to understand a language that you do not hear? The first problem is to hear it; the second, to understand it; the third, to reduce it to grammar and to rules; the fourth, to study it; the fifth (and not the least, hurdle, one which obliged St. Jerome to wear down his teeth) is to pronounce it."[27]

In his efforts at evangelizing, Vieira said that "the letters of the Chinese and Japanese are quite difficult because they are hieroglyphs, like those of the Egyptians, but after all one can learn the language of political people and study it by letter and by paper. But having to face a primitive language of savages, without books, without a teacher, without a guide, and in the midst of that darkness and dissonance to have to dig out the first foundations and to discover the primary elements of that language . . . there is no doubt that that is a most arduous task for any mind."[28]

In his Epiphany sermon, preached in the Royal Chapel before the Queen Regent, he declaimed: "When God confused the tongues at the tower of Babel, Philo the Hebrew believed that all became deaf and dumb, because even though all spoke and all heard, no one understood anyone else. In ancient Babel there were seventy-two languages; in the Babel of the Amazon River there are already more than one hundred fifty known, as different from each other as ours is from Greek; thus when we arrived there, all of us were mute and all of them deaf. See now how much study and how much work will be necessary so that these mute may speak and these deaf may hear."[29]

Vieira continued, concerning the learning of languages: "Our calling (says St. Ignatius in the beginning of his *Instituto*) is to go about and bring life to every place on the Earth where the greatest service to God and aid to souls awaits. . . . His rule states: For the greatest help to the natives of the land in which they reside, all must learn their language. Let us note well those two all-encompassing terms: all and every place. And which part or parts of the Earth, and which land or lands are those in which they reside? Japan, China, Malabar, Mogul, Mexico, Peru, Brazil, Maranhão, and if an unknown land is discovered, that one also. And who are those who are to learn the languages? Everyone, he says, without exception."

Vieira pointed out other considerations, referring to the three nonbarbaric languages in which was written the title that Jesus received on the cross: Hebrew, Greek, and Latin. He continued:

> However, after Calvary extended to all the world and upon
> it was raised the standard of the Crucified One, the title on
> the cross is now composed of all languages, no matter how
> barbaric or unknown they may be. How widely used was the
> language of Brazil in this province is well testified by its first

art or grammar, of which the author and inventor was the great Anchieta, and which can rightly be esteemed as one of his miracles. . . . The other more abbreviated ones which came out afterward and the copious vocabularies and the very exact catechism also so testify. . . . Above all it is attested by the very use of which the elders remind us, in which the native Portuguese tongue was not more general among us than the Brazilian. . . . And what shall I say to the College of Bahia, or what will they say to me, when in this community the language called the general language of Brazil is so little general, for so few are those who use it.[30]

The battle of the languages led Vieira to wonder:

Have the old refinements increased or have they become extinguished or at least cooled down this fire of languages in our province, because the general language of Brazil is less cultivated here today? . . . It is certain that the reduction to one language has been replaced by five others: the Portuguese language which by so many means is insisted upon in the reformation of the Portuguese; the Ethiopian, in which in this city alone 25,000 negroes are being indoctrinated and catechized, not to mention the infinite number of them from elsewhere; the two Tapuias, with which in the remotest hinterlands of our interior the six new Christendoms among the Paiaiá and the Chiriri have risen; and finally "general Brazilian" itself, with which in the twelve settlements closest to the sea along four hundred leagues of the coast, the Company indoctrinates and preserves the relics of the Indians of that name, which by now would have been finished if it had not preserved them. . . . And since in Brazil the number of Indians has been decreasing and that of the Portuguese increasing, with the prudence characteristic of our Institute the study of the language of the land has been reduced, so that the ages in which it is more easily learned should be applied as soon as possible to the study of rhetoric, philosophy, and theology, and the workers who need further instruction be trained more quickly. However, in the present situation, when to the obligations of this province have been added the universal conquest of the new world of Maranhão and the great sea of the Amazon River, there is no doubt that the *língua geral* of Brazil, as the only gateway through which one can enter into an understanding of the other languages, comprises the great lack and difficulty in which we find ourselves.[31]

The língua geral: its diffusion in Brazil

The Indians who spoke língua geral were always, in spite of being warlike, those who most readily submitted and made peace with the colonists. Thus orders came from His Majesty "to the Paulistas who, under the pretext of hunting the Tapuia, captured those who spoke the língua geral." They were Indians who were being domesticated by the Jesuits, and thus His Majesty decided to thwart their intentions, ordering António Luís Gonçalves de Câmara Coutinho, governor of Bahia (1690–94), to write to the Paulistas to show them "how much it behooved the service of His Majesty and the welfare of that conquest to keep the already domesticated Indians in the place in which they were situated."[32]

Like those of the coast, but valiant or more docile, the Indians of the *sertão*, who were in general called the Tapuia, were being subjected little by little. They were the ones who faced the forces of the colonists and especially of the *bandeirantes*. There were cases, in the assaults on the "barbarian" natives, when only one was captured. In one such case the authorities tried at all costs to find an interpreter, for they were faced with an unknown language. For this reason the Marquis of Angeja, Dom Pedro António de Noronha Albuquerque e Sousa, governor of Bahia (1714–18) and third viceroy, wrote to the sergeant field-master Manuel Nunes Viana, the leader of the *emboabas*, to look for an interpreter who could understand their Indian prisoner.[33]

The predominance of the língua geral became established with the bandeirantes, all or almost all of whom spoke only that language with no knowledge of Portuguese. Thus António Vieira, in his "Voto" about the doubts of the inhabitants of São Paulo regarding the administration of the Indians,[34] said it was "certain that the families of the Portuguese and Indians of São Paulo are today so closely linked that the women and children grow up mystically and domestically together, and the language which is spoken in said families is that of the Indians, and the children go to school to learn Portuguese."

Sérgio Buarque de Holanda, in a valuable note on "The Língua Geral in São Paulo,"[35] cites the solicitation made to His Majesty by the governor Artur de Sá e Menezes that the appointing of parish priests to the churches of the southern district should be made to religious who were familiar with the língua geral of the Indians, stating that "the majority of these people do not express themselves in any other language, especially the female sex and all the servants. Because of the lack of [bilingual] priests irreparable loss occurs, as we see today in São Paulo with the new vicar who came appointed to that church, who needs to have someone interpret for him."

Another example referred to by Sérgio Buarque de Holanda is taken from the report written around 1692, when the governor of Rio de Janeiro, António Pais de Sande (1693–94), stated that "the first language that children [of the Paulistas] learn is that of the natives rather than the mother tongue," i.e. Portuguese. He cites in addition the case of the inventory of the estate of Brás Esteves Leme, in which it was necessary for the Judge for Orphans "to swear in Álvaro Neto, practiced in the language of the land, in order to be able to understand the declarations of Luzia Esteves, daughter of the deceased, since she didn't know how to speak Portuguese well." Sérgio Buarque de Holanda explains that the judge, Dom Francisco Rendon de Quebedo, was a newcomer to São Paulo and thus needed an interpreter for the language that was the normal one of the populace.

Add to this the case of Domingos Jorge Velho, one of the greatest of the bandeirantes, who, visiting the Bishop of Pernambuco, provided this impression which the bishop transmitted to the king; "This man is one of the biggest savages I have ever met; when he visited me he brought an interpreter with him for he does not even know how to speak, and he is no different from the most barbarous Tapuia except to say that he is a Christian, and notwithstanding his having been married recently he has seven concubines attending him, and from this one can infer how he proceeds in everything else." [36]

Yet another instance of the need for bilingual administrators is found in Manuel da Fonseca's *Vida do Venerável Padre Belchior de Pontes.* The author writes of his subject that "the notice of his great skill in the Brazilian language was not the least reason for the prelate's being held in high regard." Farther on he says that after Pontes became a religious, the superiors considered how to put him to work. "They looked toward São Paulo, and judged him suited for that region, because he was mature in years and skilled in the Brazilian language which was so necessary in those parts that both the natives and the Portuguese who traded with the heathens . . . had co-naturalized it." [37]

Hercules Florence wrote in his diary of the expedition of the Russian consul Baron de Langsdorff "that the Apiacá speak Guarani or Brazilian língua geral. In the Portuguese missions, which are today Brazilian in Rio Grande do Sul, and in those of Paraguay, the people, and especially the indigenous race, still use that language. In São Paulo, sixty years ago [i.e., in 1768], the ladies spoke in that language, which was the language of friendship and household intimacy. I have still heard it from the mouths of old persons. In Paraguay it is common to all classes, but, just as formerly in São Paulo, it is spoken only at home, for with strangers they speak Spanish."[38]

Sérgio Buarque de Holanda, in a passage notable for synthesis and precision, wrote: "Note that the influence of the língua geral in vocabulary, pronunciation, and even in the syntactic usage of our rural population did not stop exerting itself even when the indigenous languages used were not of the great Tupi-Guarani family; that is the case of the Bororo and especially of the Pareci, who in the São Paulo of the eighteenth century had a role in all ways comparable to that of the Carijó in the 1600s, the era par excellence of the bandeirantes. The fact was that having been domesticated and catechized ordinarily in the língua geral of the coast, they could not communicate with their masters in any other language."

And immediately thereafter he wrote that "if it is true that without the very pronounced presence of the Indian, the Portuguese would not have been able to live on the plateau, with it they could not survive in a pure state. In other words, they would have to renounce many of their hereditary habits, their forms of life and society, their techniques, their aspirations and, what is quite significant, their language. And that was in fact what happened."[39]

Tupi in Pará, Maranhão, and Amazonas

The expansion and predominance of the língua geral developed above all, as we have seen, in São Paulo. The bandeirantes spoke only língua geral, and it was spoken in Amazonas generally, i.e. in Maranhão, Pará, and Amazonas. On the coast the Portuguese language prevailed, but it was primarily in São Paulo and in Amazonas that the língua geral won out in a war that lasted two and a half centuries.

In 1722 the king wrote to the commissioner-general of the Capuchins of Our Lady of the Conception in Maranhão regarding the manner in which the Indians were to be instructed: "It is my wish to recommend to you that the missionaries that you place in the villages that are delivered to you be well versed in the language of the Indians that they are to missionize, like the padres of the Company of Jesus, because if they are not knowledgeable in said language all the work that they do in indoctrinating them will be useless and without fruit, and that after they are instructed in the true faith you order them to undertake with all care that the Indians learn the Portuguese language, for thus will they more easily receive our religion with greater understanding."[40] But Portuguese suffered as a result; thus, João Francisco Lisboa pointed out that "in 1755 the Portuguese language was so corrupted, or rather, banished, that in São Luís and Belém only Tupi was spoken, even from the pulpits."[41]

More recently, commenting on articles by Jaime Cortesão (called collectively *Introdução à História das Bandeiras*), Artur Cesar Ferreira Reis, an outstanding authority on Amazonia, noted that "in the seventeenth century as in the eighteenth, not in Belém but in Amazonia, the use of Tupi was so widespread that we can safely say that without it, it was to a certain extent impossible to live integrated into that social environment or gain any benefit from it."[42]

The African languages

The Portuguese language had the língua geral and the diversity of languages spoken by the Indians as its principal enemy, but the African languages also had to be overcome for Portuguese to become victorious. It was Portugal's colonialist policy to diversify as much as possible the composition of the African people it brought to Brazil. Thus, the Portuguese prevented their unity through the diversity of languages and kept them submissive.

Africans were brought to Brazil from the outset, for Cardim speaks of Negroes from Guinea. In his "Informação da Missão do P. Christóvão Gouvêa às Partes do Brasil no ano de 1583" and his "Narrativa Epistolar de uma viagem à Missão Jesuítica" he had already declared that there were three or four thousand slaves from Guinea among three thousand Portuguese and eight thousand Christianized Indians. He said that there was also a priest who spoke the language of the slaves from Guinea.[43] In Pernambuco, at the festival of the martyrdom of Padre Ignacio de Azevedo and his companions, besides an oration in verse in the refectory, a brother of fourteen years gave another one in the language of Angola. Also in Pernambuco there is reference to the benefit that the mission gained through a padre who knew the language of the Guinean slaves. Pernambuco had, as did Bahia, many slaves from Guinea, "who must have numbered close to two thousand"[44]

Ever since the work of Varnhagen it has been known that Portugal brought different ethnic groups to Brazil, with a great variety of African languages. People came from Guinea, the Mina coast, the Congo, Angola, and Mozambique, and Varnhagen cites some words of current use in Brazil that originally derived from Africa.[45]

Writing in 1711, Antonil revealed that Ardas, Minas, and Congolese, from São Tomé, Angola, Cape Verde, and some from Mozambique, came to Brazil on board ships from India. The Ardas and the Minas were robust, he stated, while those from Cape Verde and São

Tomé were the weakest. Natives of Angola who had grown up in Luanda were more readily capable of learning mechanical trades than were those from the other places mentioned. Among the Congolese there were also some who were good and industrious, not only for working sugarcane but also in workshops and for domestic work. Some arrived in Brazil very "rough and tough" and continued that way all their lives. Others in a few years turned out to be sharp and clever, both in learning Christian doctrine and in seeking ways to make a living, fit to be entrusted with a boat, to carry messages, or to perform any task among those likely to arise.[46]

Luís dos Santos Vilhena, writing in the late eighteenth century, attempted to show in one of his letters how the troubles that afflicted society resulted as much from the introduction of the Negroes from Africa as from the depraved upbringing ordinarily given to the mulattoes and creoles born in Brazil. His information, however, was sparse, and he stated only that they are brought from diverse ports of Africa in exchange for tobacco, sugar, and rum. He wrote nothing about the languages these different groups brought to Brazil.[47]

In an exemplary book on the traffic of Negroes between the Gulf of Benin and Bahia de Todos os Santos, Pierre Verger showed with regard to Bahia alone that the traffic in Negroes could be divided into four periods: the Guinea cycle during the second half of the sixteenth century; the Angola and Congo cycle of the eighteenth century; the coast of Mina cycle of the first three-quarters of the eighteenth century; and the cycle of the Gulf of Benin between 1770 and 1850, including the period of the clandestine traffic.[48] The arrival of the Dahomeyans, called Gêge in Brazil, occurred during the last two periods. That of the Nagô-Yoruba corresponded especially to the last period. Only in Bahia was there a greater concentration of Negroes from the Mina coast, while in Rio de Janeiro, Africans arrived from everywhere, although with a predominance of people from Angola and the Congo.

The first person to study the African languages and dialects in Brazil was Nina Rodrigues in his *Os Africanos no Brasil*.[49] After recalling that Sílvio Romero lamented that in Brazil the study of the African languages spoken by the slaves had been neglected, Nina Rodrigues noted what happened once the slave trade stopped:

> The African languages spoken in Brazil soon suffered great
> alterations, both because of the learning of Portuguese on
> the part of the slaves, and because of the African language
> adopted as a língua geral by the acclimated Negroes. In fact,

no one would suppose that all of the black slaves spoke the same language. Rather, in the number of languages that were imported, in the infinite multiplicity and nuances of their dialects, they were so many that, in an almost excusable exaggeration, they could be said to be equal in number to that of the shipments of slaves brought into the country. Under such conditions, it became an urgent need for the black slaves to adopt one African language as a língua geral in which all might understand each other. Hence, upon disembarking in Brazil, the new Negro was obliged to learn Portuguese to speak with the white masters, the mestizos, and creole Negroes, and the língua geral in order to be understood by his partners or companions in slavery.[50]

It was easier, Nina Rodrigues points out, for the Africans to learn the latter language than to learn Portuguese, for which they had no teachers, nor was the example of their fellow-slaves sufficient to teach Portuguese to them, since even they hardly understood it and mangled it barbarously.

The important fact is that, just like the língua geral created to provide communication among various Tupi groups, there was a black língua geral created to provide understanding among the various African groups. The difference is that the indigenous língua geral was created by the Jesuits, while the black língua geral was created by the Africans themselves.

Nina Rodrigues attempted to determine which African languages were spoken in Brazil and cited various students of African linguistics and the classifications they adopted. He accepted a division into three groups; the Hamitic (Tuareg and Fulá); the Sudanese, with twelve groups, among which are the Mandinga, Ewe or Gêge, the Yoruba or Nagô; and the southern or Bantu group. He states that many of the languages that figured in the complete list of his classification were spoken in Brazil and that among them the ones that were adopted as línguas gerais were Nagô or Yoruba in Bahia and Kimbundu or Congolese in the north and south, that is, one a Sudanese language and the other a Bantu. He recalls that Varnhagen pointed out the importance of the Nagô language, spoken as a língua geral in Bahia, which so many slaves learned in order to understand each other.[51]

Nina Rodrigues emphasized the importance of the Nagô language, pointing out that those who compile lists of African words, especially Bantu, have mixed Yoruba or Nagô terms with Bantu. He also stressed the importance and extent of Gêge or Êuê or Ewe in Brazil, and of Haussa, spoken widely in Africa. Both Gêge and Haussa possess various dialects, the latter being generally called Sudanese as it is the language most widely spoken in Sudan. He refers also to Kanuri, spoken by the Bornu Negroes in Bahia; to Tapa, Nifê, or Nupê, also spoken in Bahia, the language of the Grunce Negroes, known in Bahia as the chicken Negroes. He states that at the time he wrote his book, in 1905, Haussa, Kanúri, Tapa, and Grunce were still spoken in Bahia.

Nina Rodrigues also dealt with the existence of Mandinga Negroes and therefore with the use of the Mandinga language, which is the língua geral of former Portuguese Guinea. In addition, he referred to the Fulá language, or the Felupian group, which he believed was spoken in Maranhão, in the north of Brazil, and in Bahia itself. Finally, he dealt with the Bantu languages, spoken with their many dialects in a vast region of Africa, including Angola and Mozambique. There were few Angolan and Congo Negroes in Bahia who abandoned their language to speak Nagô, the African língua geral of Bahia. But in Rio de Janeiro the great majority of Negro slaves were Bantu; hence the predominance of Kimbundu, Ambundu, and other languages, just a few of the many dialects of Angola, where there are ten large ethnic groups. Nina Rodrigues asserted that almost all the Bantu languages were spoken in Brazil.[52]

According to Renato de Mendonça, two strong language families exist in African linguistics: Bantu and non-Bantu, and from these two arose an infinite variety of languages or dialects. He cites Blaise Cendrars who, in his *Anthologie Nègre,* divided the African languages into six groups, each further divided into dozens of languages.[53] Thus, the Bantu group, dominant in Africa, had some 168 languages and 55 dialects. The languages of Sudan and of Guinea comprised some 16 groups.[54] In a chapter on the imported Negro peoples, Renato de Mendonça demonstrated the insufficiency of the data, the confused denominations, and the extremely varied origins of the Brazilian Negroes. In his opinion, Negroes from Guinea predominated in Bahia, while the Bantu prevailed in the state of Rio de Janeiro and in Minas Gerais, the regions with the largest Negro contingents. But the Guineans and Bantus each possessed various languages and dialects.[55] Renato de Mendonça concluded by stating that "the following languages were spoken in Brazil: Nagô or Yoruba, Kimbundu, Gêge or Eue, Kanúri or Nipê and Grunce."[56] From these languages two stood out which were adopted by the Negroes of the country as línguas gerais: Nagô or Yoruba in Bahia, and Kimbundu in the north and in the south. This conclusion is based on information from Nina Rodrigues, whose work was summarized earlier.

Edison Carneiro, who was one of the best Brazilian specialists in studies of the Negro in Brazil, wrote a splendid synthesis on the languages spoken by the various tribes that arrived there.[57] He said that there were no studies worthy of special mention, and that with respect to the Africans' presence, research involving language did not merit the same attention as that bestowed upon the religions of the Negroes. He considered Nina Rodrigues's study the best and that of Renato de Mendonça deficient; he claimed not to know what adjective Jacques Raimundo's might deserve. He emphasized that Nagô, Gêge, and Kimbundu, in the Angolan and Congo variants, were languages in current use in Bahia and that Nagô and Gêge were alive in the Xangô religion of Pernambuco and in the Tambor of Maranhão. Carneiro additionally noted that Kimbundu appellations and place-names are innumerable throughout the country. He pleaded, then, that the study of African languages spoken in Brazil be encouraged.

Thus the Babel of indigenous languages to which António Vieira referred is joined by another Babel, that of African languages. A hint of it can be found in a classified ad in the *Jornal do Comércio* of 14 May 1830 placed by a slave-owner looking for a runaway slave who was "a Fulá" and "who doesn't speak Portuguese well."[58] Indeed, this may have been the rule rather than the exception. Thus, in 1836 George Gardner noted that "many times when traveling through the interior, I saw bands of slaves whose number ranged from twenty to a hundred individuals, all of them unable to speak a word of Portuguese, herded to the *sertão* to be sold or already bought by plantation owners."[59] Robert Avé-Lallemant, too, traveling through the interior of Bahia, encountered a group of free Africans placed at the disposition of Senator and Minister Gonçalves Martins (later Baron and Viscount of São Lourenço) for the preparation of the enterprise of the Jequitinhonha. He wrote that "few Negroes spoke fluent Portuguese. Among themselves they chattered animatedly and passionately in their Nagô dialect, which sounds most unpleasant."[60]

Avé-Lallemant went on to say: "The fact that they spoke their dialect seemed to me a circumstance worthy of note, though the foreman, a rather indecisive man, was of a different opinion, not having, however, thought about it. But I certainly believe that those groups of Negroes, with a strange language, when they have no direction and do not encounter any example to imitate in the civilized world which surrounds them, can easily abuse their brute strength, of which they have full consciousness. These savage creatures, once excited, need only a resolute chief with just a few fiery remarks in their native African tongue to unleash a rapid coup." He would not be surprised, he added, if they rebelled and formed a *quilombo*, a society of rebellious

Negroes, like many others that existed.[61] Richard F. Burton, it may
be noted, wrote that the Negro slaves of Morro Velho spoke Luso-
Hamitic.[62]

The Portuguese reaction: the legislation of Pombal

In the face of this multitude of indigenous and African languages, the
defenders of Portuguese had to use all available resources to prevail.
Thus it is that in 1727 Dom João V informed the governor of the state
of Maranhão, João da Maia da Gama (1722–28), that he was ordering
the prelates of the religious orders to see to it that the Indians under
their administration should be well instructed in Portuguese, "for the
great benefit that could result from it."[63]

The royal order does not appear to have brought any results; on
the contrary, it seems to have been inoperative. In fact, the Jesuits
dominated relations with the natives and were the ones who best knew
the Tupi language as adapted by them to the língua geral. Not all of
the other religious orders, nor the recently arrived colonists, knew the
language so well as to be able to communicate and interact with the
Indians. The result was that the linguistic barrier strengthened the
dominion of the Jesuits over the Indians and of those who opposed
the imposition of the Portuguese language. The royal order thus initiated an antagonism with serious consequences involving the Crown
on the one hand and the Society of Jesus on the other.

In the "Representação dos Moradores do Estado do Maranhão"
of 12 April 1729,[64] it is stated that the Jesuit missionaries "forget the
spiritual growth of the Indians at the missions, so that whereas they
ought to be teaching them the Portuguese language and some of them
to read in order to understand the evangelical doctrine with clarity
and become more tractable and better vassals of your Majesty, they
converse with them only in the language which they call *geral* in that
state, which differs very little from the brutish language with which
they came out of the backlands; in this, colonists imitate them and
thus cannot force them to learn the Portuguese language without special orders from your Majesty; for without them they will flee to the
missions where the missionaries keep them without wishing to restrict
them to their masters." Finally, it was pleaded that His Majesty should
order the missionaries to teach the Portuguese language to the mission Indians and also to the colonists, to those who have slaves, and to
the free Indians. Thus, when the Law of the Directorate of 3 May
1757 was promulgated, which established new relations with the Indians in order to promote their emancipation and improve their con-

ditions, it had as one of its principal objectives the popularization of the Portuguese language.

It was the Directorate of 1757, which was to be observed in the Indian settlements of Pará and Maranhão, that imposed Portuguese as the official language in that vast region which comprises a third of the present territory of Brazil.[65] The Law of the Directorate stipulated: "And since it is evident that the paternal providences of Our August Sovereign are directed solely to Christianize and civilize these until-now unhappy and wretched peoples, so that leaving behind the ignorance and rusticity to which they find themselves reduced, they might be useful to themselves, to the mission dwellers, and to the state. These two virtuous and important ends which always was [sic] the heroic undertaking of the incomparable zeal of our Catholic and Most Faithful Monarchs, will be the principal object of the reflexion and care of the Directors" (Art. 3). The law further states:

> While, however, the civilizing of the Indians comprises the principal obligation of the Directors as is proper in their ministry, the latter will employ a most special care in persuading them of all those means that might be conducive to such a useful and important end, which are the ones to which I will refer (Art. 5).
>
> It was always the inalterable practice of all nations who conquered new domains, *to introduce their own language immediately* to the conquered peoples, as it is indisputable that this is one of the most efficient means for banishing from uncultured peoples the barbarity of their old customs; and experience has shown that introducing the use of the language of the Prince who conquered them established in them as well the affection, veneration, and obedience to that same Prince. Whereas all the civilized nations of the world have observed this prudent and solid system, quite the opposite was practiced in this conquest, for the first conquerors took care only to establish the use of the language which they called língua geral, a truly abominable and diabolical invention, in order that, deprived of all those means which could civilize them, the Indians would remain in the brutish and barbaric subjection under which they are kept until now. So as to banish this pernicious abuse, *it will be one of the primary concerns of the Directors to establish among their respective settlements the use of the Portuguese language, not allowing in any way the boys and girls attending the schools, and all those Indians that*

are capable of instruction in this matter, to use the language of their
nations or the one called geral, but only Portuguese, such as His
Majesty has recommended in repeated orders, which until
now have not been observed, resulting in total spiritual and
temporal ruin for the State (Art. 6).

Article 7 states that this resolution is the fundamental basis of the
civilizing process being undertaken, ordering the establishment of
public schools in all settlements, one for boys and one for girls, and in
addition providing for support for the schools, for the selection of
male and female teachers and sufficient salaries for the teachers "paid
by the parents of those same Indians, or by the persons under whose
power they live, each one contributing an amount to be determined
either in money or in goods."

The Law of the Directorate established other moral and economic
principles beyond the subject of this study, but it is worth remember-
ing that the Portuguese were prohibited from calling them (i.e., the
Indians) Negroes, "wishing perhaps through the infamy and vileness
of this name to persuade them that nature had destined them to be
slaves of the whites, as is often thought with respect to the blacks of
the African coast." It further ordered that Indians would have access
to honorable employments and that there should be no preference
for whites. It also guaranteed to the Indians the ownership of their
lands, ordered the Directors to extinguish completely "the odious and
abominable distinction" between whites and Indians, and to facilitate
and promote marriage between whites and Indians. In order to facilitate such marriages the Directors were to persuade all white people
that the Indians were not of inferior quality, so much so that His Majesty qualified the Indians for all those honors proper to the levels of
their posts, "consequently those who marry said Indians end up ob-
taining the same privileges."[66]

Through the Writ of Law of 4 April 1755, His Majesty already
had declared that his vassals in Portugal and in America who married
Indian women "would not incur any sort of infamy, rather would
make themselves worthy of My Royal Attention, and in those lands
where they establish themselves they will be given preference for
those places and occupations that befit the rank of such persons, and
their children and dependents will be able and capable for any sort of
work, honor, or dignity."[67]

On 17 August 1759 the king renewed the Law of the Directorate
with a Writ of Confirmation for all of Brazil, therewith marking the
date of the obligatory use of the Portuguese language with all its uni-

fying power, and consequently the progressive abandonment of the língua geral which by 1768 "was already restricted (in São Paulo) to the rural communities deep in the interior."[68]

On 18 May 1759 in Recife, a directive was recorded "provisionally regulating the Indians of the new villages and towns erected in the captaincy of Pernambuco."[69] Section 7 stated that "it shall be one of the principal concerns of the Directors to establish in their respective towns and villages the use of the Portuguese language, not allowing in any way the boys and girls who attend the schools nor any of the Indians . . . to use the language of their own nations or the one called *geral*, but only Portuguese, as His Majesty has recommended in repeated orders which until now have not been observed."

This codification, which was applied throughout all Brazil, was without a doubt one of the most notable administrative acts of the Marquis of Pombal. It succeeded in changing the language of Amazonas, Pará, Maranhão, and São Paulo, where Tupi or the língua geral was common, as well as in other captaincies, as we saw in the case of Pernambuco.

In Rio de Janeiro the order for the execution of the Law of the Directorate and consequently for the imposition of the Portuguese language reached Gomes Freire de Andrade, the Count of Bobadela, on 17 October 1758.[70] At that time his authority extended over the greater portion of Brazil, i.e., Rio de Janeiro, Minas Gerais, São Paulo, Goiás, Mato Grosso, Santa Catarina, Rio Grande do Sul, and Colônia do Sacramento.

Francisco Xavier de Mendonça Furtado and M. João Gomes de Araújo wrote a letter dated 18 March 1767 to the Count da Cunha, Dom António Álvares da Cunha, Viceroy of Brazil (1763–67), concerning the Indians and islanders (of Santa Catarina) who, because they had not observed the laws of His Majesty, were dispersed in the territory of Viamão, in Rio Grande do Sul. The letter stated that "little could be hoped for from the old people, but what the schools have accomplished is that today Portuguese is a familiar language in those settlements."[71]

The Royal Letter of 15 January 1774 abolished the difference between natives and whites, while the Writ of 4 April 1755 had established that Indians could marry whites, and the Writ of 8 May 1758 confirmed that Indians were the masters of their own freedom and property in every way, like those of Maranhão. Thus, conditions were created for the victory of the Portuguese language.

The Writ of 30 September 1770 declared that the correct use of the national language is one of the most noteworthy objectives for the culture of civilized peoples. Learning it by means of principles, and not merely by rote and habit, provides the way to reach its highest degree of enjoyment and perfection. The clarity, energy, and majesty with which laws ought to be established and writings made useful and pleasant depend on the correct use of the national language. The writ asserts that imposing this use on conquered peoples civilizes them and creates in them a love for the princes who have given that language to them.

The language of this writ calls to mind the words of Brandônio in the *Diálogos das Grandezas do Brasil,* written in 1618: "You must know that Brazil is a marketplace of the world, if I do not offend any kingdom or city in giving it such a name; it is at the same time a public academy where one can learn all polity with great facility, a good manner of speaking, honorable terms of courtesy, to learn how to negotiate well, and other attributes of this nature." And further on, responding to Aliviano, who had thought all to be very good speakers, Brandônio said, "So it is, for I already told you that Brazil was an academy wherein one learned good speech." [72]

In spite of the praise uttered by Brandonio in the *Diálogos,* the truth is that as late as December of 1803 the promulgation of a national tongue was far from complete. In that year the magistrate in charge of the judicial district of Porto Seguro, Francisco Dantas Barbosa, wrote in an official letter to the governor of Bahia: "The Indians of the Menhãs nation have shown themselves to have progressed only in the pronunciation of the Portuguese language but otherwise they remain savages." [73]

There were, naturally, those who objected to the Law of the Directorate, especially with respect to the official imposition of the Portuguese language. Dr. Antônio José Pestana da Silva alleged that while the mother country had to impose her own language for peoples to become civilized, she could absolutely not banish the use of the indigenous language of the country. Only by means of the latter could newly converted peoples be instructed and catechized. Only the common vernacular could serve as a vehicle to communicate the knowledge of the truth and the mysteries of the Christian religion, as the Council of Trent recommended and as was the practice of the first apostles. In his opinion, one language or the other should be used, according to the capabilities and intelligence of the listeners. After criticizing the Law of the Directorate, he recommended against its imposition and urged that there should be daily meetings and talks in the língua geral of the Indians. [74]

All this was to no avail. When the Law of the Directorate was abolished by the Royal Letter of 12 May 1798, at the recommendation of the governor of Pará, Dom Francisco Maurício de Sousa Coutinho, the Portuguese language was no longer imposed. Yet it had spread and become adopted in the typically Tupi regions of Brazil. Naturally, in Amazonia, the língua geral continued to persist as the language spoken by large groups, as Lourenço da Silva Araújo e Amazonas asserted in 1852: "Língua geral: the Tupi language, so designated not only in this district but also in all the Province of Pará and even in all of Brazil. The entire indigenous nation that interacts in the settlements speaks it. In the cities it is spoken at home; and in the villages and other settlements, except Pauxis in Lower Amazonas, it is the only language, not because Portuguese is not known but because the mestizos, being ill at ease in speaking it because of the difficulty of forming the verb tenses, which the língua geral dispenses with, respond in the latter when one questions them in the former."[75] The fact remains, however, that it seems most unlikely that large populations and the territories they inhabited would have been integrated into the colony without the provisions of Pombal's laws.

The final victory of the Portuguese language

George Friederici, in his magnificent study entitled *Caráter da Descoberta e Conquista da América pelos Europeus*, summarized the problem of language: "Though Spanish has borrowed a considerable number of words from various native dialects, no indigenous language at any time or in any of the Spanish colonies came to supersede Spanish as the current spoken language."[76]

This statement is equivocal and imprecise. Even today in various Spanish-American countries, the native languages are used by considerable portions of the population and compete with Spanish: in Paraguay, which is bilingual; Bolivia, which has an indigenous population larger than the white Spanish population; Ecuador, 40 to 50 percent of whose populace speaks indigenous languages; Guatemala, whose population is one-third indigenous; Mexico, with a significant indigenous portion; and Peru with a population one-third indigenous. Similarly, Argentina, Canada, Colombia, Costa Rica, Chile, El Salvador, the United States, the Guianas, Honduras, Nicaragua, Panama, and Venezuela all have small indigenous populations like Brazil, with their own varied languages.

Friederici further stated that in Brazil there existed a quite different situation, wherein during the first century of colonization, when the Indians were very numerous in the coastal region and many colonists lived there with their native wives on the land grants, Tupi was spoken as widely as Portuguese. We have seen that there was an indigenous predominance, and we know that the colonists and Indian women did not live on land grants, which were large gifts of land normally given to the Portuguese lesser nobility or to colonists.

He then added that "in the seventeenth century, Vieira relates that the elderly remember the time when Portuguese was not more widely spoken than Tupi. Governor Salvador Correia de Sá [e Benevides] in 1660 spoke Tupi fluently and was therefore highly esteemed by the Indians." Further on he pointed out that around 1694, the entire population of São Paulo spoke Tupi at home, the same situation prevailing in Paraná (which came into existence as such only in 1853) and further south to Rio Grande and the environs of the Paraguay River. He said further that at the beginning of the eighteenth century, three-quarters of the Brazilian population still spoke Tupi, which had become the língua geral; only a quarter spoke Portuguese. Everything that we have been discussing, based on the examination of documents, was summarized by Friederici.

He recapitulated that "in the days of the great pioneering expeditions into the interior of Brazil, almost all the backland explorers, slave hunters, and prospectors spoke the língua geral, which at that time dominated the country, and they gave Tupi names to the places they discovered." He failed to cite the great studies by Teodoro Sampaio (*O Tupi na Geografia Nacional*), by Alfredo de Carvalho (*O Tupi na Corografia Pernambucana*), and by Mário Melo (*Toponímia Pernambucana*).[77]

Friederici stated, as we have stressed, that the língua geral was the language of the "bandeiras." To these backland explorers and the mestizos that accompanied them, Brazil owes the major part of her present geographical nomenclature in the interior and also, we must add, on the coast. In the provinces of the north, Maranhão and Pará, Portuguese began to be more widely spoken only in 1755. Until then everyone there spoke only Tupi, including the priests in the churches. Thus, continued Friederici, during three centuries, Portuguese and Tupi, or língua geral, existed side by side in the captaincies of the Brazilian interior, influencing each other reciprocally, fusing together and crossing over into each other. Tupi was the domestic, familiar, and current language of the colonists, and Portuguese was the official language, which children—mestizos and the children of Indians—learned at school but did not speak at home. So explained Friederici; the reality, however, was much more complex, for we must recognize the role of the various indigenous languages and, equally, the African língua franca and the various languages spoken by the Negroes in Brazil. The victory of the Portuguese language occurred only in the second half of the eighteenth century.

At the beginning of the nineteenth century, as I wrote on the subject of speech in the chapter "Economia e Sociedade" in my book *Independência: Revoluçâo e Contra-Revolução*,[78] the language spoken in Brazil was still either very Lusitanized in the white centers of the large coastal cities or suffering from the deficiencies of the oral apprenticeship served by Negroes and Indians. The alternatives were either the pidgin Portuguese of the Negroes and the linguistic miscegenations of the Indian and Negro línguas gerais, or total submission to European Portuguese speech.

In a society divided into castes, races, and classes, in a country like Brazil where for three centuries various indigenous Indian and immigrant African languages battled against a single white language, there could be neither cultural nor linguistic peace even when the process of linguistic unification was evident.

The cultural process that imposed a single victorious language over all the others was neither peaceful nor easy. It cost unprecedented efforts, it cost the blood of rebels, it cost suicides, it cost lives. In São Paulo and Amazonas, where Tupi, the língua geral imposed by the white man, was more commonly spoken than Portuguese even after the middle of the eighteenth century, there still raged during the process of independence a dispute regarding which language would become the national tongue. The matter was grave, and the threat of linguistic fragmentation hovered for more than two and a half centuries. There were peoples who did not understand each other, or understood each other poorly and attempted with gesticulation to make up for their poverty of phrasing, just as Caminha described in the first meeting of white Portuguese and Indians.

The lack of a língua franca was still a privation, an affliction, a permanent anguish, which black slaves, arriving in ever greater numbers, experienced because of their linguistic separation. They suffered in their anticipation of the effort that they would be required to make in order to speak, to express themselves, to reveal themselves. And suffer they did as they endured the transition leading to social communication. Some Africans learned rapidly, others slowly and painfully. All those with low social status—Indians and Negroes—had to learn the Portuguese language to survive. The successful student gained a weapon that ensured military, political, and economic advantage. The value or excellence of the white Western language and culture that were being imposed was not at issue. It was a matter of seeing oneself degraded because one's ties of cultural continuity were broken. As we have seen, the variety of the Indian and Negro tribal groups facilitated the work of the Portuguese, who preferred, as a security measure, to import different dialectal groups, who did not understand one another and had to strive to find in Portuguese the means by which to make known their personal and social needs.

The German traveler C. Schlichthorst, who lived in Brazil between 1824 and 1826, shortly after independence, wrote that there was a Babel of languages in the slave markets and depots of Rio de Janeiro. "Many times I saw it was necessary to employ ten or more interpreters in order to interrogate a Negro about the symptoms of his illness. They say that the language of the Caçanjes, a creole dialect of Portuguese spoken in Angola, is the easiest of all, so that the majority of the merchants and ships' captains who frequent Africa understand it. This is why badly spoken or poorly written Portuguese is called *caçanje*." But the Negroes, added the German officer, "learn Portuguese with great facility. In three months they can, in general, make themselves more or less understood." Schlichthorst observed that "if a young Negro learns any language which he is obligated to speak, in the short period of three to four months, without any method and generally also without being beaten, a German, to whom this or that Latin language is not generally strange, will not require more time to manage Portuguese, which is not distinguished by richness or difficulty of construction or pronunciation . . . . When one knows Latin or even only French, with little practice one can make oneself understood by any Portuguese."[79]

Maria Graham, who was in Brazil between 1821 and 1823, wrote that a Negro she had contracted, the young son of a king in Africa, greatly enjoyed entertaining her by telling her stories of his land. "I greatly regret that his very imperfect knowledge of Portuguese and my complete ignorance of African languages impeded my getting more information from this very intelligent boy."[80] What is surprising in Brazil is that the triumph of linguistic unity was not a work of education but of the efforts of the people, without any official help.

By the nineteenth century Alexander Caldcleugh wrote that it no longer was a crime for Negroes to speak in their native languages. Even so, Carl Seidler, a German officer who was in military service in the era of Dom Pedro I, observed that the slave owners, as soon as they bought their Negroes, saw to it that the slaves "learn Portuguese, which as a rule they manage to do quickly."[81] Thus, even during the reign of Dom Pedro I, after independence was won, the black slaves had to learn Portuguese in order to serve their owners.

The same might be said of the Indians, who suffered terribly because their resistance was greater; they endured a tremendous amount of bloodshed before they were vanquished, which was true also of some Negro groups. They refused to learn anything, and only the ones who lived in villages and the backwoodsmen learned the língua geral and later a little Portuguese. Many groups lived without any language of communication; others who came into contact with the dominating class spoke Portuguese very poorly, though the women didn't speak it at all. Still others only understood it.

Since legislation concerning the Indians, from the fall of Pombal to the fall of Dom Pedro I, was progressively more anti-indigenous, after independence the level of imposition and aggression intensified.[82] Maria Graham, when she visited the Botocudo in September 1823, noted that the Indians there had learned a few Portuguese words, "but that among themselves they spoke their native language, which seemed to be a series of half-articulated sounds."[83]

The war against the Indians and the harsh measures and cruelty used to suppress black rebellions, which stained Brazilian soil even in the nineteenth century, constituted a linguistic and a cultural war, one that promoted a total lack of understanding and a fragmentation of cultures and languages. The situation was even more confused because the Portuguese language of Brazil and that of Portugal were already themselves considerably differentiated.

Independence established the beginning of literary autonomy, and the Portuguese language of Portugal was outmoded, unable to attend to the social demands of Brazilian life-styles. This process was well observed by travelers who made an effort to learn Portuguese and were able to recognize the divergences and even the regional differences. "The Portuguese spoken by Brazilians," observed Caldcleugh, "is easily distinguished from the Portuguese of Portugal. Their way of speaking is much slower, a particular that is noted in all colonies, and can only be attributed to the climate, which saps its inhabitants of liveliness of spirit, of which there is no deficiency in Europe, producing in fact considerable lassitude. Brazilian pronunciation is not as nasal, nor as Judaic in the sound of the s and is altogether a much more pleasant language than that in the mouths of the native Portuguese."[84]

Saint-Hilaire noted that among the men of Minas Gerais the pronunciation of Portuguese took on a gentleness which did not exist in that of the Portuguese of Europe; but in Jacarei (São Paulo) this gentleness turned into softness; the inflections were little varied, and had a certain something that reminded one of the language of the Indians.[85] While traveling through São Paulo he wrote: "Given all that which I've just explained, it should not cause any surprise that the inhabitants of the interior of the province of São Paulo speak and pronounce Portuguese very incorrectly, while those in the interior of Minas Gerais, at least in the eastern part of that province, speak, in general, correctly, and have a pronunciation which differs from that of the European Portuguese only in being more melodious and soft. The Paulistas of the interior, instead of *vossemecê*, a shortening of *vossa mercê*, by which the second person is designated, say *mecê;* their pronunciation is harsh and drawn-out." In Curitiba he did not observe that the inhabitants of the region did not pronounce Portuguese with the alterations that he had noted in the people of the backwoods.[86]

Cunha Matos, a Portuguese who had lived in Africa, pointed out: "The pronunciation of the people of Goiás is very gentle, and notwithstanding their being descendants of Paulistas they do not have that guttural harshness which was noted in the people of São Paulo, nor the feminine affectation of many people from more enlightened provinces."[87] If we do not forget the centuries-old "Tupinization" of São Paulo and its backwardness in the phase of independence, the observation of Cunha Matos is not strange.

Any investigation into the gradual evolution and the causes of the differences in speech in Brazil must take into account the historical factors and the origins of indigenous groups and newcomers alike. Such a study must start from the principle that there never was a cultural peace but a grueling struggle for dominance among all the languages, the indigenous, the African, and Portuguese. And the latter suffered the fragmentation of the different types of speech spoken by the different social groups: i.e., there was the Portuguese held as a model, the Portuguese that expressed varied social experiences and needs, and the Portuguese that had just been learned; in short, a field of daily experience which, if it was not pathological, was at least highly unusual.

Manuel Antônio de Almeida himself, writing in mid-nineteenth century, offers examples of dialogue in his novel that was not the Portuguese spoken thirty years after independence but an attempt to reconstruct its image. He senses the fragmentation, the linguistic division, and when he refers to a practical joker who was the perfect type of rogue, he writes that "he spoke the language of a Negro."[88] Aside from the evident prejudice, the characterization reveals that the Negroes spoke poorly, because most of them were still learning the language.

The real and true victory of Portuguese came only when the representatives of the various Brazilian provinces spoke with one another at the Constituent Assembly of 1823 and noted that though there were differences in pronunciation they were all speaking the same language.[89]

Notes

1. *A Carta de Pero Vaz de Caminha*, ed. Jaime Cortesão (Rio de Janeiro: Livros de Portugal, 1943), pp. 202, 216–17, 220, 238.

2. Pero de Magalhães Gândavo, *História da Província de Santa Cruz* (Rio de Janeiro: Annuario do Brasil, 1912), pp. 124–25.

3. *Diário de Navegação de Pero Lopes de Sousa*, ed. Eugênio de Castro, preface by Capistrano de Abreu (Rio de Janeiro: Comissão Brasileira dos Centenários Portugueses, 1940), p. 210.

4. Manuel da Nóbrega, *Cartas do Brasil, 1549–1560* (Rio de Janeiro: Academia Brasileira de Letras, 1931), p. 73.

5. Ibid., pp. 92–93, 105.

6. Ibid., pp. 141, 145.

7. José de Anchieta, *Arte da Gramática da Língua mais usada na Costa do Brasil* (Coimbra, 1595). There are various editions and translations, including a new facsimile edition (Salvador: Universidade da Bahia, 1980).

8. António Vieira, "Exhortaçam I em vespora do Espirito Santo, na Capella interior do Colegio da Bahia, 1688," in *Sermões do P. António Vieira* (Lisbon, 1690), pp. 514–34.

9. José de Anchieta, letter from São Vicente, 1554, in *Cartas, Informações, Fragmentos Históricos e Sermões, 1554–94* (Rio de Janeiro: Biblioteca Nacional, 1933), pp. 64, 329

10. Ibid., pp. 404, 478

11. *Cartas Avulsas, 1550–1568* (Rio de Janeiro: Academia Brasileira de Letras, 1931), p. 253.

12. Ibid., p. 270.

13. Fernão Cardim, "Do Principio e Origem dos Indios do Brasil e de seus Costumes, adoração e cerimonias," in *Tratado da Terra e da Gente do Brasil* (São Paulo: Companhia Editora Nacional, 1939), pp. 170–81.

14. Ibid., pp. 180–81.

15. Fernão Cardim, "Informação da Missão do P. Christóvão Gouvêa às Partes do Brasil, Ano de 83," in *Tratado da Terra e da Gente do Brasil*, pp. 247–326.

16. Ibid., p. 272.

17. Ibid., pp. 278–79.

18. Gabriel Soares de Sousa, *Tratado Descritivo do Brasil em 1587*, 3d ed. (São Paulo: Companhia Editora Nacional, 1938), pp. 23–24, 33–36, 58.

19. Ibid., pp. 71, 83–84.

20. Ibid., p. 102.

21. Ibid., pp. 110–11.

22. Ibid., pp. 364–65.

23. Ambrósio Fernandes Brandão, *Diálogos das Grandezas do Brasil* (1618) (Rio de Janeiro: Academia Brasileira de Letras, 1930), p. 266.

24. Ibid., p. 289.

25. António Vieira, "Sermão do Espírito Santo," in *Sermões Pregados no Brasil* (Lisbon: Edição Hernani Cidade, 1940), 3: 320.

26. Ibid., p. 331.

27. Ibid., p. 332.

28. Ibid., p. 333.

29. Ibid., p. 378.

30. António Vieira, "Exortação Primeira em Véspora do Espírito Santo Pregado na Capella interior do Colegio em 1688," in *Sermões Pregados no Brasil*, pp. 423–26.

31. Ibid., pp. 426–28.

32. "Carta da Bahia, de 19 de julho de 1693," in *Documentos Históricos, 1692–1712* (Rio de Janeiro: Biblioteca Nacional, 1936), 34: 84–86.

33. "Carta para o sargento-mor do Rio das Caravelas sobre o assalto do gentio barbaro, e intérprete, que procura para o aprisionado de 22 de julho de 1717," in *Documentos Históricos, 1716–1720*, 43: 66–67.

34. Bahia, 12 de junho de 1694, in António Vieira, *Obras Várias* (1856), pp. 239–51.

35. Sérgio Buarque de Holanda, *Raízes do Brasil*, 2d ed. rev. and amplified (Rio de Janeiro: José Olympio, 1948), pp. 179–93.

36. Documento no. 57, "Consulta da Junta das Missões, de 29 de outubro de 1697, sobre as Cartas do Bispo e Governador de Pernambuco," in Ernesto Ennes, *As Guerras dos Palmares* (São Paulo: Companhia Editora Nacional, 1938), pp. 352–53.

37. Manuel da Fonseca, *Vida do Venerável Padre Belchior de Pontes* (Lisbon, 1752; São Paulo: Companhia Melhoramentos, n.d.), pp. 25, 27.

38. Hercules Florence, *Viagem Fluvial do Tiete ao Amazonas, de 1825 a 1829* (São Paulo: Edições Melhoramentos, n.d.), p. 174.

39. Sérgio Buarque de Holanda, pp. 189, 191.

40. "Livro Grosso do Maranhão," in *Anais da Biblioteca Nacional do Rio de Janeiro*, 67: 190–91.

41. João Francisco Lisboa, *Obras* (Lisbon, 1902), p. 223.

42. Artur Cesar Ferreira Reis, "Família Luso-Tupi," *A Manhã*, 18 June 1948.

43. Fernão Cardim, *Tratado da Terra e da Gente do Brasil* (see note 13), pp. 255, 282.

44. Ibid., pp. 289, 292, 294.

45. F. A. Varnhagen, *História Geral do Brasil*, 3d ed. (São Paulo: Melhoramentos, n.d.), 1:281, 282

46. Antonil, *Cultura e Opulência do Brasil por suas drogas e minas* (Lisbon, 1711), notes by J. A. G. de Melo Neto (facsimile ed., Pernambuco, 1969), pp. 22–23.

47. Luís dos Santos Vilhena, *Cartas de Vilhena. Notícias Soteropolitanas e Brasílicas* (Bahia, 1922), vol. 1. Edison Carneiro has prepared a more recent three-volume edition (Bahia, 1969).

48. Pierre Verger, *Flux et Reflux de la Traite de Nègres entre le Golfe de Bénin et Bahia de Todos os Santos du XVII' siècle au XIX' siècle* (Paris: Mouton, 1968).

49. Nina Rodrigues, *Os Africanos no Brasil*, 3d ed. (São Paulo: Companhia Editora Nacional, 1945; 1st ed. 1932), pp. 205–48.

50. Ibid., p. 207.

51. Varnhagen, 1:281 (see note 45).

52. Nina Rodrigues, *Os Africanos*, pp. 205–48.

53. Renato de Mendonça, *A influência africana no português do Brasil* (Porto, 1948); Blaise Cendrars, *Anthologie Nègre* (Paris, 1947).

54. Mendonça, *A influência africana*, pp. 39–54.

55. Ibid., p. 82.

56. Ibid., p. 87.

57. Edison Carneiro, *Ladinos e Crioulos* (Rio de Janeiro: Civilização Brasileira, 1964).

58. Reproduced in the *Jornal do Comércio*, 14 May 1980 in the section entitled "Há 150 anos."

59. George Gardner, *Viagens ao Brasil* (São Paulo: Editora Nacional, 1942), Brasiliana, 223:13.

60. Robert Avé-Lallemant, *Viagem pelo Norte do Brasil no Ano de 1859* (Rio de Janeiro, 1961), pp. 128–29.

61. Ibid., p. 129.

62. Richard F. Burton, *Explorations of the Highlands of Brazil* (1868), trans. as *Viagens ao planalto do Brasil* (São Paulo: Companhia Editora Nacional, 1941), 1: 381.

63. Dom João V to João da Maia da Gama, in *Annaes da Biblioteca e Archivo Público do Pará* (ed. of 1968), pp. 190–91.

64. "Representação dos Moradores do Estado do Maranhão," 12 April 1729, in Melo Moraes, *Corografia histórica, genealógica, nobiliária e política do Império do Brasil* (Rio de Janeiro, 1860), 5: 297–300, especially p. 299.

65. "Diretório, que se deve observar nas povoações dos Indios do Pará e Maranhão em quanto sua Magestade não mandar o contrário," in *Coleção da Legislação Portugueza desde a ultima compilação das Ordenações*, redigida pelo dezembargador Antonio Delgado da Silva, vol. 1750– 62 (Lisbon, 1830), pp. 507–30.

66. Ibid., Articles 10, 17, 81, 82, 84, 87, 88, 89.

67. Ibid., pp. 367–68.

68. Serafim Silva Neto, *Introdução ao Estudo da Língua Portuguesa no Brasil* (Rio de Janeiro: Instituto Nacional do Livro, 1950), p. 68.

69. *Revista do Instituto Histórico e Geográfico Brasileiro* 46(1) (1883): 121–71.

70. *Archivo do Distrito Federal* (January 1896), p. 353, and (January 1897), pp. 36–40.

71. "Relação das instruções e ordens que se expediram ao Conde da

Cunha," *Revista do Instituto Histórico e Geográfico Brasileiro* 35(1) (1872): 217 (see note 69).

72. Brandão, *Diálogos das Grandezas do Brasil*, pp. 142, 264 (see note 23).

73. "Offício do Ouvidor interino de Porto Seguro Francisco Dantas Barbosa para o Governador da Bahia, sobre o estado da civilização dos Índios da sua comarca Porto Seguro, 20 de dezembro de 1803," in *Anais da Biblioteca Nacional do Rio de Janeiro* 37 (1918): 179.

74. Antônio José Pestana da Silva, "Meios de dirigir o governo temporal dos Índios" (1778), in Melo Moraes, *Corografia Histórica*, 5: 122–85.

75. Cited by Silva Neto in *Introdução ao Estudo da Língua Portuguesa*, pp. 76–77.

76. George Friederici, *Caráter da Descoberta e Conquista da América pelos Europeus* (Rio de Janeiro: Instituto Nacional do Livro, 1967), pp. 122–23.

77. Teodoro Sampaio, *O Tupi na Geographia Nacional*, 4th ed. (Salvador, 1955; 1st ed., São Paulo, 1901); Alfredo de Carvalho, *O Tupi na Corografia Pernambucana* (Recife, 1907); Mário Melo, *Toponímia Pernambucana* (Recife, 1931).

78. José Honório Rodrigues, "Economia e Sociedade," in *Independência: Revolução e Contra-Revolução* (Rio de Janeiro: Livraria Francisco Alves, 1976), pp. 156–60.

79. Carl Schlichthorst, *O Rio de Janeiro como é. 1824–1826. Huma vez e nunca mais* (Rio de Janeiro, n.d.), pp. 139–40, 67–68.

80. See "Escorço Biográfico de D. Pedro I," *Anais da Biblioteca Nacional* 60 (1940): 138–39.

81. Alexander Caldcleugh, *Travels in South America, during the years 1819–20–21* (London, 1825), 1: 82; Carl Seidler, *Dez Anos no Brasil* (São Paulo: Livraria Martins, 1941), p. 235.

82. See Carlos de Araújo Moreira Neto, "A Política Indigenista Brasileira durante o século XIX" (Ph.D. diss., Rio Claro, São Paulo, 1971).

83. Maria Graham [Callcott], *Diário de uma viagem ao Brasil* (São Paulo: Companhia Editora Nacional, 1956), p. 333.

84. Caldcleugh, *Travels*, p. 66.

85. Augustin de Saint-Hilaire, *Segunda Viagem do Rio de Janeiro a Minas Gerais e a São Paulo* (1822), 2d ed. (São Paulo: Companhia Editora Nacional, 1938), p. 155.

86. Saint-Hilaire, *Viagem à Comarca de Curitiba* (São Paulo, 1964), p. 120.

87. Cunha Matos, "Corografia Histórica da Província de Goiás," *Revista do Instituto Histórico e Geográfico Brasileiro* 37(1): 213; 38(1) (1875): 5, 311.

88. See chap. 43 of Manuel Antônio de Almeida, *Memórias de um sargento de milícias* (Rio de Janeiro: Instituto Nacional do Livro), p. 262.

89. See José Honório Rodrigues, "A Assembléia e a língua portuguesa," in *A Assembléia Constituinte de 1823* (Petrópolis: Vozes, 1974), pp. 277–78.

An Epic Birth Certificate: Pero Vaz de Caminha's *Carta* to Dom Manuel

Irwin Stern

I

JAIME CORTESÃO has provided an overview of the research which has been carried out on Pero Vaz de Caminha's *Carta do achamento do Brasil,* as well as a detailed summary of Caminha's life.[1] More recently, Adrien Roig has added several other biographical facts.[2] Briefly, Caminha was the son of an *escrivão,*[3] Vasco Fernandes, who later became a treasurer of the kingdom ("recebedor dos dinheiros do ultramar"). Pero Vaz had probably been an escrivão on other Portuguese explorations prior to that of Pedro Álvares Cabral, although no definitive documents attest to this. His significance within Portuguese culture rests with his *Carta* to Dom Manuel from 1500.

Since its rediscovery in 1817, the *Carta* (which I will call the narrative) has been studied as a historical, anthropological, and geographical document, notable for the author's extreme accuracy.[4] It has been considered only superficially as part of the literature that flourished during the epoch of Portuguese expansion. The general comments on the narrative as literature refer to the author's possession of a "humanistic knowledge," i.e., the influence of Petrarch, Plutarch, and Quintilian, with little specificity. In this brief study I will attempt to shed light on Caminha's cultural background as revealed through analysis of the narrative. Such an analysis may further clarify the breadth and depth of the knowledge of a late medieval/early Renaissance *escrivão a bordo.*[5]

II

The inherent literary value of the narrative is attributable to Caminha's vision and understanding of the event in which he was participating.[6] In the presentation of the event, he was influenced by his awareness of two major literary sources of the Middle Ages—the Bible and the epic narrative form.

As an educated Portuguese Catholic, Caminha was no doubt well acquainted with the Bible. The narrative reflects this religious background as well as the religious aims of the explorations. Caminha evaluates the natives' qualities and encourages the king to proselytize them.[7] He states that since they have no apparent religion, proselytization would be extremely simple. He describes the natives at Easter Mass comprehending the relationship of the altar to heaven (139). Specific biblical echoes can be seen in the relation of the events of nine days, reminding one of the seven days of creation. Each day's encounters supposedly brought forth new understandings between the natives and the Portuguese. Caminha's descriptions of the close of each day's activities are as simple and as brief as those contained in Genesis.[8] The idea that the Portuguese had discovered some sort of Garden of Eden is also implied in the narrative. The constant references to the extreme beauty of the area, the abundance of food, the innocence of the inhabitants, especially their unabashed nudity (which so shocks Caminha), could have been inspired by the story of Adam and Eve. Caminha, in fact, states, "asy S^{or} que ajnocẽ/cia desta jemte he tal que a dadam nõ seria majs quanta em vergonha" (171). The only other religious reference is the surprising comparison of the state of an old native's body to that of Saint Sebastian (137), which indicates the author's knowledge of the iconography of the medieval lives of saints.

The predominant epic tone and influences apparent in the narrative probably result from Caminha's familiarity with the prose translations of episodes of the *Iliad* and the *Aeneid* that circulated in Europe during the late Middle Ages.[9] Caminha was also probably acquainted with the heroic poetry written in commemoration of the Portuguese conquests during the fifteenth century and with medieval novels of chivalry, both of which reveal epic qualities. In his use of an epic orientation, Caminha follows a pattern set in Portuguese prose by Fernão Lopes.[10]

The *Carta* presents two conditions that often appear in epic accounts: it presents facts that Caminha saw and in which he participated, and it belongs to the oral tradition because it was to be read to

Dom Manuel.[11] Epic literary devices appear throughout. The narrative begins with a proposition, followed vaguely by an invocation and a dedication, which includes a very humble *captata benevolentia:*

> Sñor—
> posto queo capitam moor desta vossa frota e asy os outros
> capitaães screpuam avossa alteza anova do acha mento desta
> vossa terra noua que se ora neesta naue gaçam achou. nom
> leixarey tam bem de dar disso minha comta avossa alteza asi
> como eu milhor poder ajmda que perao bem contar e falar o
> saiba pior que todos fazer./pero tome vossa alteza minha in-
> oramçia por boa vomtade, aqual bem çerto crea q̄ por af-
> remosentar nem afear aja aquy de poer ma is caaquilo que
> vy e me pareçeo. (123)

The body of the narrative is a series of short episodes together with many descriptions of the land and its inhabitants. The presentation of many of these episodes assumes epic structures. For example, there are councils of the captains to determine the actions of the Portuguese (125, 143). The second council may be considered the epic climax, for it is here that a decision is made to leave behind two *degredados* to learn the ways of the natives.

The epic catalogue was a means of honoring all those who participated in an event. Thus, similar to the catalogue of the ships in the *Iliad* are the two brief catalogues that Caminha presents regarding the captains of the fleet (129–31, 165). Minute, repetitious descriptions of the people, places, and things are recurrent in the epic, as well as a necessary requirement for an efficient chronicler.[12] Caminha's narrative is replete with repetitions of the descriptions of both the natives and the landscapes. In a dozen descriptions of the Indians, Caminha discusses the color of their skin, their pierced lips, their bows and arrows, and their highly praised *vergonhas*.[13] There are also seven descriptions of the land itself in which the abundance of water is almost always pointed out.[14] It is through these repetitions that *ufania,* the pride and glory in the discovery, takes shape. This ufania, this amazement with the new land, became the major theme of later chroniclers and commentators on Brazil: Brandão, Frei Vicente de Salvador, Botelho de Oliveira, Rocha Pita, and the Brazilian writers.

Caminha's Indian is an emotionally and psychologically pure being; the adjective *inocente,* with all its possible connotations, is the one he most frequently applied to them. He considered them extremely friendly, well-built, almost like children in their attitude toward the newcomers, and with rather extraordinary "bird-like" sanitary habits. In his descriptions of the land, he constantly uses the words *muito,* or *mui* and *grande,* or others which express size. This usage is most noticeable in the final description (italics mine):

> Esta trra S^{or} me pareçe que dapomta q̃ mais cont^a osul vimos ataa out^a pomta que cont^a onorte vem de que nos deste porto ouuvemos vista./sera *tamanha* que auera neela bem xx ou xxb legoas per cota./traz ao lomgo do mar em algũas partes *grandes* bareiras delas vermelhas e delas bramcas e a terra per cima toda chaã e *mujto* chea de *grandes* aruoredos./ depomta apomta he toda praya parma *mujto* chaã e *mujto* fremosa.
>
> pelo sartaão nos pareceo do mar *mujto grande* por que aestender olhos nõ podiamos veer se nõ tera earuoredos que nos pareçia *muy longa* tera. (173)

He uses the same modifiers to describe the intensity of the winds and the abundance of water.

Perhaps the most widely known and discussed facet of the epic form is its hero. Caminha's *Carta* presents no figure with the qualities required of a classical epic hero.[15] Indeed, his characterization of the Portuguese voyagers is extremely limited. Although Caminha views the new discovery as a collective effort, the figure of Pedro Álvares Cabral is highlighted. His distinction rests with his passive presence. Neither his authority nor his wisdom is discussed by Caminha. Cabral does not take an active part in the relationship with the natives; he only gives orders (the verb *mandar* is most often used with his name), directs the meetings of the captains, and makes plans for the Portuguese. Dom Manuel, to whom the narrative is directed, is present as a guiding spirit; Caminha always addresses him as *Vossa Alteza,* although several times throughout the narrative he does use the word *Senhor,* with a capital *S.*

The degredado Afonso Ribeiro appears as the only other barely developed character. We never discover why he is a degredado, but, surely owing to his extreme intelligence, he is one of the men left behind to learn the language of the natives, to study their habits, and to begin their religious indoctrination. The popular idea that the degredado was the first to be "sacrificed" would not fit with Caminha's idealistic view of the natives. He views Ribeiro's duty as more of an honor than the do-or-die obligation of a sentenced man. Caminha worries, needlessly he decides, about the treatment the Portuguese will receive from the Indians.[16]

III

To place Pero Vaz de Caminha's *Carta* within the literary perspective of his epoch, it has been necessary to consider him as a direct descendant of Fernão Lopes's epic orientation toward Portuguese history. Fernão Lopes's chronicles, similar to the *Iliad,* are based on secondary sources; although Homer almost never comments in the first person on events, Fernão Lopes repeatedly makes judgments about personalities and happenings. Pero Vaz is an eye-witness narrator; thus his perspective is unique and allows him to interpret words and signs of the native that he does not really understand, and to offer quite freely his opinions about the circumstances.[17] No other chronicler or escrivão a bordo of the fifteenth century takes an epic view of the events he narrates. We might compare the dry, factual prose of Zurara's *Crónica da Tomada de Ceuta* (1450), or the equally uninspired *Roteiro da Viagem de Vasco da Gama,* by its supposed author Álvaro Velho, which is one of the few other surviving contemporaneous documents.

Further, we might justly evaluate the *Carta* in light of Garcia de Resende's *Cancioneiro Geral* (1516) and Gil Vicente's theatre. Resende's prologue laments the inability or failure of the Portuguese to set their achievements to paper in a manner befitting their significance.[18] As if in support of this statement, the *Cancioneiro Geral* contains only one poem, "De luys Anriquez ao duque de Bragança quando tomou azamor em q̃ conta como foy,"[19] which approximates the epic or heroic style of poetry. It shares the biblical and epic references of Caminha's narrative as well as the authorial stance within the oral tradition. Anriquez's descriptions of the preparations and the battle are rather bland and barely poetic. Gil Vicente's tragicomedy *Exortação da Guerra* (1514) also treats this same 1513 expedition with both epic and religious inspiration. In addition, Vicente censures the commercial aims and profit motive of the explorations,[20] which also received Caminha's rather noncommittal attention (131, 132, 135, 173).

Thus, Caminha's *Carta* is *the* striking prose narrative of its time. Although an explicit literary intention was probably of secondary or even doubtful interest to the author, thematically and technically the *Carta* expresses the prime literary concerns of the epoch. Through the *Carta,* Caminha reveals his own cultural background, that required of an escrivão a bordo, and also suggests the Portuguese Renaissance mentality that would lead to Camões's *Os Lusíadas.* Rather than describe battle or conquest, Caminha relates a discovery, which he himself attempts to comprehend. He confronts the Old World with the New World. His astonishment forces him to describe the new land through his knowledge of Portugal and to extol the former's superiority. The climate of the new land and the homes of the natives surprisingly remind him of his own Entre Douro e Minho (156, 173). The trees and birds are similar to those in Portugal but bigger and with a greater number of species. Caminha is also enthusiastic about the natives' rejection of the foods of the Old World and their preference for a natural diet of fruits and seeds, which makes them "taaes e tam rrijos e tã nedeos. queo nõ somosnos tamto com quanto trigo e legumes comemos" (165).[21]

I believe that it would be just to say that Caminha planted a seed with his *Carta*. This seed would grow throughout the sixteenth century in the chronicles, *cartas,* and *roteiros* about the new Portuguese territories. Some of these would share Caminha's epic view and his sincerity about the Portuguese aims, while others would reflect complete cynicism. All, however, would blossom into Camões's *Os Lusíadas*.

Notes

1. Jaime Cortesão, *A Carta de Pero Vaz de Caminha*, 2d ed. (Lisbon: Portugália Editora, 1969; 1st ed., 1943).

2. Adrien Roig, "La biographie de Pero Vaz de Caminha d'après de nouveaux documents," *Arquivos do Centro Cultural Português* 10 (1976): 449–92.

3. For an explanation of the different types of escrivães, see the articles by Rui d'Abreu Torres in *Dicionário de História de Portugal,* ed. Joel Serrão (Lisbon: Iniciativas Editoriais, 1970), 2: 84–86.

4. The most interesting exception is the philological study of the narrative by João Ribeiro, "A Carta de Vaz de Caminha," in *O Fabordão,* 2d ed. (Rio de Janeiro: São José, 1964), pp. 227–73. See also António Baião, *Os sete únicos documentos de 1500, conservados em Lisboa, referentes à viagem de Pedro Álvares Cabral* (Lisbon: Agência Geral das Colónias, 1940), p. 64. Jaime Cortesão cites and summarizes an interesting article by Pedro Calmon, "A Carta de Caminha," *A Noite* (Rio de Janeiro), 26 September 1942, which I was unable to locate.

5. For information on the cultural background of the Portuguese chroniclers, see summary of Calmon, "A Carta de Caminha," in *Cortesão,* p. 69; António José Saraiva, *Fernão Lopes,* 2d ed. (Lisbon: Publicações Europa-America, 1965), pp. 14–15; Joaquim de Carvalho, "Sobre a erudição de Gomes Eannes de Zurara," *Estudos sobre a Cultura Portuguesa do século XV* (Coimbra: Por ordem da Universidade, 1949), 1: 1–241.

6. See Manuel Rodrigues Lapa, "Fernão Lopes e os cronistas," *Lições de Literatura Portuguesa: Época Medieval*, 6th ed. (Coimbra: Coimbra Editora, Limitada, 1966), pp. 351–407.

7. Pedro Vaz de Caminha, *Carta a El-Rei D. Manuel*, in *Vocabulário da Carta de Pedro Vaz de Caminha* (Rio de Janeiro: Instituto Nacional do Livro, 1964), pp. 163, 167–69. Other references, where feasible, will appear in the text.

8. Ibid., pp. 125, 133, 138, 151, 155, 159, 161, 165–67. For another perspective on the religious tone of the *Carta* see Margarida Barradas de Carvalho, "L'idéologie religieuse dans la 'Carta' de Pero Vaz de Caminha," *Bulletin des études portugaises*, new series 22 (1959–60): 21–29.

9. The earliest prose translations of the *Iliad* into Portuguese that I have been able to verify were done after 1450 and may have been in the Royal Library. Carolina Michaëlis de Vasconcelos notes that the legend of Troy was popular during the Middle Ages; see *Notas Vicentinas* (Lisbon: Edição da Revista de Ocidente, 1947), 4: 348.

10. A close study of Fernão Lopes's chronicles, principally *D. João I*, reveals that he was quite aware of the epic tradition and influenced by it. See António José Saraiva and Oscar Lopes, *História da Literatura Portuguesa* (Porto: Porto Editora, n.d.), pp. 105–21.

11. Cecil M. Bowra, *Tradition and Design in the Iliad* (Oxford: The Clarendon Press, 1930).

12. Ibid., p. 67.

13. Caminha, pp. 123–25, 129, 135, 137, 141, 145, 147, 151, 153, 163.

14. Ibid., pp. 123–25, 127, 137, 141, 155, 171, 173.

15. Cecil Bowra, *Heroic Poetry* (London: Macmillan, 1952), p. 2.

16. Caminha, pp. 125, 131, 134, 139, 145, 149, 153, 155, 163, 167.

17. Ibid., pp. 129, 131, 169, etc.

18. See "Prologuo de Garçia de Resende," in *Cancioneiro Geral*, Lisbon, 1516 (Lisbon: Livros do Brasil, 1973), 1: 1.

19. Ibid., 3: fols. 104–5.

20. In *Obras Completas de Gil Vicente*, ed. Marques Braga (Lisbon: Sá da Costa Editora, 1953), 4: 148, 154.

21. See also Caminha, p. 131.

"Estes Têm Alma Como Nós?" Manuel da Nóbrega's View of the Brazilian Indians

Fred Gillette Sturm

WHEN Luís de Camões left Goa to assume his new assignment in Macao, Padre Manuel da Nóbrega was engaged in writing his well-known *Diálogo Sôbre a Conversão do Gentio.*[1] The year was 1557. Nóbrega had come to Brazil nine years earlier in the company of Thomé de Souza, the first governor-general of all Brazil, to direct the work of Jesuit missions among the Brazilian Indians. At that time the Portuguese crown had made clear that priority was to be given Christian missions in the work of colonization of the New World: "Take good care of the Indians, because the principal reason for populating Brazil is to bring the *gentio* to the Catholic faith . . . to attract them to peace for the sake of the propagation of the Faith and the increase of settlement and commerce."[2] In the papal bull "Sublimis Deus" of 1537, Paul II had condemned the ill treatment—"como animais brutos"—to the point of severe oppression which had been visited upon the indigenous people of the Americas by Spanish conquistadores and colonists, declaring that "those same Indians, as true humans, are not only capable of Faith in Christ, but even eager for it," and decreeing that the Indians should not be deprived of their liberty or their goods and should not be reduced to slavery.[3] In light of the royal *regulamento* and the papal bull, the question of the humanity of the Indians and their rights under natural law should not have been raised by the Portuguese settlers and missionaries in Brazil. The appearance of Nóbrega's *Diálogo* demonstrates, however, that even among the Jesuits there had arisen doubts about whether the inhabitants of this "New World" did in fact possess a human nature. At the same time,

72

contrary to the expressed command of the papacy, Portuguese colonists, and even some of the missionaries,[4] were taking Indians as slaves, a practice which Nóbrega opposed and which he was to address vehemently ten years after the appearance of the *Diálogo*. The *Diálogo* itself was not concerned with slavery, except for indirect references, but was written to clarify a different problem closely related to the question of the nature of the Indians, namely, whether the Brazilian Indians were sufficiently human to possess the capacity for genuine conversion to the Christian faith.

The central question appears halfway through the *Diálogo:* "Estes têm alma como nós?" Were the reply in the negative, the mission would be futile, but there would no longer be either legal or moral strictures against the exploitation of the Indians, including total enslavement, and the expropriation of their land and resources. There is no evidence that the doubts being expressed by some of Nóbrega's fellow Jesuits had been initiated or encouraged by colonists eager to be freed from restraints imposed by state and church that impeded their exploitation of the native population. It is fairly clear that the doubts concerning the humanity of the Brazilian Indians were experientially based, growing out of an increasing sense of frustration and futility as hopes for the rapid and successful evangelization of Brazil's native population began to fade. Nóbrega's *Diálogo* demonstrates these feelings. The two participants are both affiliated with the Jesuit mission, and the focus of their discourse is, as the title indicates, the problems associated with the conversion of the gentios, these newly discovered "gentiles" or "pagans."

In the *Diálogo*, Nóbrega's own viewpoint seems to be mediated through the remarks of one of the participants, Mateus Nogueira. He was an ex-soldier, a veteran of the North African wars and, later, of military service in the Captaincy of Espírito Santo. He had entered the service of the Company of Jesus, serving as a blacksmith.[5] The doubts and concerns of the Jesuit fathers that had prompted Nóbrega to write the *Diálogo* are expressed through the words of Brother Gonçalo Álvares. Serafim Leite, the renowned historian of the Society of Jesus in Brazil, notes that although the name Gonçalo Álvares does appear in two letters of the period, along with mention of his linguistic skill in having acquired fluency in the Tupi language, there is no mention of him in any of the official documents of the company.[6] Leite concludes that "one cannot give the title of 'Brother' to Gonçalo Álvares," since he apparently was a layman who served as a kind of "curador dos Índios." In a brief introductory paragraph Nóbrega characterizes the two interlocutors as "my Brother Gonçalo Álvares, to whom God gave the grace and talent to be a trumpet of his word in the Captaincy of Espírito Santo, and . . . my Brother Mateus Nogueira, blacksmith for Jesus Christ, who, although he doesn't preach with words, does so with works and hammerblows" (73).

The dialogue opens with the entrance of Gonçalo Álvares, presumably into Mateus Nogueira's blacksmith shop. He is described as having been nettled by the "Negros do Gato"[7] and despondent about the prospects of their conversion. "I've had it!" he begins. The Negros do Gato are so bestial that nothing divine can enter their hearts. They are bloodthirsty, happiest when they are killing and eating other persons. Preaching the gospel to them is no different from preaching to the stones in a desert. The response by Mateus Nogueira to this outburst expresses a prevalent diagnosis of the problem: "If they had a king, they could be converted" (74). The implication, and it is very important to the argument of the *Diálogo,* is that the social conditions are lacking that would provide the necessary context for successful communication of the gospel. The difficulty is not with the people's inherent nature, then, but rather with the level of their sociocultural development. Although Gonçalo Álvares replies, "Well said!" he obviously misses the point. He proceeds to talk about the rapid spread of Christianity during the days described in the Book of Acts and the early years of the Church during which whole cities and kingdoms were converted. This rapid evangelization was possible, he claimed, "because they were people of judgment" (75). The point he is making is clear: the Brazilian Indians are not people of judgment. It is the possession of reason that has led humans, despite the corruption of that reason in the Fall, to create social and political institutions and to be receptive to rational persuasion. The Indians did not live in cities, had not developed complex political and social structures, and were not receptive to the persuasive powers of Jesuit missionaries. Therefore, they lacked the rational nature that is characteristic of the rest of humanity.

On the surface Mateus Nogueira's response seems to be sympathetic to this analysis. Referring to Matthew 7:6 he suggests that these, more than any others, are the insensitive people about whom Jesus was talking:[8] "We see that they are dogs in eating and killing, and hogs in their vices and manner of living." However, he continues with an indirect criticism of the missionaries. "Some Fathers," he notes, "become ill trying to convert all 'Brazil' in an hour and finding that they cannot convert even one in a year because of their rusticity and bestiality" (75). He agrees, then, that the level of cultural attainment is extremely low and that the customary behavior patterns are "bestial."

But once again he insists that this does not indicate that the Brazilian Indians lack the inherent capacity for rationality and conversion. The difficulty may lie in the impatience of those who have been sent for the purpose of civilizing and Christianizing them.

Gonçalo Álvares reveals that his arrival on the field has been recent, an indication, perhaps, that it was the newer members of the company who were questioning the classification of the native population as human. Does Mateus Nogueira, who has been living and working with the natives for several years, view them as "neighbors"? "I've heard from well-informed people," Gonçalo Álvares says, "that these are not 'neighbors,' and they argue strongly that these are not humans like us." "Well," Mateus Nogueira responds, "if they aren't human, they aren't 'neighbors'." Nonetheless, he has taken them to be his "neighbors" in his daily contact with them (81–82).

Gonçalo Álvares next quizzes Mateus Nogueira about what the Jesuit Brothers say concerning the task of converting the Indians. The response is that they are determined to die in the attempt because of their vows of obedience but that some see little hope of accomplishing the task given the rusticity of their charges. This conclusion is based on their belief that "to become Christian one needs a good understanding . . . which these people lack," whereas these pagans are extremely vicious, lack rational judgment, and are cut off by nature from the faith (83). Only direct intervention by God could possibly open them to the gospel. Gonçalo Álvares is convinced that these are good reasons for not expecting results, but he asks whether "there aren't any among my Brothers and Fathers who take the side of those negroes." The reply is interesting: they *all* take the side of the Indians, not because they are confident that the Indians are human but rather because "all desire to convert them," given their orders which have placed them in the new world (83).

At this point in the *Diálogo*, the subject of conversation seems to shift rather abruptly to the question of forcible conversion. It is apparent from this that some of Nóbrega's colleagues who despaired of persuading the Indians of the truth of the gospel had begun to advocate the use of force to "Christianize" these less-than-human pagans. It is not stated explicitly, yet Mateus Nogueira suddenly asks whether anything is to be gained through forcing the Indians to become Christian. They would remain gentios or pagans in their "life, customs, and will"(85). Gonçalo Álvares's response expresses what must have been a common rationale in defense of forcible conversion: little would be gained if one refers only to the present generation of adults, but there would be hope of civilizing the behavior of their children and grandchildren (85). Later he seems to question this rationale, however, insisting that the former king, Dom Manuel, was mistaken when, after the massacre of 1506, he forced the Jews to become Christians (87). Indeed, he notes that there is an inconsistency in the reasoning. If persuasion cannot succeed because of the lack of rational ability on the part of the Indians, there seem to be no grounds for believing that the children and grandchildren of these same Indians can be nurtured in the faith.

It is at this juncture that Nóbrega makes his basic statement about the nature of the Brazilian Indians through the words attributed to Mateus Nogueira: "Imagine all the souls of human beings as being composed of one and the same metal, made in the image of God, capable of glory and created by it. In the presence of God the soul of the Pope would be of equal value with the soul of your Papaná slave" (88). He evokes the response that articulates the underlying topic of the dialogue: "Estes têm alma como nós?" (88). The answer is unambiguous: "That is clear, since the soul has three powers: understanding, memory, will—which all possess" (89). Mateus Nogueira continues: "After Adam sinned . . .he became similar to the beast, so that all of us, both Portuguese and Spaniards, along with Tamoios and Aimorés are similar to beasts through a corrupt nature, and in this all of us are equal" (89–90). The full impact of the statement becomes clear when the reader learns that there is a significant difference between the two indigenous peoples mentioned. The Aimorés are non-Tupi-speakers who were considered by the Tupi-speaking Tamoios to be savage barbarians. There is considerable irony in this declaration!

If this be the case, Gonçalo Álvares replies, that all of us possess the same kind of soul and are, by virtue of the Fall, bestial by nature, so that apart from saving grace we are all one, how can it be explained that other pagans have developed sophisticated cultures, while the Indians have remained so patently bestial (91)? Mateus Nogueira, while admitting that this is a good question, nonetheless suggests that there is a clear answer, namely that every pagan culture has manifested a certain level of bestiality, including the Jews themselves, "who were the people possessing the highest degree of reason in the world." "If you want to compare point to point, blindness to blindness, bestiality to bestiality," Mateus Nogueira continues, "then you will find that all have the same trappings, which stems from the same blindness . . ." (92). This does not satisfy Gonçalo Álvares, who wants to know why the other pagans have become more polished, with a knowledge of how to read and write, capable of doing philosophy and inventing sciences, whereas the Indians "never know more than how to walk around nude and make arrows" (93).

Mateus Nogueira returns to his central contention, the necessity of distinguishing between nature and nurture. The Indians do not differ essentially from other humans. The difference lies rather in the social milieux. "The Romans and other pagans," he says, "had more political organization than these people, which did not lead them to possess a better understanding, but to have a better upbringing. They were brought up more politically" (93). He still fails to satisfy Gonçalo Álvares, who demands to know why the Brazilian Indians have chanced to have a worse upbringing; why nature has not provided them with a similar penchant for political organization (93). Mateus Nogueira responds with reference to the biblical account of Noah and his three sons, a passage that has been used traditionally not only to explain ethnic and racial differences but also to justify enslavement of certain peoples by others. "We believe these to be the descendants of Ham," says Mateus Nogueira, while the other pagans trace their ancestry to Shem and Japheth (94). It will be recalled that Shem and Japheth received Noah's blessing, but the son of Ham, Canaan, was subject to the curse of being a "slave of slaves" to the others. Nogueira proceeds to insist, however, that all descendants of Noah possess the same kind of soul along with the power of understanding. The contrast between societies with advanced political structures and people with simpler social units is traced back to the differences between Cain and Abel, between Isaac and Ishmael. In each case there are two brothers with the same natural ability to reason, but the uses to which reasoning is put differ radically according to the environment. "Even though they have different upbringing, both have a natural understanding exercised according to their upbringing," (94) he insists.

The *Diálogo* ends with Mateus Nogueira interweaving two separate arguments on behalf of the Indians of Brazil. In the first place he argues that a distinction must be made between individuals of genius within a given society and the general level of ability and accomplishment achieved by the population of that society considered as a whole. The philosophic and scientific achievements associated with the Greeks, the Romans, and the Europeans were accomplished by a tiny elite, recipients of a "special grace given by God" (94). It must be noted that there are individuals within Indian societies who are outstanding also, recipients themselves of a special divine grace. In a moving passage, we are presented with a roll-call of Brazilian Indians who became willing martyrs to the faith, this despite the failure of the Jesuit missioners to exhibit the traits deemed necessary for successful evangelization, namely, acquaintance with the indigenous languages, comprehension of indigenous cultures, ability to work miracles, confidence in God, and charity (97–100). "Yet we have seen Indians," he declares, "who have given clear signs of having true faith in their hearts" (97). It is important to note that the martyrs cited represent distinct societies along the coast.[9]

The objection might be raised that the examples of individuals who exhibited an extraordinary degree of rationality are European, whereas the examples of outstanding tenacity of faith are Brazilian Indians. This view leads to the second argument: It is easier to communicate the gospel to someone who is naïve and ignorant than to someone who is highly intelligent and proud. Indeed, many of the articles of faith—the Trinity, the Incarnation, the mystery of the Sacraments—cannot be proved by demonstrative reason; they are beyond the ken of human rationality (95). In a delightful passage Mateus Nogueira compares the "evil" that must be overcome in a typical Indian with the "evil" that poses the challenge in a Roman philosopher (101). The former does not follow the precepts of natural law, taking pleasure in such an unhuman practice as cannibalism. The latter also does not keep the precepts of natural law, although he understands them. Very wise, he is also very vain. He is concerned with his own reputation and well-being, and this concern leads him to "hide the truth God taught him" (101). The task of the evangelist will vary depending on which type of pagan he is trying to convert. In the case of the Brazilian Indians, it will be necessary to provide means of comprehending natural law; in the case of the philosopher the corrupting influence of prideful rationalization must be vanquished. Gonçalo Álvares responds to the question about which of the two would pose the more difficult challenge to an evangelist, saying that there seems to be no real choice between the two, although he confesses that the matter remains unclear in his own mind (102). Mateus Nogueira concludes the conversation by insisting that the case is clearly and adequately stated in what has been said already in the dialogue (102).

Nóbrega's view of the nature of the Brazilian Indian is clearly articulated in the *Diálogo*. That nature is, in his opinion, decidedly human. It does not differ *essentially* from Portuguese nature or European nature in general. The Indian has a soul, made in the image of God, the same image in which the Portuguese soul has been made. The ability to reason is present, although contrasts in environment and historical development have resulted in a wide divergence as far as directions taken and levels of attainment of that rationality are concerned. If there has been a peculiar difficulty in effecting large-scale and lasting conversion of the peoples of the New World, the reasons should be sought not in the lack of capacity on the part of the Indians of Brazil to comprehend the gospel and respond to rational persuasion but rather in the attitudes and practices of the missionaries themselves. Through Mateus Nogueira he notes that "up until now the Indians haven't been able to see the difference between the Fathers and the other Christians" (97). To Gonçalo Álvares, who seems to personify the missionary community in general, Mateus Nogueira remarks that "yesterday you asked him [the Indian] to provide his son to be a slave, and on this other day you look about for ways to deceive them. They have good reason to fear that you intend to deceive them since this is how the 'bad Christians' commonly treat them" (96).

Nóbrega's stance regarding the right of the Portuguese to enslave these fellow human beings remains ambiguous in the *Diálogo*. When Mateus Nogueira referred to the curse of Noah against the son of Ham and declared that "we believe these to be descendants of Canaan," was he voicing Nóbrega's own understanding or merely articulating the commonly held view that the "primitive peoples" of the world are intended to perform menial tasks for the more developed peoples? We have to wait ten years for the full answer.[10] In 1567, the same year that Camões left Asia to return home, Nóbrega wrote a second essay in which the issue of slavery is treated directly.[11] The crown of Portugal was disturbed at reports of abuses in the treatment of the Indians, especially regarding their enslavement. It was revealed that many were being sold into slavery by persons falsely claiming to be their parents. Nóbrega was unable to participate in the consultation ordered by the king to make recommendations to the Mesa de Consciência e Ordens concerning the matter. The result of the consultation was a decree from the Mesa to the effect that, except for capture in a just war, an Indian could not be taken into slavery unless his parents sold him because of extreme or great necessity or, as an adult over twenty years of age, he sold himself. Both Quirício Caxa, professor of moral theology at the Colégio da Baía, and Nóbrega were asked to comment on the decree. Caxa agreed fully with the terms of the decree, specifying that the use of the word "great" extended the range of circumstances within which parents could legally sell children into slavery. Nóbrega reacted negatively.

In addressing himself to the legitimacy of parental sale of children, Nóbrega insisted that it could be justified only in instances of *extreme* necessity. If the Mesa used the word "great," then it could be interpreted only as a synonym of "extreme," and not as an extension of circumstances.[12] In the course of his *quid iuris* argument, Nóbrega cited Gregory's *De Iustitia et Iure: "contra naturam est homines hominibus dominari."* In the following paragraph he then dealt with the question of how to interpret Genesis 9:25–27, the account of Noah's blessing and curse on his three sons, as well as Genesis 27:37–40, where Isaac informs Esau that he has been given to his brother Jacob as a servant. The biblical text, he declared, "does not speak of slaves in the way we do." [13] He added: "it would be a great absurdity to say that the entire generation of Ham are slaves to other generations *iure perpetuo*." [14]

In his *quid facti* argument, citing a particular case in which the Potiguares Indians faced a situation of famine not brought on by any intervention from outside, he admitted that the sale of their children in order to obtain food was legitimate. This was a clear instance of "extreme" necessity. [15] Such cases are rare, however. He insisted that he never had witnessed an instance in which a genuine parent freely offered his own child for sale. It was only out of fear of consequences that Indian parents agreed to sell their own children. There was no evidence that, prior to Portuguese settlement, the Brazilian Indians were accustomed to selling members of their family into slavery. The practice is contrary to the law of natural reason, which decrees parental love for children. Nóbrega strongly urged the crown to prevent the introduction of a practice into Brazil that ran counter to natural law as well as to the traditional customs of the indigenous population. [16]

In his refutation of the decree permitting an adult to sell himself into slavery, Nóbrega makes very clear his position concerning the full and equal status of the Brazilian Indians as humans. His argument is based on an appeal to natural law. By such an appeal Nóbrega equates the Brazilian Indians, on whose behalf he is arguing, with all other human beings. The liberty of an individual human being is given in natural law. It cannot be removed through tyranny or deceit, but only when reason, founded on natural law, permits. [17] The only instance in which this could occur would be one in which there is a conflict between the natural law of self-preservation and the natural law of the conservation of individual freedom. This represented the "extreme necessity" that Nóbrega was willing to recognize as legitimizing the sale of children into slavery. [18] The vast majority of cases of enslavement of Brazilian Indians are condemned as illegitimate in a series of corollaries appended to the argument.

Throughout this second essay, Nóbrega interprets the Indians as being fully human. Whether he accepted the theory that they were descended from Ham and Canaan, he rejects in straightforward manner the notion that they are inferior in any way. They have the same right to life and liberty that natural law gives to humanity in general. It is their life-style that is deplorable. Nomadism does not provide the stable environment within which learning, conversion, and nurture in the faith can flourish. Therefore he favored the establishment of villages and schools for the settlement of the Indians and the full development of their human potential. He was disturbed, as well, by cannibalism and other practices that involved violence against other humans, and he recommended that measures be taken to dissuade Brazilian Indians from pursuing such inhumane customs, which flew in the face of natural law.

The composition of the two essays demonstrates that Nóbrega was in the minority among among the Portuguese in the New World concerning these matters. Colleagues either denied that the Brazilian Indians were human or insisted that they were inferior, descended from Ham and Canaan and therefore consigned by historic fate to a status of servitude. Perhaps these controversial issues concerning the nature and enslavement of the Indians did not generate the same intensity of debate in Brazil and Portugal as they did in Spanish America and Spain, due largely to the labors of Bartolomé de las Casas; but they were debated, and the essays of Nóbrega provide a glimpse into the substance of that debate. His was certainly the most articulate voice in the Portuguese world of the time to be raised in favor of a view of the Brazilian Indian as fully human, of equal status in nature to the Portuguese, and therefore possessing the same rights and deserving the same protection under natural law as the Portuguese.

Notes

1. Nóbrega was born 18 October 1517 and died 18 October 1570. The manuscript text of the *Diálogo* is in the Biblioteca de Évora (cod. 116, 1–33, fols. 208r–215r). Recent editions include: *Revista do Instituto Histórico e Geográfico Brasileiro* (Rio de Janeiro, 1880), 43 (1): 133–52; Serafim Leite, ed., *Cartas do Brasil (1549–1560) de Manuel da Nóbrega* (Rio de Janeiro: Oficina Industrial Gráfica, 1931), pp. 229–45; Serafim Leite, ed., *Diálogo Sôbre a Conversão do Gentio pelo P. Manuel da Nóbrega, Com Preliminares e Anotações Históricas e Críticas* (Lisbon: Comissão do IV Centenário da Fundação de São Paulo, 1954), pp. 53–70; Serafim Leite, ed., *Cartas do Brasil e Mais Escritos do P. Manuel da Nóbrega (Opera Omnia)* (Coimbra: Universidade de Coimbra, 1955), pp. 215–50.

2. Regulamento Real de 17 de dezembro de 1548.

3. See Francisco Javier Hernáez, *Colleción de bulas, breves y otros documentos relativos a la Iglesia de América y Filipinas* (Brussels, 1879), 1:101f.; Mariano Cuevas, *Documentos inéditos del siglo XVI para la historia de México* (Mexico, 1914), pp. 84ff.

4. Several references to slaveholding by Jesuit priests and brothers appear in Nóbrega's *Diálogo*.

5. See Serafim Leite, *Artes e ofícios dos Jesuítas no Brasil, 1549–1760* (Lisbon and Rio de Janeiro, 1953).

6. Serafim Leite, ed., *Diálogo Sôbre a Conversão do Gentio*, pp. 45ff. Subsequent page references to this work are incorporated in the text and refer to Leite's "Texto Actualizado."

7. The reference is to the Maracajá Indians. "Negro" is used to refer to the Brazilian Indians in contradistinction to the "branco" Portuguese.

8. "Do not give dogs what is holy; and do not throw your pearls before swine, lest they trample them underfoot and turn to attack you" (Revised Standard Version).

9. Pero Lopes was from the Capitania de São Vicente; the "velho Caiubi" had come to Piratininga from a place two leagues distant; Fernão Correia was a "Maniçoba" (Carijó) from the south.

10. In a lengthy letter to the former governor-general, Thomé de Souza, dated 5 July 1559, Nóbrega did complain that Portuguese Christians were committing the sin of encouraging the Indians to practice self-betrayal by selling themselves into slavery.

11. The manuscript text of this document is in the Biblioteca de Évora (cod. 116, 1–33, fols. 145r–152v). Recent editions include: Serafim Leite, "Primeiro documento importante jurídico-moral escrito no Brasil (1567)," in *Jornal do Comércio* (Rio de Janeiro), 20 November 1938; Serafim Leite, ed., *Novas Cartas Jesuíticas—de Nóbrega a Vieira* (São Paulo, 1940), pp. 113–29; *Revista do Instituto Histórico e Geográfico do Rio Grande do Sul* (Pôrto Alegre, 1941), pp. 518–30; Serafim Leite, *Cartas do Brasil e Mais Escritos do P. Manuel da Nóbrega*, pp. 397–429.

12. Ibid., par. 5–8.

13. Ibid., par. 9, lines 270f., and par. 10, line 27.

14. Ibid., par. 10, lines 280ff.

15. Ibid., par. 13.

16. Ibid., par. 16.

17. Ibid., par. 23.

18. Ibid., par. 19.

Estrutura e Temas da *Prosopopéia* de Bento Teixeira

Frederick C. H. Garcia

Nos DIAS em que era costume atribuir a Bento Teixeira livros que o poeta nunca escrevera, sua única obra, pouquíssimo estudada, era quase sempe lembrada com a pecha infamante: profanadora do altar de São Camões.[1] À falta de informações seguras sobre o autor da *Prosopopéia*, nos dias em que a biografia imperava, arranjavam-se alguns dados, repetidos sem maior exame.

Felizmente tudo isso vem mudando. Já temos uma biografia baseada em documentos, razoavelmente digna de confiança e útil para a compreensão do poema; os *Diálogos das Grandezas do Brasil* e a *Relação do Naufrágio* e seus respectivos autores finalmente se encontraram outra vez.[2] Paralelamente a esses progressos, chegou-se a uma visão serena do poeta em sua relação com a obra de Camões e de Bento Teixeira nas letras do Brasil.[3] Não há unanimidade quanto ao valor artístico da *Prosopopéia*, porém muitos dos juízos que lemos hoje em dia são ditados por princípios estéticos. A contraposição do poemeto à biografia de Jorge de Albuquerque Coelho, por outro lado, elimina em parte o aspecto de elogio oco, inseparável durante muitas décadas de todas as discussões da *Prosopopéia*.[4] E, para completar este quadro da boa maré em que anda navegando Bento Teixeira, finalmente o poema deixou de ser raridade bibliográfica. Num período de três anos apareceram duas edições que, de certo modo, se completam.[5] A da Universidade Federal de Pernambuco, não inteiramente cega a realidades literárias, atribui maior importância a aspectos históricos. A edição do Instituto Nacional do Livro, com a orientação basicamente filológica que lhe deram Celso Cunha e Carlos Duval (e não era sem tempo que se tivesse um texto apurado) não ignora os aspectos históricos, mitológicos e estéticos indispensáveis à compreensão do poema.

Com todos os bons sinais ligados a Bento Teixeira—e a bibliografia está crescendo—a discussão de aspectos literários ainda não alcançou o nível dos estudos biográficos e de fundo histórico. A esperança de poder oferecer uma contribuição nessa área menos explorada é a força animadora deste estudo, que examina a estrutura da *Prosopopéia* e os temas dos três episódios centrais da obra.

Terá sido talvez um tanto extensa esta introdução, mas fica declarado o objetivo do estudo que, se não pretende resolver todos os problemas ainda sem solução ligados a Bento Teixeira (e muito menos dar palavra final sobre nenhum deles), procura ainda determinar as relações entre a matéria utilizada pelo poeta e as transformações por que passou essa matéria no processo de criação literária.

No desenvolvimento poucas vezes aparecerá o nome de Luís Vaz de Camões, mas, discutindo um poema dos muitos derivados de *Os Lusíadas,* mantemo-nos nos limites do Mundo Português ao tempo de Camões.

1. A Construção do Poema

As estrofes iniciais da *Prosopopéia* seguem o esquema clássico do poema épico: Proposição (I), Invocação (II), e Dedicatória (III–VI). Esta serve para reforçar e ampliar os propósitos já declarados do poeta, que, contrariando as intenções anunciadas de só pedir ajuda a Deus e de não se valer das "Délficas Irmãs," agarra-se com Talia e embarca nas águas de Aganipe. Na Narração, que vai da sétima estrofe à penúltima, três oitavas descrevem o anoitecer (VII–IX); chega Tritão quando já escurece e convoca os deuses para um concílio (X–XIV); vem logo a conhecida "Descrição do Recife de Pernambuco" (XVII–XXI), ao fim da qual anuncia-se o "Canto de Proteu," que vai da estrofe XXII à oitava XCIII.

Finda a narraçao das ações de Jorge e de seu irmão Duarte na Batalha de Alcácer-Quibir, o velho oráculo declara-se cansado. O poeta podia, quinhentistamente, preparar-se para encerrar o canto. Proteu não se esquece de chamar a atenção dos circunstantes para o fato de que já amanhece. E é tempo de Netuno penitenciar-se pelos males causados a Jorge de Albuquerque (XCIII), e chegamos ao "Epílogo" (XCIV), com a partida da "cerúlea gente" e com a intervenção final do poeta.

O cerne do poema é o "Canto de Proteu," que começa logo depois do anoitecer e que encerra com o raiar do dia. Com o nascer do sol terá ficado evidente a glória do herói. Assim espera Proteu; assim esperava o poeta. A maneira como Bento Teixeira balizou os pontos extremos da profecia, iniciada no começo da noite, e o cansaço do cantor quando amanhece e a missão está cumprida, evidenciam intencionalidade. A aproximação de pintores e poetas, evocada por Bento Teixeira,[6] justifica até falarmos no "Canto de Proteu" como um quadro, e os limites dados no poema ajustam o foco e dão um senso dinâmico à narrativa.

Não entra nesta discussão o soneto escrito em castelhano que se segue ao poema. É discutível a autoria de Bento Teixeira, cujo verso está livre do rebuscado trocadilhista desses arroubos gratulatórios. De qualquer modo, é de pouco valor para a interpretação da *Prosopopéia*.

2. O Poema dentro do Poema

Visto o esquema geral do poema, passemos ao exame da prosopopéia que justifica o título. É o "Canto de Proteu," que abrange 560 versos. Os demais, 192 ao todo, emolduram a série de profecias. Verdadeiramente, o "Canto de Proteu" é um poema dentro de um poema, ou, talvez mais rigorosamente, um poema dentro de uma estrutura. Nesse poema interno vem glorificado o governador de Pernambuco, a quem a obra é dedicada. Poeta menos conhecedor dos cânones clássicos teria, partindo das mesmas informações, simplesmente metrificado a crônica das façanhas de Jorge de Albuquerque em dois continentes e numa travessia trágica.

Na composição do canto profético, Bento Teixeira se valeu mais uma vez dos elementos estruturais do poema épico. O "Canto de Proteu" abre com uma proposição (XXII–XXIII), seguida de uma invocação (XXIV–XXV). Não há dedicatória, nem havia lugar para tal. Filho legítimo de seu criador, que não queria invocar as "Délficas Irmãs," o deus-profeta não deseja ajuda das "nove moradoras do Parnaso," assistência dispensável, saiba o ouvinte, já que seu canto dirá apenas a verdade.

Começam as profecias, que apresentam problemas ténicos nem sempre resolvidos com felicidade. Um destes é a presença de parentes do herói, também cantados, ou pelo menos mencionados em termos de alto respeito: Duarte Coelho Pereira, primeiro donatário de Pernambuco, pai do herói, em luta contra os selvagens e também contra franceses invasores (XXVII-XXVIII); D. Beatriz, esposa do primeiro capitão-mor (XXIX); Jerônimo de Albuquerque, tio de Jorge, apresentado como vassalo leal, homem religioso e bom soldado (XXXIII–XXXVIII). Com todo o seu valor, Jerônimo foi (ou será), de acordo com Proteu, privado do reconhecimento a que tinha direito. Isso explica, diz-nos o vaticinador, a ausência de seus filhos na campanha africana de D. Sebastião. Outro parente louvado no poema é Duarte, o primogênito. O cadete é o herói, mas não falta ao morgado o seu momento de grande glória (LXXXIII–LXXXVII).

Partindo de uma concepção razoável para elaborar o seu "Canto de Proteu," que poderia estabelecer o quadro projetado, mais de uma vez, por desejo de originalidade ou por imperícia, o poeta destrói a atmosfera que pretende criar, fazendo intervenções que prejudicam a unidade do poema dentro do poema (XXV.1; XXXIX.1; XLII.1; XLIII.5–8; XLIV.1; LXX.1–8; XCIII.1–3). E em alguns passos, como nos que prometem novos cantos sobre a mesma matéria (LXXXII; XCI–XCII) ou nos protestos de dizer somente a verdade (XXIV.6–8), não se sabe se fala Proteu, se o poeta, esquecido do disfarce épico.

A mitologia, razoável na estética em que está enquadrado o poema, mais de uma vez cresce descontroladamente. É ver o catálogo de ninfas que chegam, acompanhadas de sereias, ao Recife de Pernambuco (XVI). No "Canto de Proteu" a arrancada mitológica que explica a ira de Vulcano contra Jorge de Albuquerque (XLVIII–LIII), pela ação deste contra os índios, chega a prejudicar a continuidade da narrativa. No meio das durezas do naufrágio, o eloqüente Jorge lembra aos companheiros que, embora forças inimigas "que se parcialidam com Vulcano" causem perigos e desgraças, o "Soberano" divino não deixará de socorrê-los (LXI). É simplesmente a invasão de um plano da narrativa por matéria que pertence a outro plano. Sem negar que aí temos sério defeito de elaboração, podemos sempre imaginar que um dos motivos desse tratamento do sobrenatural era o desejo de eliminar dúvidas que os zelosos inquisidores pudessem ter a respeito do poeta, que deixava bem clara a fraqueza dos deuses do gentio diante da fé católica.

As profecias de Proteu relatam inicialmente a ação de Jorge e de seus parentes na capitania, em sua conquista territorial, catequese e luta contra protestantes e selvagens (XXVI–XXXVIII). O império e a fé—nesta ordem ou ao contrário—ainda eram as duas direções da expansão ultramarina. Após um interlúdio (XXXIX–XLI) e uma intrusão do poeta (XLIII–XLIV) recomeça a narrativa, e a ira de Vulcano leva Netuno a causar o naufrágio em que Jorge, mercê de sua coragem e enorme confiança na Providência, consegue sobreviver com parte de seus companheiros (LV–LXVIII). Vem logo a campanha africana (LXIX–XCI); morre Duarte e, com o luto de Olinda (XCII) a capitania muda de mãos e passa ao filho segundo. O donatário morreu. Viva o donatário. Encerra-se o "Canto de Proteu" e Netuno se penitencia por ter dado ouvidos a Vulcano. Sabe-se logo que o futuro conhecerá a glória do grande Albuquerque.

Neste passo final do canto profético há um elemento de tempo mais que ambíguo: Proteu profetiza o naufrágio; Netuno se arrepende de ter atendido ao pedido de Vulcano e de ter cometido os atos profetizados. E o poeta remata, declarando-se testemunha presencial de tudo quanto acaba de descrever. Evidentemente o poeta não sustém o disfarce épico.

Na discussão dos vaticínios, é quase inevitável, pela ligação de Bento Teixeira à épica camoniana, o cotejo da visão de Proteu e das profecias de Tétis.[7] Sem ser necessário dar ênfase à superioridade poética de Camões, tinha este ainda a vantagem de lidar com espectro muito mais amplo. Ainda mais, no texto camoniano a visão do futuro é para completar um panorama já apresentado, abrangedor de séculos e vivido por vasto elenco. Em Bento Teixeira a profecia é o poema.

3. Os Três Temas do "Canto de Proteu"

Eliminados os figurantes mitológicos, isolada uma ou outra moralização, postos de lado os elementos de pura carpintaria, restam-nos no "Canto de Proteu" três episódios da biografia de Jorge de Albuquerque Coelho, em cada um desses episódios louvando uma ou mais virtudes do herói. São essas virtudes os temas do poeta.

A narrative se baseia em fatos reais. O donatário não se ofenderia com um ou outro exagero na relação de seus atos, e é lícito imaginar que Bento Teixeira terá composto as suas estrofes com essa noção em mente. Embora seja inegável a intenção glorificadora, é pela apresentação no poema—pelo tratamento da matéria e não pela intenção bajuladora—que se deve fazer o julgamento do mérito literário da *Prosopopéia,* verdade simples nem sempre respeitada. O exame da estrutura do poema e o estudo de seus temas nos dão elementos para uma valoração estética da obra.

O primeiro tema é a coragem, que se manifesta na atividade colonial, lembrada de maneira muito esquemática. Intencionalmente ou não, Bento Teixeira acertou nessa apresentação mais evocativa que alistadora. Fosse por pressa de composição, fosse de caso pensado, sem oferecer riqueza de pormenores o poeta conseguiu apresentar uma família de homens valentes nas lutas contra os bárbaros e os luteranos (os termos são da *Prosopopéia*). Um dos defeitos básicos de muitos dos poemas seguidores de Camões é a preocupação de "fidelidade minuciosa,"[8] causadora de inevitável monotonia. Desse crime de esmiuçar não foi réu Bento Teixeira.

A narração da travessia é superficial, porém menos esquemática que a relação das atividades na capitania. O poeta evoca as tempestades e a fome, que levou alguns dos tripulantes a formular idéias de antropofagia. São todos dissuadidos pela eloqüência de Jorge, disposto a morrer defendendo o seu ponto de vista. Reconfirmada a coragem, fica também estabelecida sua confiança na Providência. O herói nunca duvida: com a ajuda de Deus chegará ao destino. O devoto que aqui vemos não parece o mesmo já apresentado na luta contra os protestantes e na obra de catequese, aspectos tratados de maneira bastante remota. Pouco interesse do cristão-novo Bento Teixeira quanto à obra missionária e por essa religião tão militante como militar? E já que entrou na discussão o caso do cristão-novo, fique bem claro que, falando tantas vezes na Providência, não se menciona jamais o nome de Cristo e em nenhum passo aparece a cruz simbólica da fé do fidalgo, pormenor que terá escapado aos censores, sem dúvida informados do catolicismo muito limitado do poeta.

Quando comparamos os eventos da travessia narrados por Bento Teixeira e os que vêm no *Naufrágio*, nota-se no poema a ausência da atitude intransigente de Jorge diante de protestantes, que não lhe inspiravam nenhum espírito de conciliação.[9] No "Canto de Proteu" nem de longe vem mencionado o episódio dos corsários franceses, cuja presença no poema ajudaria a glorificar o herói e daria maior ênfase a sua coragem e ao seu sentimento religioso, de que a intolerância era, naquelas alturas, verdadeiramente inseparável. Ou a *Prosopopéia* foi composta sem conhecimento do texto do *Naufrágio*, hipótese muito viável, ou aqui o cristão-novo, mais tolerante que os antigos, preferiu abster-se de glorificar a intolerância, hipótese tentadora, mas de base frágil, pela falta de sutileza do poeta.

Dadas as ações de graças em Lisboa (LXVIII), Jorge se reúne a Duarte, e, quase sem transição, lá se vão a caminho do desastre africano. A coragem e a fé de Jorge aqui se conjugam com uma virtude: a lealdade ao rei, personificação da Pátria—e chegamos ao terceiro tema do "Canto de Proteu."

Não pode ficar sem comentário a maneira como D. Sebastião, que põe em prova as virtudes do fidalgo, passa pelas páginas da profecia. O rei está presente na estrofe LXIX, em que se anuncia a campanha marroquina. Continua diante do leitor até a estrofe LXXVIII, em que o fidalgo se despede de seu soberano. A batalha continua, e D. Sebastião só é novamente mencionado na imprecação de Duarte contra os que fugiam (LXXXVI). Nas seis estrofes em que não se menciona o monarca, este não deixa de estar presente na memória do leitor. Embora o rei derrotado esteja visível em toda a evocação da jornada africana, que abrange vinte e três estâncias, jamais se menciona de maneira directa o seu nome. Bem diferente de *Os Lusíadas*, em que, na rememoração dos reis passados, são todos lembrados com menção de nome, até mesmo os mais obscuros (III.28–IV.104). Na *Prosopopéia* D. Sebastião é o "Rei sublime" na fala de Duarte (LXXXVI); na dis-

cussão do planejamento da expedição é o "Rei altivo imperioso,"
pouco antes chamado "Sebasto lusitano," que é a expressão mais próxima de seu nome em todo o poema (LXIX); antes mesmo do com-
bate é o "mal afortunado Rei ufano" (LXXII); na batalha, no meio de
todos os perigos, encontramos o "Rei das gentes lusitanas" (LXXIV).
Na estrofe seguinte, "será visto por Jorge sublimado," ficando bem
claro que a ausência de sujeito corre por conta de Bento Teixeira. O
governador transfere sua montada a D. Sebastião, chamando-lhe
"infelice Rei" (LXXVI) ao formular o oferecimento. E continua,
dirigindo-se ao monarca:

> Vejo-vos co cavalo já cansado,
> A vós, nunca cansado, mas ferido,
> Salvai em este meu a vossa vida,
> Que a minha pouco vai em ser perdida.

Justifica-se a transferência, aparentemente não aceita sem relutância por parte do rei, de cuja coragem fanática nunca se duvidou,
como também nunca se negou a sua inépcia em matéria estratégica.
Diz ainda o fidalgo que, se D. Sebastião não morrer, manter-se-á o
"Luso Reino" (LXXVII). E, feita a troca, Proteu comenta, louvando a
virtude de Jorge: "Ó Portuguesa/Lealdade do tempo florentíssimo!"
(LXXVIII).

Durante muito tempo discutiu-se a questão da nacionalidade do
poeta e do poema. A leitura vagarosa deste passo teria poupado muita
tinta e muito papel. Nascido em Olinda, Jorge era ainda um fidalgo
português. Esta a apresentação do poeta. O Brasil era parte de Portugal; patriotismo era sinônimo de lealdade ao Rei de Portugal.

Intencionalmente ou não, as exclamaçãoes sobre a lealdade de
Jorge a seu monarca fazem eco da "grã fidelidade portuguesa" de
Egas Moniz (*Lusíadas*, III.41). Há a diferença de que Egas se sacri-
ficava no início do Reino de Portugal, enquanto que no heroísmo do
"sublime Jorge" testemunhamos o holocausto:

> O Rei promete, se de tal empresa
> Sai vivo, o fará senhor grandíssimo,
> Mas 'té nisto lhe será avara a sorte,
> Pois tudo cubrirá com sombra a morte.

> [LXXVIII.5–8]

Morreu o rei quase anônimo, apresentado em tom de nênia e em
termos que retratam um súdito leal. Bem diferente, a propósito, de

alguns poemas elegíacos castelhanos, que quase apostrofam o rei pela
insânia causadora de sua morte e do domínio espanhol. Veja-se o epi-
táfio escrito por Lope de Vega;[10] examinem-se vários passos de Fernando de Herrera.[11] Contrastem-se esses escritos com a descrição da
Batalha de Alcácer-Quibir na *Elegíada*, de 1588, e no *Afonso Africano*,
impresso em 1614. Nesses poemas portugueses[12] não há apenas a la-
mentação da independência perdida; há o luto pela perda do monarca. Bento Teixeira e dois outros continuadores de Camões vibra-
vam na mesma freqüência quando evocavam D. Sebastião.

Feita a rememoração da campanha africana, em que a coragem e
a lealdade de Jorge não conseguiram salvar o rei e, com ele, a Pátria (a
primeira idéia vem quase dita por extenso e a segunda está implícita),
Proteu lamenta a velhice e o cansaço que quase o levam a esquecer o
irmão do protagonista (LXXXII), fidalgo também corajoso, cuja rea-
ção diante de portugueses em fuga só podia levar à recriminação:

—Donde vos is, homens insanos?
Que digo: homens, estátuas sem sentido,
Pois não sentis o bem que haveis perdido?

[LXXXIII.6–8]

A coragem é decididamente um dos temas desse episódio secundário. A raridade desta virtude teria decretado a morte do rei e a
queda de Portugal. Encarecem-se a coragem e a lealdade dos dois
irmãos.

Com a perda da batalha, que o poeta não tenta descrever minu-
ciosamente, chega logo o fim do "Canto de Proteu." Sem delongas encerra-se o poema.

O herói fica marcado pela coragem, implícita no primeiro episódio; pela fé em Deus, manifesta na travessia; e pela lealdade a seu
rei, mais que evidenciada na guerra marroquina. As três virtudes do
fidalgo—que são as mesmas de seu tio Jerônimo—não se negam e se
completam.

A *Prosopopéia* não entra na questão da perda da independência de
Portugal. Saía isso a seu objectivo e, de qualquer maneira, pela data de
composição,[13] bem como pela distância geográfica, ainda não se fizera
sentir na colônia o domínio espanhol. De qualquer modo, a lealdade
do fidalgo é ao rei perdido, mas só com exagero veríamos no texto
intenção autonomista e até mesmo anticastelhana. O poeta não era,
evidentemente, alheio às realidades políticas e militares. Sabia fazer
sugestões construtivas às autoridades, e é bem conhecida a estrofe que
fala da necessidade de uma fortificação para proteger a entrada do

Recife (XX.1–4). Era capaz ainda de acusar os poderosos que não reconheciam os seus melhores súditos, e o melhor exemplo é, na apresentação de Jorge de Albuquerque, a maneira como fala do nenhum prêmio de suas qualidades de bom católico, militar de valor e súdito leal.

4. Encerramento

Deste exame temático e estrutural da *Prosopopéia* terá ficado evidente que, se o poema pode dar a impressão inicial de elogio oco—rótulo que José Veríssimo e outros aplicaram a todo o texto—é na verdade uma visão condensada da carreira de Jorge de Albuquerque Coelho, com exposição de suas qualidades de militar, de crente em Deus e de vassalo leal. A qualidade literária de cada um dos três episódios é proporcional ao grau de interesse humano dos aspectos descritos, ao potencial heróico de cada um e à força criadora de Bento Teixeira. Poeta de maior estro teria, com matéria idêntica, escrito obra melhor. Por outro lado, formação humanística mais disciplinada teria levado o cantor de Jorge a domínio mais completo do seu múnus e a evitar alguns dos defeitos evidentes da *Prosopopéia*.

Em vários momentos (com o disfarce de Proteu e em seu próprio nome) Bento Teixeira descreve o poema como texto provisório, sujeito a reformas e ajustes.[14] Se eram protestos sinceros, não podemos saber ao certo; eram, em parte, mesuras retóricas.

A análise temática e estrutural do poema evidencia que o poeta levou a cabo o seu plano, anunciado na estrofe de abertura, ao definir o seu herói como "Albuquerque soberano,/Da fé, da cara Pátria firme muro,/Cujo valor . . ./Pode estancar a Lácia e Grega lira." É evidente que não estancou a grega nem a romana. E nem de longe abalou o pedestal de *Os Lusíadas*. Indiscutivelmente, porém, seja qual for nossa opinião sobre a qualidade do poema, a rememoração dos feitos de Jorge de Albuquerque Coelho desenvolveu os temas anunciados na proposição: coragem, fé, patriotismo.

Como encerramento desta visão parcial da *Prosopopéia*, damos uma volta ao ponto de partida. Temos aqui uma análise de dois aspectos do poema, um dos primeiros caudatários de *Os Lusíadas*. Com toda a modéstia do texto de Bento Teixeira, seu estudo pode ajudar-nos a explorar o Mundo Português ao Tempo de Camões.

Notas

1. Se José Veríssimo não foi o primeiro crítico a condenar a *Prosopopéia*, foi sem dúvida o que demonstrou mais pronunciada má vontade, muito de

ser notada num intelectual geralmente sereno e objetivo. Segundo este crítico, o poema era sem "mérito algum de inspiração, poesia ou forma." Veríssimo ataca o poeta ainda chamando-o engrossador e dando a impressão de que a profecia ex post facto seria defeito imperdoável. Chega até a se valer de erro de imprensa ("primeiras primícias") para fundamentar a apresentação vitri-ólica. Alguns críticos e diversos manuais ecoaram e ainda ecoam o ataque da *História da Literatura Brasileira* (citada pela terceira edição, Rio de Janeiro: José Olympio, 1954, pp. 36–41), e dos *Estudos de Literatura Brasileira*, Quarta Série (Paris e Rio de Janeiro: H. Garnier, 1904, pp. 25–64).

2. Para conhecimento da biografia e de quanto já se fez no estudo de Bento Teixeira, consulte-se a lista bibliográfica de J. Galante de Sousa, *Em torno do Poeta Bento Teixeira* (São Paulo: Instituto de Estudos Brasileiros [da Universidade de São Paulo], 1972), pp. 92–106, abundante de fontes para o estudo de aspectos históricos, biográficos e literários. Vejam-se ainda: José Antônio Gonçalves de Mello, *Estudos Pernambucanos* (Recife: Imprensa Universitária, 1960), pp. 5–43; Rubens Borba de Moraes, "Muitas Perguntas e Poucas Respostas sobre o Autor da *Prosopopéia*," *Comentário* 5 (1964): i, 77–88.

3. Quanto ao primeiro aspecto, veja-se Antônio Soares Amora, "A *Prosopopéia*, de Bento Teixeira, à Luz da Moderna Camonologia," *Miscelânea de Estudos em Honra do Prof. Hernâni Cidade* (Lisboa: Universidade de Lisboa, 1957), pp. 402–8; reimpresso com novo título ("Bento Teixeira e a *Prosopopéia*") e mínimas alterações de texto em *Classicismo e Romantismo no Brasil* (São Paulo: Conselho Estadual de Cultura, 1966), pp. 25–31. Quanto aos dois aspectos, veja-se Wilson Martins, *História da Inteligência Brasileira* (São Paulo: Cultrix, 1977), 1: 105–9. Consulte-se ainda José Aderaldo Castello, "Bento Teixeira, um Iniciador," *Estado de São Paulo: Suplemento Literário*, 26 de janeiro de 1957, p. 4. Do mesmo, leia-se *Manifestações Literárias na Era Colonial*, 2ª edição (São Paulo: Cultrix, 1965), especialmente pp. 64–68. Veja-se ainda Antônio Soares Amora, "A *Prosopopéia* e seus Temas de Interesse," *Estado de São Paulo: Suplemento Literário*, 22 de dezembro de 1956, p. 4.

4. Veja-se, no livro de J. Galante de Sousa, o capítulo "O Donatário Zeloso da Própria Glória," pp. 37–44. Além da narração do naufrágio (v. nota seguinte), leia-se também Jerônimo de Mendonça, *Jornada de África* (Lisboa, 1785), p. 63. A folha de rosto nos diz que o texto era "copiado fielmente da edição de 1607 por Bento J. de Sousa Farinha."

5. A primeira a aparecer foi [Afonso Luís Piloto e Bento Teixeira] *Naufrágio e Prosopopéia* (Recife: Universidade Federal de Pernambuco, 1969); a introdução e as notas, e mais o glossário são de Fernando de Oliveira Mota; o prefácio é de José Gonsalves de Mello. Referências ao *Naufrágio* por esta edição. Mais recente é o texto com introdução e comentários de Celso Cunha e Carlos Duval, com o título de *Prosopopéia* (Rio de Janeiro: Instituto Nacional do Livro, 1972). Este o texto usado nas citações do poema.

6. Na primeira linha do "Prólogo" (pp. 14–15). Veja-se *Ars Poetica*, 9–10 (comparação de poetas e pintores) e 360 (identificações entre poema e quadro). Citado pela edição *Satires, Epistles and Ars Poetica* [de Horácio] (Londres: W. Heinemann, 1926), pp. 450–89.

7. *Lusíadas,* IX,86 e X,10–73. Citado por Camões, *Obra Completa,* Organização de Hernâni Cidade, 5 vols. (Lisboa: Sá da Costa, várias datas).

8. A expressão é de Fidelino de Figueiredo, em generalização formulada na discussão do *Primeiro Cerco de Diu,* em *A Épica Portuguesa no Século XVI* (São Paulo: Universidade de São Paulo, 1950), p. 387.

9. Veja-se *Naufrágio,* Cap IV, pp. 69–71.

10. Transcrito em José Maria Viqueira Barreiro, *El lusitanismo de Lope de Vega* (Coimbra: Coimbra Editora, 1950), p. 161.

11. Veja-se a "Canción por la pérdida de Don Sebastián," *Poesías* (Madri: La Lectura, 1914), pp. 80–88. Considerem-se também a canção "Si alguna vez mi pena" (pp. 108–13) e o soneto "Ya qu'el sujeto reino lusitano" (p. 198) e a elegia "Estoy pensando en medio de mi engaño" (pp. 261–71). Quanto à presença de D. Sebastião nos escritos de Herrera, consulte-se ainda Oreste Macrí, *Fernando de Herrera* (Madri: Gredos, 1971), pp. 183, 184, 508, 509, 604 e 608.

12. Em J. Cabral do Nascimento, *Poemas Narrativos Portugueses* (Lisboa: Minerva, 1947). Amostra do poema de Luís Pereira Brandão, pp. 155–56. "Antevisão de Alcácer-Quibir," do poema de Vasco Mousinho de Quevedo, pp. 163–67.

13. O poema teria sido composto entre 1584 e 1593. Para discussão minuciosa deste aspecto, veja-se J. Galante de Sousa, *Em torno do Poeta Bento Teixeira,* pp. 25–29. Vale lembrar que os anos finais do poeta, falecido em 1600, não teriam sido propícios à criação literária, pelos muitos problemas vividos por Bento Teixeira.

14. Veja-se o "Prólogo" e mais as estrofes LXXXII, XCI e XCII. Sobre este aspecto, consultem-se os trabalhos de José Aderaldo Castello citados (nota 3).

III

The Portuguese in
Africa and Asia

Grumbling Veterans of an Empire

Gerald M. Moser

Heroica Lusitania . . .
Mas si tanto has podido
Resplandecer con bélicos Poderes;
Bien te has escurecido
Con negar, por los términos de Ceres,
De Thetis por la espuma,
Tanto a la Espada honor, como a la
    pluma.

Manuel de Faria e Sousa
Rimas, Pt. III, Ode 15 (1627)

("Heroic Lusitania . . . who has been
able to shine so brightly in the wars,
you have tarnished your glory within
the bounds of Ceres and Tethys's
foamy realm when you refused to
honor sword or pen.")

I N THE Portuguese literature of the times, criticism frequently took
the form of a veteran soldier's complaint that his faithful service
was not being rewarded as it should have been. In a way, it was a self-
criticism: in an intensely personal manner, it implied a condemnation
of the methods of colonization by the colonizers themselves. And anyone who knows a little about Portuguese literature is familiar with at
least one of the complainers, Luís de Camões, who served the king for
many years as a soldier, first in Morocco, then in the East Indies. Since
little is known of his life, nothing can dispel the image of the luckless
man that he created through his poetry. This pathetic figure, "alone,
abandoned / by friends, by king and country / unworthy of the singer

97

of his Lusiads," as young Almeida Garrett presented him in 1825
(Garrett, *Camões*, pp. 123–24), is the Camões who lives on in the
minds of his countrymen. [References are to bibliography at the end
of the chapter; English translations are the author's.] Yet, the poet, a
member of the lesser gentry, actually subdued his criticism. The loud-
est and also the most listened to complaints of any of the soldiers came
from members of the high nobility. First to be voiced, they have to be
mentioned first. Camões then introduced a new view by taking up the
grievances of humbler folk as well. Simultaneously and for a century
to come, we find anonymous soldiers also recording their woes—or so
it was made to appear.

Complaining noblemen and their hangers-on were legion, with
many heading the procession who had served as governors or viceroys. Those who pestered the king and his councilors the most would
often get what they wanted, as Diogo do Couto has an unnamed veteran observe, whereas untitled petitioners were put into the common
jail for making nuisances of themselves, *por enfadonho(s)* (Couto, *Soldado*, p. 201). The appeals hot-tempered Afonso de Albuquerque directed to King Manuel in his letters are well known, as are his last
words uttered on his sickbed when he had learned that his candidates
for important Indian positions had been ignored in Lisbon.

Others who remonstrated were merely anxious to enrich themselves. The claims made, for example, by greedy governor Martim
Afonso de Sousa are still preserved. The official historians, who tried
hard to be fair, saw through such maneuvers. By the same token, they
were revolted by the shabby treatment given to the few good and honest commanders, upright men such as viceroy Nuno da Cunha, son of
that old captain Tristão da Cunha whose name is perpetuated in that
of an island in the South Atlantic. The drama of royal ingratitude
with its demoralizing effects moved Diogo do Couto to write a page
ringing with indignation: Cunha was expecting to reap the reward for
fitting out a powerful fleet that was to break the Turkish blockade of
Diu, the most important stronghold of the Portuguese in northern India, when he learned that he had been recalled and that his successor,
indecisive, seventy-year-old Garcia de Noronha, had already arrived
in Goa. "Nuno da Cunha," Couto writes,

> was deeply hurt by the royal offense, having been informed
> by his father Tristão what had happened when the latter had
> questioned the king about the matter. He became so de-
> pressed that no one saw him in a happy mood ever after. . . .

When the homeward bound ships had already rounded
the Cape, Nuno da Cunha came down with a grave illness,
from which he was to die. It may well be that it had been
caused by the profound depression and sorrow that ate his
heart out as he thought about the poor reward he had
received. . . .

As he lay dying he started to breathe so hard that everyone thought his last moment had come. This continued for
quite a while. Then he reopened his eyes and repeated the
words of the Roman in a somewhat cavernous voice: "In-
grata patria, ossa mea non possidebis!" That's how shocked
he still was by the poor reward he had received for ten years
of service as governor of India and for building three fortresses, Chale (near Kozhikode, the Calicut of the Portuguese), Basein and Dive (Diu). And to this day, whenever
the conversation turns to good government, only Nuno da
Cunha's is mentioned. What would he have felt had he
known that jealousy [of him] had reached such a point that
he was being awaited in the Azores with a pair of the heav-
iest handcuffs to shackle him and thus take him to the castle
in Lisbon and from there to the Mansos Gatetower in Santarém, made ready to receive him on the king's orders. Such
was the triumphant reception he was to get for all the victories he had won in the Orient.

Couto, Década quinta, bk. III, chap. 9, fol. 88b,
and bk. V, chap. 6, fols. 136a–37a.

Camões knew at first hand the lives led by the upper classes and
by the common people both in Portugal as well as in the colonies. He
joined the historians of the overseas expansion in putting in a good
word for the soldiers who bore the brunt of the campaigns, whether
as commanders or in the ranks.

In the final canto of the *Lusiads,* where Tethys sings her prophetic
verses of the heroic exploits to be expected, she first praises Duarte
Pacheco Pereira as a greater commander of his little band of a hundred Portuguese than any that ancient Greece or Rome had produced.
And like the historian Damião de Góis, Camões, through Tethys, accuses the king, Dom Manuel, of ingratitude, stinginess, and injustice
because he lent an ear to Pacheco's enemies. Lowering her voice, the
goddess foretells what would happen and sheds tears as she reaches

the end of the story, the poor reward Pacheco received for all his bravery:

> Cantando em baxa voz, envolta em choro,
> O grande esforço mal agradecido.

Lus., X, 22, vv. 3–4

Nor was it the first time that this had happened. The poet cites the Roman Belisarius and Homer's hero Aias as classic examples. Perhaps he did not mean to include himself in their numbers, but the lines

> In you [Pacheco] and in him [Belisarius], we see stout-
>   hearted men
> Fall to a low estate, humble, obscure,
> Ending their lives in wretched paupers' beds

Lus., X, 23, vv. 3–5

would remind his readers of the poet's own last years.

A few stanzas further on, the goddess, having praised and mourned Almeida, extols Albuquerque, but not without giving vent to a complaint of his soldiers, who had always been obedient to his orders—*a tudo obedientes*—about his exceeding harshness when he punished one of them in a fit of anger.

In the seventeenth century, a commentator of unusual sensitivity, Faria e Sousa, had already perceived a deeper significance in his favorite poet's complaints. Commenting on the honors reserved for Gama's expedition on the Isle of Love, he wrote:

> By saying that [Tethys], the greatest of the goddesses, espoused Gama, the Poet shows how attentive he was to justice when he made her, the foremost of the goddesses, wed Gama, the foremost of the ship's company, while they, the company, were to be wed to her subordinates. And by mentioning him last, the Poet showed that the reward for the men through whose efforts captains achieve great victories must not come last, even though it should not be the same, for without the men nothing could be achieved. The Poet arranged it this way because he objected to what he saw being practiced in his lifetime (as it is today and always will be), which is, to give everything to the chiefs, instead of dividing it among them and the men. . . . Likewise, he will say

in stanza 94 that after all, it is only fair not to give to the
great what is due to the rank and file.

Faria e Sousa, ed., *Os Lusíadas,* IV: col. 256

Diogo do Couto, himself discontented since he resented the scant
recognition he received from the king for his services, repeatedly
pointed out in his *Décadas* that great men, such as Vasco da Gama's son
Estêvão, were not rewarded properly by the country they served so
well in India. He called this "the careless handling of India" (*o descuido
da Índia*) (Couto, *Décadas,* I: xl, lxxii, cxxiv, 64; 2: 95). Diogo do
Couto's work of 1612, *O soldado prático* ("The experienced soldier"),
stands as the most comprehensive indictment of colonial practice in
India. But lest Portugal be made a whipping boy for imperialism, one
should remember what an Englishman, H. E. J. Stanley, had to say in
the introduction to his translation of Gaspar Correia's similar accusa-
tions in his first *Lenda:* "It is necessary to point out how much of Diogo
do Couto's observations upon the defects of the Portuguese administration in his time applies to our Indian administration. Those who
have served in India or in other Asiatic territories of the British
Crown will be able to make the application for themselves" (Correia,
The Three Voyages, pp. lxxv–lxxvi).

I shall make only two points about Couto's unique book. First, all
of his complaints are put into the mouth of a single one of the three
persons who talk about the rotten state of India, an unnamed, poverty-
stricken veteran, sixty years old, who had served there for twelve
years, on top of three years' service in the home fleet. The other point
is that the bill of particulars drawn up by the veteran goes beyond anything alleged by others while it includes the criticisms Camões made
his own.

Couto was neither the first nor the last to speak up in behalf of the
common soldier. I know of nine other works in which this is done. All
were probably written by men in responsible positions, who could
draw on extensive firsthand experience. One of the earliest was Gaspar Correia's *Lendas da Índia.* It contains a bitter outburst of indignation over the poor recompense the privates received while the glory
and the perquisites went to the gentlemen. Correia illustrates this with
what happened to the small troop of Cristóvão Justarte and his thirty-
seven brave men, who relieved the beleaguered fort at Calicut in 1525.
"Their feat," he writes, "would have been talked about had they been
nobles. But they were not. I saw some of them, who had been crippled
and were dogged by poverty, die in the charity wards, while those who

survived were removed from the pay and relief rolls" (Correia, *Lendas,* 2: 912). Correia raised his protest in 1563 or 1564, at a time when Camões was completing his epic.

There is an anonymous work, *Primor e honra da vida soldadesca* ("Excellence and honor of soldierly life"), written in Goa, probably in 1585, according to Charles R. Boxer. The author, a veteran himself, who is filled with religious zeal, blames on the one hand the king, for his ingratitude toward the men serving him best in the Indies (Anon., *Primor,* fol. 39r and v), and on the other the men because of their lack of discipline (fols. 55r and 56r).

Between 1580 and 1590, a Dutch visitor to India, Jan Huygen van Linschoten, confirmed the truth of the Portuguese allegations of niggardly pay, which, however, did not prevent the soldiers from wanting to appear magnificent and noble to the public eye (Linschoten, *Itinerario,* 1: 136–37).

Couto's *Soldado prático* of 1612 is followed by the work of a persistent and ingenuous reformer of the seventeenth-century variety, Francisco Rodrigues Silveira. His "Reformação da milícia e governo do estado da Índia Oriental" ("Reform of the military and the governance of the state of East India") was the revised text of the memorandum he had addressed to the Council of Portugal in Madrid six times in succession between 1600 and 1619, changing it each time. Having served as a soldier in India for twelve years beginning in 1585, he was deeply hurt when the council paid no attention to his suggestions. All he heard was the mocking remark "Well now, won't this pegleg ever leave us alone with his pile of papers?" (Silveira, "Reformação," fol. 3r). Silveira's indictment can stand comparison with Couto's or Correia's.

Very different from Silveira's is the fanciful but rather uninspired work *El soldado quexoso* ("The complaining soldier") by a certain João Franco Barreto, who had had some college training. He wrote it in the form of a rogue story, whose principal antihero is the complaining soldier. A printing permit had been secured in 1628, but the manuscript was never published. Among the verses Barreto interspersed in the story is a poem addressed boldly to a viceroy. It contrasts the glory of the discovery with the present disorder in India. The illustrious personage is accused of disastrous military tactics, of promulgating rules and regulations that make life impossible for the soldiers, and of entrusting inexperienced officers with the command of the troops (Barreto, "El soldado quexoso," fols. 29r–33v).

The series of protests continues with at least four more writings. One is an anonymous satirical poem with the burden "Such is the good regime of Portugal" (*Este é o bom governo de Portugal*) which was attributed to Tomás Pinto Brandão, an imitator of Gregório de Matos, with the date 1713. Three or four of its forty to forty-six stanzas, depending on the version, take up the theme of the soldiers' neglect by the government. The ninth in particular condemns the War Council for not considering services rendered when it decides on promotions, while the twenty-sixth attacks the king for compelling the miserable soldiery to be on duty in garrisons or in the field without pay—*sempre de fome morrendo / sem lhe darem um real: / este é o bom governo de Portugal* (Anon., "Este é o bom governo," st. 26).

Another text is represented by Father António Vieira's sermon of Mary's Visitation, which he preached in Bahia on 2 July 1640. In the presence of a newly arrived viceroy, the Jesuit preacher pleads the cause of the ragged, demoralized infantry.

More substantial was Captain João Ribeiro's account of how the Portuguese lost Ceylon to the Dutch, the *Fatalidade histórica da ilha de Ceilão* of 1685. Ribeiro had been in the military service for forty years, eighteen of them in Ceylon. Aside from greed, he pointed to lack of foresight as the reason for the mistakes that were committed. His work has a very modern ring since he attached much importance to economic factors. Something else is new in his treatment of the topic of the grumbling soldier: he does not speak *for* the common soldier. Though telling of the soldier's troubles he knows him too well to idealize him.

The series concludes with the "Primer for thieves" (*Arte de furtar*), published in the eighteenth century but in the main referring to events of the seventeenth. It includes numerous pages denouncing abuses, among them the pressing of men into the Indian service by unscrupulous recruiters (Anon., *Arte de furtar,* pp. 87–89).

All except one of the authors, Silveira, were anything but common soldiers. Why did they adopt the ordinary private's viewpoint in so many instances? Perhaps it was out of a sense of justice and morality. Being illiterate for the most part, the privates could not write in their own behalf. However, it seems unlikely that they would not have coined proverbial sayings, told stories, or composed songs about their plight, as soldiers did in other countries. Perhaps such stories have been lost because folklore was collected late in Portugal, or perhaps they still exist unrecognized. I only know of a few vestiges. One is a proverb among the several that Ferreira de Vasconcelos put into his play *Eufrosina* in the sixteenth century. It recalls the veterans' grumblings: "The hospitals are full of loyal fools" (*Dos leais estão cheios os hospitais*). Another is ballad no. 128 in Leite de Vasconcellos's collection: "Come here, my Manuel; song of the hungry soldier" (*Anda cá, ó meu Manel*) (Vasconcellos, *Romanceiro português*, 2:471). A third is a *trova* or quatrain collected by Agostinho de Campos and Alberto d'Oliveira: *Ó meu pai, ó minha mãe, / não me chameis vosso filho: / Eu sou um triste soldado, / Por trinta réis vou vendido!* ("Oh, father dear, oh, mother dear, I am your son no more but a miserable serviceman sold for thirty silver pieces") (*Mil trovas*, p. 24). The fact remains that we do not really know what the common Portuguese soldier said or sang.

The main object of this study has been to show that Luís de Camões was not alone in taking up the complaints of the Portuguese soldiery of his time, although he remains unique in attributing his own misfortunes to an adverse fate (*má Fortuna*) and rarely to other men. The complaints are part and parcel of a tradition of criticizing imperial practice, to the point of creating a literary commonplace, the grumbling soldier (*o soldado quexoso*).

As for modern echoes, one has only to turn to the African veterans, beginning with officers such as Mousinho de Albuquerque and Paiva Couceiro or, writing from a very different viewpoint, Henrique Galvão and Manuel dos Santos Lima, to see that the tradition continues.

Author's note: This paper is an abridged version of a chapter in a projected work on the Portuguese critics of their own empire.

References

Anon. *Arte de furtar,* ed. Jaime Brasil. Lisbon: Livraria Peninsular Editora, 1937.

_____. "Este é o bom governo de Portugal." In the miscellany ms. 399, Biblioteca da Universidade, Coimbra, fols. 196–202 (dated 1713, copied in 1783).

_____. *Primor e honra da vida soldadesca no Estado da Índia.* Lisbon: Jorge Rodrigues, 1630.

Barreto, João Franco. "El soldado quexoso." First part. Biblioteca da Ajuda, Lisbon, ms. 50–I–54.

Camões, Luís de. *Os Lusíadas,* ed. Emanuel Paulo Ramos. 6th ed. Porto: Porto Editora; Lisbon: Empresa Literária Fluminense, n.d.

_____. *Os Lusíadas,* ed. Manuel de Faria e Sousa. 4 vols. Facsimile reproduction of the 1639 ed. Lisbon: Imprensa Nacional–Casa da Moeda, 1972.

Campos, Agostinho de, and Alberto d'Oliveira, eds. *Mil trovas populares portuguesas.* 4th ed. Lisbon: Imprensa Nacional, 1937.

Correia, Gaspar. *Lendas da Índia.* Reproduction of R. J. de Lima Felner's ed. of 1858 ff. 4 vols. Porto: Lello e Irmão, 1975.

_____. *The Three Voyages of Vasco da Gama and His Viceroyalty*, trans. H. E. J. Stanley. London: The Hakluyt Society, 1869.

Couto, Diogo do. *Década quinta da "Ásia"*, ed. Marcus de Jong. Coimbra: Biblioteca da Universidade, 1937.

_____. *Décadas*, ed. A. Baião. 2 vols. Lisbon: Sá da Costa, 1947.

_____. *O soldado prático*, ed. M. Rodrigues Lapa. Lisbon: Sá da Costa, 1937.

Garrett, J. B. Almeida. *Camões*. Porto: Lello e Irmão, 1945.

Linschoten, Jan Huygen van. *Itinerario (1579–1592)*. 2 vols. The Hague, Nijhoff, 1910.

Ribeiro, João. *Fatalidade histórica da ilha de Ceilão*. Lisbon: Academia das Ciências, 1836. (Besides the printed text, I used the ms., dated Lisbon, 8 January 1685, FG 518 / 530 / 531; Biblioteca Nacional, Lisbon.)

Silveira, Francisco Rodrigues. "Reformação da milícia e governo do estado da Índia Oriental." British Museum, London, add. mss. no. 25:419. (Compared with its partial publication by A. de S. S. Costa Lobo as *Memórias de um soldado da Índia;* Lisbon: Imprensa Nacional, 1877.)

Vasconcellos, José Leite de, ed. *Romanceiro português*. 2 vols. Coimbra: Universidade, 1960.

Vasconcelos, Jorge Ferreira de. *Eufrosina*, ed. Eugenio Asensio. Madrid: Consejo Superior de Investigaciones Científicas, 1951.

Vieira, António. *Obras escolhidas*, ed. A. Sérgio and H. Cidade. Vol. 10, *Sermões* (I). Lisbon: Sá da Costa, 1954. (A critical edition has been consulted, *António Vieiras Predigt über "Marias Heimsuchung,"* by Radegundis Leopold, Münster, Westphalia: Aschendorff, 1978.)

The Portuguese Asian "Decadência," Revisited

George Winius

FOR BETTER or for worse, the notion that the Portuguese empire in Asia went into eclipse because of the malfeasance of its public officialdom is no longer in fashion. The first edition of Diogo do Couto's *Soldado prático,* printed in 1790, was entitled "Observations on the principal causes of decadence of the Portuguese in India"; for a century and a half thereafter, the idea was accepted without question that the reasons for its collapse had more to do with moral depravity than with anything else. Not only did the German historian Justus Strandes and the English historian E. Denison Ross think so, but even the *Grande Enciclopédia Portuguesa e Brasileira* carried a heading under "*D*" for "Decadência," which added that during this period the participants were "no longer worthy of the name Portuguese."

Since World War II, however, morality has become unfashionable, international drug smuggling is a thousand times bigger a business than the whole sixteenth-century spice trade, and an American vice-president has been sacked for accepting bribes. No wonder, then, that the idea of the *decadência* has all but disappeared, too: a viceroy who sailed home with a fortune in tainted wealth might seem no worse than Spiro Agnew or even the hometown girl who uncovered for *Playboy.* Hence, I think we are in an ideal position to view Portuguese Asian history objectively—not too moralistically, possibly just a shade sympathetically, but still unwilling to allow the deceitful to tread on the weak. If we can accept C. R. Boxer's view that it was not Portuguese corruption but Dutch superiority that turned the tables in Asia during the first half of the seventeenth century, I think we are ready to begin.

First of all we will need a working definition of corruption, at-

106

tuned to our time period. The English author J. Hurstfield, writing on political corruption in early modern England, has offered an explanation that may serve our need: "If we assume that the object of the state is the welfare of all its members, we may define corruption as the subversion of that object to other ends."[1] To him, the modern state and the existence of a bureaucracy are identical, but he feels that there is a weak link in the system, namely the lack of sufficient state revenues to pay bureaucrats decent salaries. They then helped themselves to the substance of the commonweal to make up the difference. Another writer, the Australian M. N. Pearson, goes further when he adds that this lack of adequate salaries was compensated by the addition to practically all offices of so-called perquisites, i.e., the creation and retention of certain fees not specifically authorized by the Crown, but more or less tolerated.[2] He adds that distinctions between the "ethical" perks and the more nearly rapacious ones easily became vague. Finally, a Dutch writer, Jacob van Klaveren, has remarked that in feudal times the perks may have been deemed proper and legitimate, but that when the bureaucracies took over administrative tasks from the feudatories, the same perks, or some like them, became illegal and therefore corrupt except when enjoyed by the Crown itself.[3] At any rate, holding these possible interpretations of corruption in mind, it is time to move on to some concepts of a different nature, those regarding the early overseas empires with which I will be dealing.

The three groups of Europeans who established extensive empires in Asia between 1500 and 1700 were of course the Portuguese, who arrived in India in 1498, and the English and Dutch, who arrived at the end of the sixteenth century and did not establish real footholds until the beginning of the seventeenth. We might add the Spaniards in the Philippines, though they were not strictly comparable because they did not use the Cape route but came from Mexico across the Pacific. Moreover, though they had a short-lived station on Formosa and briefly occupied parts of the Moluccas for defensive purposes, their empire cannot really be called extensive. Our ends will perhaps best be served if we stick mostly to the Portuguese and the empires of the two northern European powers, for they illustrate the basic differences I wish to suggest. However, it may be useful to allude to one or two administrative aspects of the Spanish empire in America for comparative purposes.

In *Carracks, Caravans and Companies*, published in 1972, Niels Steensgaard, of Copenhagen, makes a fundamental distinction between the way in which the Portuguese empire earned its wealth within Asia and the way in which the English and Dutch East India companies did. (I said "within Asia," because by no means were all their incomes derived from the long-distance spice trade to Europe, though it is the trade for which they are best known.) He remarks that the basic Portuguese revenues were derived from "redistribution"—a polite word for a policy based upon force, or the threat of it, rather than upon the ability to transmit goods and sell them competitively. By holding such strategically placed fortresses as those at Hormuz, Diu, Goa, Cochin, Colombo, and Malacca and by operating fleets to patrol the sea lanes between them, the Portuguese could oblige all native vessels peddling wares up and down the Indian west coast and in the vicinity of the Straits of Malacca to purchase *cartazes*, laissez-passer documents. These additionally obliged the bearers to call in at all the Portuguese fortresses along their routes and pay ad valorem customs duties, thereby producing even more revenue.[4] Finally, because the Portuguese encountered resistance to this system, notably from the Kunjali pirates who were sheltered by the hostile Samorin of Calicut, they had to organize the cartaz-carrying peddlers in convoys, for which they also charged a tax. These incomes, as one can readily see, were not the results of buying and selling per se, but rather of syphoning some of the proceeds therefrom into the Portuguese treasury. The closest the Estado da Índia Oriental, as the areas administered by the viceroy in Goa were called, ever came to becoming an actual merchant itself within Asia was through the concession of annual voyage rights to individual Portuguese *fidalgos*, or traders, for a single trip to Japan and China, the Moluccas, or Pegu, among other places—in return for a percentage of the profits. In addition, it is worth noting that a number of ex-soldiers who had left service to the Portuguese state went into activities for themselves. They were, however, an informal aspect of the Estado, linked to it only by language, perhaps by residence (they did not always reside in areas under Portuguese jurisdiction), and also perhaps by capital illegally invested by Portuguese officials, invariably under another's name. At any rate, the Estado da Índia was in no sense itself a merchant save for the concession voyages and also for some horses sold to interior Indian states, a trade it had inherited from the rulers of Goa prior to 1510.

By contrast, the two East India companies, the English (founded in 1600) and the Dutch (founded in 1602), were truly mercantile in that the essence of their operations was buying and selling. Unlike the Portuguese, whose fees added to the net price of doing business, their well-capitalized superpeddling operations in Asia actually reduced the price of doing business in a given region—as shown by comparative figures Steensgaard has collected for the Persian Gulf trade.

The two companies both possessed armaments, but they were commanded by merchants, not soldiers, and, aside from a few esquires in English service, there were hardly any noblemen at all in the Dutch and English management structure. One can hardly say the same for the Estado da Índia, which was the almost exclusive province of nobles. And no wonder.

The whole history of the Iberian Peninsula is bucolic and military, not commercial, and there was almost no exchanging of products between the ports and the hinterland. There are no river systems of any kind to compare with the Rhine or the Maas and no canals whatsoever, and internal agricultural products largely duplicate one another, although in early modern times Portugal did import some Castilian grain. What merchants there were in Lisbon and Oporto hardly played the dynamic role in Portuguese society that their counterparts played in London, Amsterdam, Antwerp, or the other national societies in the north. Instead, through the fifteenth century, the Portuguese fit better into the warrior tradition of the *Reconquista* than into the merchant tradition of England or Flanders. In 1415, the attack on Ceuta had taken place because they were spoiling for a fight and booty, and all during the fifteenth century they had honed their martial skills in Morocco.

Of the perhaps million and a quarter souls in Portugal at the time the sea route to Asia was discovered, there may have been about 20,000 nobles of any kind, and these were grouped into a few score important families. Probably because the country was so small, one does not find the king struggling to offset them by creating an administrative bureaucracy as a counterweight as in other European countries, but only to find sufficiently educated men of any background to fill the upper and middle administrative posts. One reason the house of Aviz did not seem to fear the nobility as much as did, say, the Trastamaras in Spain is that after the revolution of the 1380s the founder of the house, João I, had elevated all his supporters, including some Lisbon merchants, incidentally, to the highest ranks of the land. He left the old nobility, who had opposed him, in isolation. Hence the fortunes of the powerful "new" nobility and the new ruling house were intertwined. To make matters more complicated, the nobility frequently invested spare income in trading activities, to the extent that some historians even believe it slowed the growth of the middle classes.[5] But perhaps the simplest explanation will serve just as well: in such a small country, the kings thought they knew whom to appoint and whom not to, because they knew everybody. Favoring the bourgeoisie as officeholders probably did not seem especially effective or necessary, and in a country where the bourgeoisie were almost as scarce as the nobility, they may not have constituted an alternative, anyhow. One will remember how many Genoese merchants came to settle in Lisbon: the Portuguese commercial classes were not really very large. The net result was that the nobles were allowed to run the administration.

The Portuguese overseas empire was created in a surprisingly few years after da Gama's discovery of the Cape route. In fact, the Estado da Índia Oriental was virtually complete in 1515, only sixteen years after da Gama first returned from Calicut. Because of the special circumstances, its creation was essentially a job for conquistadores, and that meant that the nobility played the essential role. They faced hostile Muslim merchants and rulers, who reminded them of the Moors nearer home and put up an equally sharp fight. With sure military instinct, the Portuguese went for the jugular, the strategic Asian trade emporia. They captured Goa in 1510, Malacca in 1511, and Hormuz in 1515, and all the while they sailed around the Indian Ocean, looking for victims and booty. Thus from a rapid string of conquests and a series of hijackings their redistributive system emerged. I cannot imagine how the Portuguese could have created anything else with what circumstances and materials they had at hand. Even while conquering they were faced with innovating a scheme for management and exploitation of their new gains. They had little time to decide. They appointed a governor, later often with a viceroy's title, they named captains to command each important fortress, appointed a *feitor,* or factor, a business manager, to handle the king's business and trade in each port, created *alfândegas,* or customhouses, on the medieval Portuguese model, threw in some judges and treasury officials, and put them all, including the governor-viceroy, on three-year terms. Then, to establish ranking priority for jobs, they passed them out according to degrees of the applicants' nobility. In this respect, there came to exist in Portuguese overseas society a microcosm of what prevailed in the metropolis. It was to prove a mistake, for the nobles, even though they may have had some administrative experience from their estates, were not given to clerical pursuits.

Obviously, what the Crown needed was a loyal bureaucracy, with a mercantile background, keeping exact books of exact piles of money in the royal treasury. But the people who volunteered for India service were wild, proud, and less than completely qualified fidalgos, who would rather board a Muslim vessel than push a quill pen; after all, they were conquistadores, only doing what came naturally. From the start there were rumors and anonymous letters to Lisbon claiming gross irregularity, matched by wild deeds that might make excellent fare for Hollywood westerns with minimal alteration of topography and costume. Some, however, might seem too cruel even for adult audiences. The nasty shoot-out in Goa between the factions of Lopo Vaz de Sampaio and Pero Mascarenhas, occasioned by Mascarenhas's absence in Malacca when he was appointed viceroy, could easily be reenacted in Tombstone Gulch; but Diogo Lopes de Mesquita's murder of the sultan of Ternate, when the ruler caught onto his graft involving the royal monopoly, might prove too vile an act even for the baddest bad man of the West. Refusing the sultan's relatives even possession of the murdered man's corpse, he cut it into chunks and hurled them into the sea. This happened in 1568.

On the other hand, even though Lisbon might have liked to dilute this kind of behavior by giving partial authority to civilian judicial types, like the *oidores* of the Spanish colonial *audiencias,* there was probably no way it dared to. As Couto wrote, Asia was a place where one must go about "with sword in hand"—meaning that the Portuguese holdings there were surrounded by enemies who might attack at any moment; it would not do to have the viceroy's power subject to a council that could communicate directly with the king. (The heartland of Spanish America was all but immune to attack; hence, Madrid could afford a greater diffusion of power there.) I also suspect that even had the king chosen to make the legally trained civilian *letrados* coresponsible with the military managers, it is doubtful whether this would have restrained the fidalgos. The judges of Goan courts were notoriously corrupt; it is doubtful the letrados as a class would have been any better. Moreover, the letrado class was fully as closed as the fidalgo, and in most cases the letrados were of noble origin themselves.[6] Thanks to the small numbers of the aristocracy, it is doubtful whether a letrado looking over his shoulder would necessarily have kept a fidalgo honest when both found out they came from Viseu or that they both had the same great-grandfather. In short, even if rule by civilian administrators might have been theoretically desirable, it was probably not a real alternative in Portuguese Asia.

At any rate, the foul deeds of the *fidalguia* are not the acts of merchants but of a class long bred to use of the rapier and pike. (In all the annals of the Dutch and English companies, one will find little violence so imaginative.) Prior to about 1575 in the Portuguese empire, there had been plenty of foul deeds committed, as the letters of Dom João de Castro, Simão Botelho, and St. Francis Xavier will attest.[7] But in 1571, Viceroy D. Luís de Ataíde and his soldiers could still turn in a spectacular martial performance against the combined armies of Bijapur, Ahmadnagar, Achin, and the Samorin, and this shows that the spirit of Albuquerque and Almeida was not entirely dead. But soon thereafter, during the closing decades of the sixteenth century, everything went, as two Portuguese witnesses were convinced, straight to hell.

These witnesses were Diogo do Couto and Francisco Rodrigues de Silveira, who both served as soldiers based in Goa during the last two decades of the sixteenth century; Couto later became an official of middling rank and a chronicler. It is not known what office, if any, Silveira filled; he was probably only the equivalent of a noncommissioned officer. Both have written typical *arbítrios,* that is, they are to be identified with the *arbitristas,* the patriotic self-appointed tract writers who realized that something was going seriously wrong with Iberian society soon after the turn of the seventeenth century (or even earlier) and set out to memorialize the Crown with analyses and solutions.

Couto's *O soldado prático,* of course, is well known to Lusitanists not only as a historical but as a literary work. Silveira is much less known, undoubtedly because his 408-page manuscript, the "Reformação da milícia e governo do estado da Índia Oriental" was bowdlerized by A. de S. S. Costa Lobo, a nineteenth-century amateur scholar.[8] He was attracted to Rodrigues de Silveira's description of his experiences but turned off by his arbitrista side. As a result he ignored it almost completely and selected and strung together the descriptive material under such chapter headings as "Expedição ao Mar Roxo," filling in gaps in the text with his own narrative, publishing it in 1877 under the misleading title *Memórias de um Soldado da Índia.* No one reading the book would know what the manuscript really contained.

What it does contain is a revelation surprisingly similar in kind to that of the *Soldado Prático* but somewhat different in scope. Couto, the experienced officeholder, knew the workings of the administration better than Rodrigues de Silveira, but he had either forgotten how it was to be a soldier or, more probable, he thought what he had to say about the inner workings of government more important. Silveira had no other experience: soldiering was all he knew, and being more than ordinarily perceptive he knew the military system from top to bottom.

Couto's and Silveira's testimony indicates that not only was Hurstfield's commonweal clearly subverted, but it was deliberately flouted by a mass conspiracy. Nor was it even M. N. Pearson's ideas of perquisites or profiteering that was at issue. It was no less than mass criminality involving all the highest officers of the state. They routinely acted in collusion to mulct the royal treasury and to shake one another down, much as do today's *mafiosi*. Most rackets like the *dívidas velhas*, or "old debts," had counterparts in Europe where the viceroy would regularly confiscate property on the false pretext of state emergency, issue certificates of generous value for the owners' goods taken, then avoid payment until the viceroy's entourage had acquired the certificates from the victims for a fraction of their face value. Then the certificates were paid in full out of the royal treasury. But many abuses went far beyond European practice. The viceroys, for example, privately minted money for their own use, sold all offices illegally, and personally pocketed the proceeds.[9] The treasury overseas procured all supplies for the state, many of them unnecessary, at exorbitant prices and always, of course, from their friends. They routinely bought full ships of luxury goods with treasury money for resale on their own accounts. Fortress captains confiscated passing vessels on flimsy pretexts, unmercifully stole from the natives under their jurisdiction, traded privately with the kings' ships, committed acts of piracy, and regularly extracted two or three times the customs taxes levied by the state. Then the viceroys made a personal voyage to inspect their books, or so their visits were advertised. Their real end was to shake down the captains in return for viceregal silence. Elsewhere, justice was sold to the highest bidder by judges of the courts or used to back up the seizures and illegal acts of the administration.

Couto had only disdain for the quality of the once formidable Portuguese soldiery. He says that where once they were called "frangues" or "Franks"—the Arab nickname for Crusaders in the Middle Ages—now they were called *frangãos* (chickens).[10] He does not tell why, but Silveira does: the viceroys out of "insáciavel cubiça" (insatiable greed) refused to pay their troops. The soldiers consequently did not show up for service, whereupon the viceroys sent out squads to arrest them and force them to work.[11] Aside from these squads themselves and a few other hoodlums, the troops were undernourished and had either no arms or very poor ones and no training whatsoever. In battle they frequently threw down their weapons and fled if the going became rough. Most of the soldiers who came out from Portugal every year simply disappeared within a year or two and were never seen again, either taking service under Indian rulers, marrying native women and melting into the depressed Indian peasantry, or simply becoming undernourished and dying of disease. Meanwhile, the viceroys pocketed the money and called upon the king for new levies of men to be sent yearly from Portugal.

There is amply detailed corroboration for all of this in the *Itinerario* of Jan Huighen van Linschoten and the *Voyages* of François

Pyrard de Laval, and to a lesser extent in the writings of another
Frenchman, Jean Mocquet. These accounts written by foreign visitors
and exact contemporaries indicate that the malfeasance was common
knowledge, obvious to even the casual foreign visitor. As written testimony, it would constitute ample evidence of the most damning kind in
a court of Roman law. Incidentally, there are also hundreds of tattle-
tale letters to the Crown, but since the motives are obviously to get an
enemy in trouble, I have excluded them as permissible evidence.

Yet the fact remains that the extent and the depth of the problem
has never been appreciated or understood by recent historians, for
three reasons. The first is that they wonder how the king of Portugal
could really ever have received the valuable cargoes from Asia that he
did or seen the scrupulous handling of the bullion he sent out to purchase spices if things had really been that crooked. If Portuguese Asia
was really so corrupt, why did the Crown not suffer more than it did?
The answer is, I think, rather simple: the pilfering was at the expense
of the redistributive income, generated in Asia, but not of the king's
trade. In both Iberian empires, Spanish and Portuguese, local income
from taxes raised in the separate Crowns, vice-royalties, and other administrative units was routinely absorbed in the same areas for their
administration and defense,[12] while the bulk of the royal revenues was
derived from import of spices or specie. The worms could, and undoubtedly did, eat up the entire redistributive revenue of Portuguese
Asia without directly affecting the king's profits (or losses) in the spice
trade. There is evidence that this trade was tightly overseen, and at
any rate it would have only been discreet to leave alone what directly
affected the king.

A second reason the magnitude of the decadência has probably
never been appreciated is that it has not been compared intelligently
with the corruption of the contemporary European empires in the
same Indian Ocean. There is the tendency to dismiss the shenanigans
of the Portuguese as no worse than anyone else's—weren't the Dutch
and the English just as bad, to say nothing of the Spanish? The answer
must be "Not to the same extent." The commercial companies paid
very generous salaries to their officers, promoted commoners to the
highest posts, and were centered around trading activities, not redis-
tributions. As one might expect, corruption was at the expense of
trade, mostly the peddler trade, and in modern terms might be described as involving moonlighting and even "sunlighting" with company equipment.[13] It did not involve the highest officers ordinarily: so
far as I know, there is not a single case of malfeasance affecting a governor-general, nor did any of it exhibit the conspiratorial nature of

the Portuguese misdoing—which required the consent and participation of nearly everybody, especially at the top. When one of the few honest viceroys of his time, Dom Vasco Mascarenhas, the first Count of Óbidos and Viceroy of Portuguese India, tried to clean up the corruption, he was overthrown by what appear to have been his own councilors. Usually the viceroys themselves pocketed the lion's share of the military payroll and required bribes from the fortress captains. By contrast, in Spanish America at the nadir of metropolitan control during the seventeenth century, it was not the viceroys or the *audiencias* who were so notoriously and openly corrupt but the *corregidores de indios,* officers who administered the remote Indian districts.

The third and final reason the peculiar character of the decadência has not been generally recognized by recent historians as a uniquely depraved period in the history of colonialism is that nobody has been able to explain why it, or something like it, should have taken place when it did; hence it does not seem to fit into any interpretive matrix. I have already ventured that the military and redistributive nature of the imperial operation and its exclusively noble upper leadership predisposed it to rapine. But one factor seems necessary to explain the peculiar depravity after 1580: upheaval in Portugal itself.

What I believe must have brought out all the weaknesses inherent in the structure of the Asian empire and its leadership was not an Asian event at all but something closer to home. Portugal was economically in poor condition in 1557 when the boy king, Sebastian, inherited it. The circumstances of his death at the Battle of El-Ksar-el-Kebir in 1578 are well known, but what is more important to this story was the death or capture of practically the whole force of around 14,000 men, including some 7,000 of Portugal's fittest fidalgos and troops. The expedition cost half of Portugal's annual state budget, and when El Mansur, the emergent Moorish victor, got around to assessing ransoms on the surviving fidalgos (and even on their corpses), it all but ruined whole noble clans. Mansur built El-Bedi, "The Wonderful," the most lavish palace of his time with these proceeds and even had money left over to make loans to European monarchs.

Two years later, even while the ransoming was still going on, King Philip II marched into Portugal to claim its vacant throne by force. The upper nobility, those with bases in Lisbon for the most part, welcomed him and the Spanish connections—only because his ambassador, Don Cristóbal de Moura, himself a Portuguese, had distributed money where it would most help defray the heavy ransoms. To the ambitious among the Portuguese city nobility, the Spanish connection in itself meant greater opportunity and wider horizons. Not so with lower and middle classes and the country nobility, where national feeling was strong.

These classes were not merely depressed and disillusioned by the death of their king, their growing impoverishment, and their subjection by a Spanish army; the peasants even lost their sense of reality and expected Sebastian to return in miraculous form. The nobility, not so ignorant, seem to have had a different reaction. Rodrigues de Silveira, when he returned to Portugal in 1598, was quick to notice the difference: the bureaucracy there, in its own way, showed the same grasping, totally unfeeling hardness he knew all about in Goa, and he topped off his tract on reform of India with one on reform in Portugal itself.

The period of greatest corruption in the Dutch East India Company in Asia during the eighteenth century exactly coincided with a period of corruption and economic depression at home. Surely it was no coincidence that the same thing had happened earlier in Portugal and in India when penniless, disillusioned nobles, who felt no compensatory loyalty to a Spanish king, went to the colonies to recoup their fortunes, and, thanks to the system, were given preferred jobs.[14] Their form of Sebastianism was not a longing for ghosts but for something more substantial. Their legacy was to leave Portuguese Asia without resources to resist invasion from Europe, just as Linschoten wrote in his *Itinerario,* published in 1592. Of this book Rodrigues de Silveira observed: "Our disorders [in India] are painted in living colors . . . for Italy, Flanders [the Dutch], France, and England to affirm. If the enemy nations compose books about our discomfiture and our bad government in order to attack us . . . how is it possible that the Portuguese do not awake now from their slumber and do something about it?"[15]

We have now come full circle back to what C. R. Boxer said. It was not corruption per se, but the Dutch who ruined the Portuguese. But it seems equally true that the internal pillage of the decadência made their work much easier.

Notes

1. J. Hurstfield, "Political Corruption in Modern England," *History* 52(1967):19.

2. Michael N. Pearson, "Corruption and Corsairs in Sixteenth-Century Western India: A Functional Analysis," in Blair B. Kling and M. N. Pearson, eds., *The Age of Partnership: Europeans in Asia before Dominion* (Honolulu: University Press of Hawaii, 1979), pp. 19 ff.

3. Jan Jacob van Klaveren, "Die Historische Erscheinung der Korruption in ihrer Zusammenhang mit der Staats- und Gesellschaftstruktur betrachtet," *Vierteljahrschrift für Sozial- und Wirtschaftsgeschichte* 44–45 (1957–58).

4. Niels Steens Steensgaard, *Carracks, Caravans and Companies: The Structural Crisis in the European-Asian Trade in the Early Seventeenth Century,* Scandinavian Institute of Asian Studies Monograph Series, No. 17 (Copenhagen: Studentlitteratur, 1972), pp. 86–90; also, M. N. Pearson, *Merchants and Rulers in Gujarat* (Los Angeles and Berkeley: University of California Press, 1977), chap. 2.

5. A. H. de Oliveira Marques, *History of Portugal,* 2 vols. (New York and London: Columbia University Press, 1972), vol. 1, *From Lusitania to Empire,* pp. 180–81.

6. Henrique da Gama Barros, *História da Administração Pública em Portugal nos Séculos XII à XV,* ed. Torquato de Sousa Soares, 2d ed., 9 vols. (Lisbon: Sá da Costa, 1945), 3: 257n.4.

7. These are conveniently summarized in Richard S. Whiteway, *The Rise of the Portuguese Power in India, 1497–1550* (London, 1899; London and Santiago de Compostela: Susil Gupta, 1967), pp. 22–23, 290–96.

8. Francisco Rodrigues de Silveira, "Reformação da milícia e governo do estado da Índia Oriental," no. 25:419 in the Additional Manuscripts Collection, British Museum, London.

9. The Hapsburgs sold all offices in their Spanish empire but did not try introducing the practice into the Estado da Índia until 1616. Apparently, the viceroys sabotaged it in order to keep the money themselves. See Luís Augusto Rebello da Silva, *História de Portugal nos Séculos XVII e XVIII,* 5 vols. (Lisbon, 1860–71), 3: 283.

10. Diogo do Couto, *O soldado prático,* ed. M. Rodrigues Lapa (Lisbon: Sá da Costa, 1937), p. xxiii. For examples of Couto's disdain for the latter-day Portuguese soldiery, see pp. 115, 145, 149, 153, 215, among others.

11. Silveira, "Reformação," fols. 7, 72v.

12. For example, see Helmut G. Koenigsberger, *The Practice of Empire* (Ithaca, N. Y.: Cornell University Press, 1969), pp. 43–58.

13. Note that I have not seen fit to mention the period of Clive and Hastings in India. I do not think it applies, for one will remember that this epoch was one of conquest and its booty—and on a far grander scale than anything the Portuguese ever achieved. The Portuguese decadência occurred in a time of stagnation and contraction, both in the metropolis and in the empire.

14. Ironically enough, the Hapsburgs, in seeking to exert better control over Portugal after the takeover, tried to downgrade the role of the court nobility and promote regionalism by favoring for employment the country nobility, who had the least training and felt the least loyalty to the Spanish connection. See *Dicionário de História de Portugal,* ed. Joel Serrão, 4 vols. (Lisbon: Iniciativas Editoriais, [1971]), 3: 154–55.

15. Silveira, "Reformação," fols. 151v.–152.

Angola in the Sixteenth Century— Um Mundo que o Português Encontrou

Joseph C. Miller

WHAT CAN an Anglophone Africanist add to the proceedings of a conference in celebration of the quadricentennial of the death of Luís de Camões? Portugal's two largest modern colonies in Africa, Angola and Mozambique, were the remnants of an empire that descended from the sixteenth-century imperial glories that the great poet witnessed and extolled four centuries ago. These African territories were also the primary tropical possessions where twentieth-century Portuguese ideologues claimed to be putting into practice the distinctively open, pragmatic, and catholic attitude toward tropical peoples that Camões had proclaimed and that their Brazilian contemporary, Gilberto Freyre, celebrated in his evocations of the science he called "Lusotropicology," or the study of Portuguese adaptability in the tropics, their openness to the new knowledge and the exotic sensibilities of peoples whom they met there.[1]

Freyre also praised Portuguese contributions to that modern Lusophone paradise in the tropics, a spiritual and cultural space that he termed "the world the Portuguese created" (*o mundo que o português criou*).[2] Freyre's Portuguese thus gave as much as to the cultural amalgam of the twentieth-century empire as they received. The peculiarity of the position of the Anglophone Africanist confronting Camões, whom Freyre praised also as the pioneer articulator of this Portuguese creativity in the tropics,[3] derives from his own heritage to a disparaging countercurrent in English and American scholarship with regard to the Portuguese in tropical Africa. This drift flows almost as deep among writers in English as the notion of a "Lusotropical" initiative runs among speakers of Portuguese. It arose almost as its necessary complement in the nineteenth and twentieth centuries as Portuguese emphasis on their adaptability across wide cultural gulfs grew to stress also their responsibility for the assimilative culture of the empire to which they clung, eventually to the near-total exclusion of African contributions.

English writers on Portuguese West Africa from the time of David Livingstone[4] have exerted themselves in condemning what they have perceived as the falsity of this "myth of Lusotropicalism." Their reaction intensified particularly against the highly politicized formulation of Freyre's Lusotropicology as a Portuguese civilizing mission that developed in the late Salazar-Caetano government in Lisbon during the 1960s and early 1970s.[5] Rather than this Salazarist donation of Lusitanian culture to a largely passive Africa, Anglophone Africanists preferred to see a set of vital, autonomous tropical worlds that Camões and his countrymen had found abroad, worlds from which they took much more in people, wealth, and human suffering than they gave in language, religion, or knowledge, and even worlds not so different from what they had known at home. In this sense, Angola becomes a *mundo que o português encontrou,* a not unfamiliar world that the Portuguese encountered, and into which they easily fit without making the great adaptive leaps that later Lusotropicologists attributed to them. The image of Africa as alien and passive, a place out of which they "created" a new tropical world according to Freyre's perspective, in fact grew more from the closed minds of modern Portuguese eulogizers than from the true experiences of Camões's early explorers.

It may in fact represent a modest return toward Camões's own inquiring spirit that an Anglophone Africanist like myself should attempt to reduce the appearance of dissimilarity between the Portuguese and the people and civilizations that the poet's contemporaries found in western central Africa. The vigor and agility of the sixteenth-century Portuguese consisted of recognizing the well-defined human geography and the established political and economic institutions of this Angolan world and in directing their energies along lines set at least as much by the Africans as by themselves.

One can appreciate how the divergence of focus between Anglophone and Lusophile scholarship on Africa has made an essay of this sort possible even without going into the details of discussions between writers of Portuguese and their English and American antagonists about the complex reasons for their differences of opinion. Their debates have stimulated both careful documentary critiques by Lusophone scholars[6] and a tenaciously countervailing interpretive effort among English, American, and other non-Portuguese students. The dialectic has generated a reconstruction of the sixteenth-century Angolan world that is unusually clear and complete by Africanist standards, according to what some have called an "African perspective." Historians can now glimpse at least the general outlines of the African side of this world, discerning who was living where, what they were doing, and perhaps something of why they were doing it, on occasion hundreds of miles into the interior of the continent. Even these limited conclusions frame and add dimension to better known detailed events among the Portuguese and their closest African associates along the not necessarily typical coastal fringes of the region.

The Angola to which I refer is the Angola *senso largo* of the eighteenth-century English: the entire southwestern coast of Africa running southward nearly seventeen degrees of latitude from equatorial Cape Lopes to the mouth of the Kunene River, and its hinterlands. It is a part of Africa that Camões never knew personally at all and of which he did not write directly, since his outbound route to India passed far to the south. Although the usual return course from Asia ran northward not far off the Angolan shoreline, few *naus* called there in the 1560s, at the time when Camões presumably returned to Portugal from the East. Even before Camões's time, however, since the first arrival of Diogo Cão in the Zaire River estuary between 1482 and 1484, other Portuguese had been exploring these parts of southwestern Africa, and some had become well acquainted with the inhabitants of its littoral.

For them, the name "Angola" referred to only the small region inland along the lower Kwanza River behind a sheltered bay known as Luanda. The area just to the north of the Zaire mouth they came to call Loango. The coasts farther south beyond the Kwanza they termed Benguela, and they applied other names particularly to the peoples living along bays and estuaries nearer the Kunene River to the lands there. They knew best the region between the Zaire and Kwanza rivers and named those lands after kings of the Kongo state claiming dominion over the farmers in the vicinity. Much of what the Portuguese discovered—indeed one sometimes suspects that nearly all of their discoveries—they learned from the African lords and merchants with whom they struck up commercial dealings, whose courts and compounds they frequented, and whose trading routes they eventually followed into the interior.[7]

African farmers of that era along the coast preferred to live in the best-watered portions of a generally sandy and arid terrain. Vegetation cover thinned rapidly from relatively moist woods and grasslands near the mouth of the Zaire River to the dry scrub beyond the Kwanza and to almost wholly barren desert at the mouth of the Kunene. Inland, beyond a forested mountainous scarp that rose up to the great plateau dominating the center of the continent, most people probably congregated in a band of fertile lowlands running east-west at about the latitude of the Zaire River estuary. To the south of them, high, sabulous, lightly populated plains declined toward the Kalahari Desert, where only sparse human populations herded cattle to survive the prevailing dryness. Life there particularly revolved around water, and the only settlements of any size occupied isolated riverine oases along the middle Kunene and the lower Okavango rivers.

The Kongo kingdom, where the Portuguese concentrated their attention in the early sixteenth century, consisted of provinces centered on plains along the lower Zaire and in the adjoining river valleys and probably contained the greatest density of people living anywhere near the Angolan coast.[8] Other Africans who lived in the valleys of the Kwanza and Lukala rivers inland from Luanda Bay, perhaps as far as the basin of the middle Kwango, began to find a few Portuguese in their midst not long after. Whatever those southerners might have called themselves at the time,[9] the Portuguese adopted the Kongo appellation for them: Mbundu. Ovimbundu-speaking farmers on the broad central highlands upland from the southerly open bay known later as the Benguela and Nkhumbi-speaking herders along the remote lower course of the Kunene as yet had encountered no Europeans. The widening band of increasingly arid desert along that part of the coast largely insulated these interior peoples from the sea until later in the seventeenth century. The Portuguese of the time were hardly even rumors in the ears of the smaller and still less maritime-oriented nuclei of relatively dense habitation farther to the east. The Kongo and the Mbundu, the largest African populations living near the sea, led the first Portuguese to set foot on Angolan soils mostly along paths they had already trod.

We have no reason to believe that the ethnic identities of these Angolans were more tradition-bound, less responsive to geographical movement, less malleable at the hands of unknown African creative geniuses like that of Camões, or less pliable in the aggregate, than the culture of the Portuguese. All those African communities had coalesced in preceding centuries as farmers and herders had modified an ancient cultural heritage brought into the region by pioneer ancestors from the north and east, who had made their way into unknown Angolan lands much as the Portuguese later probed the adjoining oceans. They all spoke closely related languages belonging to the single large family of tongues known as Bantu,[10] and they were creating an expressive fund of widespread and symbolic representations of their philosophical speculations, even as Camões defined canons of subsequent Portuguese thought and expression.[11]

In the agriculturally marginal terrain of southwestern central Africa, where irregular and insufficient rainfall often made the availability of millet and sorghum an uncertain proposition at best,[12] the farmers and herders had multiplied in the widely separated pockets of moister land along the lower Zaire, in the valleys of the Lukala, Kwanza, and Kwango rivers, and also in the central highland areas where they later attracted Portuguese attention. Where settlers had taken up the herding of cattle beyond the limits of dependable agriculture, they always anchored their grazing patterns in river valleys that carried at least seasonal supplies of good water through the dry southern deserts. Only in the higher hills and plains of the watershed east of the Kwanza and Kunene, where hardy frontiersmen had combined a flexible shifting agriculture with hunting and gathering of the natural produce of the woods there, did the inhabitants lack clearly defined geographical anchors of this sort.

The residents of each such distinct population nucleus already differed profoundly from the others by the sixteenth century, owing to distinctive historical experiences that may have reached back over as much as a millenium.[13] The considerable distances separating these groups encouraged people in each of them to elaborate distinctive living and linguistic habits, specialized social and political institutions, and other innovative practices that had given specific ecologically influenced cultural identities to these ethnocultural communities by the time the Portuguese encountered them. Although some of these identities survived to become bases for the ethnic communities of the twentieth century, others faded, still other new ones coalesced, and individual Africans then, as later, moved from culture to culture with no less flexibility than some Portuguese exhibited overseas. African cultures exhibited the same plasticity (as Freyre would have put the matter) that Camões claimed for his own compatriots.

One of the great creations of the Portuguese in this sixteenth-century Angolan world, as modern Lusotropicologists viewed the issue, was their Christianization of the kingdom of Kongo. The conversion to Catholicism of the Kongo monarch who became famous in Europe under his Christian name, Afonso I (1506–43), is a cornerstone in the edifice of Lusotropicalism. This conversion allowed missionaries and diplomats to claim credit for profound cultural change among the Africans. Indeed, much of the aristocracy of the Kongo kingdom assumed Christian names, sponsored the practice of the Christian religion at their courts, and took Christian European titles of nobility.

Less well known than this apparent Portuguese-inspired shift in the bases of politics in Kongo, but equally important, were even deeper continuities in terms of Kongo religious thought, political action, and institutional history that Afonso and his court asserted through their conversion to Catholicism.[14] Afonso in fact used the missionaries and the Christian faith to pursue thoroughly Kongo political aims of consolidating royal power, not unlike the contemporary monarchs in Europe, synthesized the new religion with local ideas familiar to his subjects, and left it as the ideological framework through which later Kongo worked out political conflicts born of equally local circumstances well into the nineteenth century. The sixteenth-century mission Christianity taken to Kongo may, in any case, have differed less from Kongo beliefs than modern Catholicism did later.[15] Viewed in terms of ongoing African cultural change and the ideological level of Kongo politics, Afonso's imaginative use of Christianity absorbed Portuguese culture into the tropics.

African historical processes similarly oriented the economic level of Euro-African contact. Afonso's aggressive strategies in Kongo and subsequent internal struggles against his centralization of power fed captives into the beginnings of the export trade in slaves, which only later acquired a momentum and destructiveness of its own beyond the pace of African political developments. Afonso and his sixteenth-century royal successors provoked hostile reactions among the local African lords as they attempted to consolidate royal control over the semi-autonomous provinces of the previously segmented Kongo polity and to extend their personal power into bordering regions. Such resistance to Kongo expansiveness appears to have driven rulers of the Ngola kingdom among the Mbundu between the Kwanza and Lukala rivers to assert their authority to the east and south by mounting wars of their own.

Captives taken in these Mbundu wars drew Portuguese slavers from the nearby island of São Tomé in the Gulf of Guinea and led to a second and growing southern branch of the slave export trade. By mid-century these slaves supported a commercial settlement at Luanda Bay, and the growing power of the Ngola eventually brought a crown-appointed representative from Portugal, Paulo Dias de Novaes, to the scene in the 1560s.[16] Refugees from the Ngola kings' expansive militarism fled south beyond the Kwanza toward the central highlands, where some established themselves as warlords in their own right. Their heirs in turn acted as future poles of attraction to seventeenth-century Portuguese slavers. African political tensions thus spread warfare out of control at the end of the sixteenth century and created new militaristic African polities from the Kwanza River all the way south to the sources of the Kunene, with the increasing numbers of captives they took beckoning Portuguese opportunists to the scenes of their conflicts.

The rhythm of conflict, warfare, and slaving in sixteenth-century Angola—as also in later centuries virtually to the present—was as much African as European in another sense as well. Armies marched to the cadence of recurrent droughts more than to any other single factor.[17] Portuguese bellicosity consequently rose and fell also with waves of hunger and disease that swept over African sorghum and millet farmers who crowded together in the moister valleys when the rains failed. Starving refugees sold their children as slaves to foreigners who could at least feed them. Competition for dwindling food supplies at such times drove the more assertive to fight one another and others to support themselves by assailing Portuguese trading caravans along hinterland trails. The Portuguese responded in kind to such assaults, but seldom with lasting effect on their enemies. Though repeated Portuguese military forays gradually increased their influence over one African state after another, they seldom won definitive victories in the sixteenth century. Portuguese forces only briefly occupied the capital of the Kongo in the 1570s, and in the 1580s and 1590s Dias de Novaes's captains still strained unsuccessfully to carve out a territorial conquest eastward from their bayside fortification at Luanda.

The definitive establishment of Portuguese military rule, which came only between 1610 and 1620, and then only as a secondary consequence of warfare among the Africans, exemplified the great extent to which their armed activities responded to drought and to domestic African politics.[18] Intrepid as some European commanders may have been, the territorial conquests of that decade came about less because of intensified Portuguese military efforts than because a series of governors at Luanda managed to ride the momentum of desperate African warriors who swarmed out of the hills in mobile bands of fighters whom contemporaries called Jagas (but whom recent historians have termed Imbangala).[19] Refugees from the military expansion of the Ngola kingdom beginning in the 1550s and 1560s had disturbed the lands of farmers whose families had lived on the central plateau for generations. The pressure they must have put on that limited cropland would have forced younger men to form roving gangs of landless bandits, youths cast loose from their agricultural origins and displaced from the densely inhabited valleys of their birth by the violence of slaving.

A period of extended drought in the 1580s and 1590s added to the growing distress attending these refugees' flight into less fertile areas. Hunger swelled the bandits' ranks to form hordes of marauders who streamed down from the central highland areas toward the coast and into the lower river valleys in search of food and booty. These Imbangala, spurred on after 1610 by renewed drought and by then supported by the Portuguese governors at Luanda, crossed the Kwanza, reduced the old Ngola kingdom to a shambles, threatened the Kongo, and by selling their captives to waiting Portuguese drove the whole region across the watershed toward two and one-half centuries of systematic slaving. Throughout those later centuries, the endemic warfare and violence of slaving in the Angolan interior repeatedly reached epidemic proportions in the wake of serious drought and the consequent famine and disease. Portuguese military exploits conducted in the venturesome spirit of Camões frequently followed the upheavals arising from African ecological stress.[20]

The commercial activity of the Portuguese in sixteenth-century Angola, which had mainly exploited an established regional commodity trading system centered on the Kongo kingdom, followed African patterns even more than did their successors' nearly exclusive concentration on slaving.[21] The resident communities of Portuguese at São Tomé and Luanda established themselves as important brokers in trade linking the forested regions of the Zaire basin in the north and east, the coast on the west, and the grassy woodlands and cattle-raising steppes to the south. Hardwoods, animal and fiber products, livestock, salt, dried fish, shells, and other commodities from all of these ecologically distinctive zones had moved earlier in quantities sufficient to support the growth of the pre-Christian Kongo monarchy. Portuguese sailing vessels and maritime skills doubtless increased the volume of goods flowing between these African markets through a complex web of exchanges that at times produced slaves as hardly more than a by-product. It was only after the late sixteenth-century droughts, the depredations of the Imbangala, and the arrival of metropolitan merchants following in the wake of Dias de Novaes at Luanda that slaving began to replace cattle from the southern coasts, dyewoods, copper, and raffia palm cloths of the Loango region, and salt and shells from the Kongo coastlands as the core of the coastal trade.

The local communities of "Portuguese" who entered so deeply

into the circuits of Kongo commerce were themselves not much more
Portuguese than the intra-African trade they conducted. Many of
them, including community leaders and others who set cultural trends
and fashions, had been born from marriages between Portuguese
males and African women. By such unions, the Portuguese continued
African practices in still another way, but they also thus expressed
their own appreciation of the fundamental importance of marriages
in confirming and consolidating relationships with prominent economic and political dimensions. Hence their trading contacts, turned
into marital unions, produced a composite Creole world in both a
physical and a spiritual sense, perhaps the only world that the Portuguese helped the Africans to create.[22] Portuguese fathers in Angola
performed the same procreative role that generations of Arab and
Persian merchants had filled on the east coast of Africa, where those
immigrants and their African women had generated a Muslim Swahili
community of similarly mixed ancestry and culture, and one similarly
unacknowledged as the indigenous society that it was.[23] Such a Luso-
African community surely formed early in the sixteenth century at
the Kongo court and soon expanded to the island of São Tomé, where
men of Luso-Kongo backgrounds became influential sugar planters
and government officials.[24] These Luso-African Creoles promoted the
varied commodity trade of the sixteenth century, employing their
powerful Kongo relatives and in-laws to secure sources of both goods
and slaves. They married their daughters to later immigrant Portuguese, sometimes to exiled criminals with no ties to Europe but on
other occasions to influential merchants who brought contacts in the
metropolitan markets useful for disposing of the sugar that their
slaves grew on the plantations of São Tomé. The same Luso-Africans
almost certainly extended their policies of marriage alliances to the
Ngola polity in the sixteenth century, and they continued such strategies into the eighteenth and nineteenth centuries throughout the Angolan interior.[25]

Thus was created a world of bilingual people who married on the
one hand African nobility and whose children became darker in
physical appearance but who married immigrant Europeans on the
other and thereby received a continuing infusion of Portuguese ideas,
trading goods, and credit. It was these Creoles and their culture that
modern Lusotropicologists have claimed as principal examples of the
Lusitanian genius in the tropics, thanks to their retention of a kind of
Portuguese as the language of commerce and government alongside
the African languages they spoke at home. Another nominally Portuguese aspect of this community was their Catholicism, though prob-

ably by the end of the sixteenth century the religion was hardly more Portuguese than it was Kongo.[26] But the same people whom Lisbon later claimed as countrymen and -women the Portuguese often despised as daughters and sons of Kongo nobility. From the point of view of sixteenth-century Kongo they must have appeared as much Kongo colonists in São Tomé and elsewhere as they would have seemed "Portuguese."

Though some of the Angolan Creoles, or Luso-Africans, later became merchant intermediaries arbitrating between both parent cultures and economies as commercial links between the two continents of Africa and Europe grew tighter, in the middle decades of the sixteenth century these people depended to only a limited extent on European Portugal. They employed the slaves they brought from Kongo and Ngola in significant part on the island of São Tomé, and they collected from adjacent parts of Angola many of the trade goods with which they acquired these captives. Like other Africans, they helped to open the way for metropolitan advances. It was this group's southward probings in search of shells from Luanda Bay that put metropolitan governors in touch with the Mbundu of the lower Kwanza River valley and with their Ngola overlords. The initiatives of the São Tomé Creoles in developing these contacts between the 1520s and 1570s give them credit for bringing to the attention of European Portuguese the name by which the entire coast, later the colony, and now the independent nation of Angola became known.

Their descendants in and around Luanda, and later at Benguela and elsewhere, remained distinct from their business associates and rulers in Portugal. From their perspective, they endured exactly four centuries of colonial rule, from the arrival of Dias de Novaes's expedition in 1575, through the vicissitudes of Dutch occupation in the 1640s, growing metropolitan mercantile intervention in the eighteenth century, and immigration of colonial settlers from Europe in the nineteenth and twentieth centuries, to independence four hundred years later in 1975. The Luso-Africans' was a community of people who, despite their sometimes intimate ties with later generations of Portuguese governors and traders from the world beyond the seas, never lost their equally close connections with their African associates and in-laws to the east.[27]

The dynamic African world of sixteenth-century Angola was in many ways a place not as different from Camões's Portuguese world of adventure and cultural change as later Lusotropicologists have imagined it. In some ways, in fact, the two were so similar that Portuguese immigrants readily understood African commerce, marriage politics, and religious beliefs without having to call upon the extraordinary cultural pliancy that modern pretenders to these alleged qualities subsequently credited to them. The "Portuguese" Creole world of São Tomé and Luanda was not entirely unlike Christian noble circles in Kongo after the conversion of the king, Afonso I. Africans had for a long time creatively modified their own cultural backgrounds before they carried on to meet the Portuguese at least halfway in the sixteenth century. Camões's compatriots often followed African initiatives and survived only by drawing on recognizable African analogues of their own practices, thereby fitting into, more than modifying, the ongoing world they had found.

Only much more recently did misperceiving modern Portuguese find it necessary to explain the early congruences by inventing a Lusotropical myth of plasticity. Ideologues of the twentieth century had by then grown as far removed in spirit from their own ancestors as they had from the residents of the tropics. Though not necessarily more set in their ways, they had lost sight of the similarities between the Africans and those sixteenth-century Portuguese contemporaries of Camões, and so they had to invent a peculiar "openness" to their forebears to explain the contact the first Portuguese had achieved in terms of their own closed Eurocentrism. Angolan domestic politics, droughts, local marriages, trade in regional products, and a resilient Creole community of Luso-Africans had remained an African world that later metropolitan Portuguese continued to encounter in the tropics but one they could no more claim credit for even comprehending than the sixteenth-century Portuguese could lay claim to have created.

Notes

1. Gilberto Freyre, *Le portugais et les tropiques* (Lisbon: Commission exécutive des commémorations du Vᵉ centenaire de la mort du prince Henri, 1961), pp. 5 ff. Also Freyre, *Integração portuguesa nos trópicos* (Lisbon: Junta de Investigações do Ultramar, 1958).

2. Gilberto Freyre, *O mundo que o Português criou: Aspectos das relações sociaes e de cultura do Brasil com Portugal e as colônias portuguesas* (Rio de Janeiro: J. Olympio, 1940).

3. Freyre, *Integração portuguesa*, pp. 31, 35.

4. David Livingstone, *Missionary Travels and Researches in South Africa* (London: J. Murray, 1857).

5. This critical line runs through Henry Nevinson, *A Modern Slavery* (London: Harper and Bros., 1906), William A. Cadbury, *Labour in Portuguese West Africa* (London: George Routledge, 1910), and other studies on the *ser-*

viçal labor recruiting system for São Tomé cocoa estates early in the twentieth century, and on through the various works of Basil Davidson, especially *Which Way Africa?*, also titled *The African Awakening* (London: Cape, 1955), James Duffy, *Portuguese Africa* (Cambridge, Mass.: Harvard University Press, 1959), and *A Question of Slavery* (Oxford: Clarendon, 1967), Charles R. Boxer, *Race Relations in the Portuguese Colonial Empire* (London: Clarendon Press, 1963), and Gerald J. Bender, *Angola under the Portuguese: The Myth and the Reality* (Berkeley and Los Angeles: University of California Press, 1978).

6. E.g., António Brasio, ed., *Monumenta missionaria africana*, 11 vols. (Lisbon: Agência Geraldo Ultramar, 1952–71), Alfredo de Albuquerque Felner, *Angola: Apontamentos sobre a ocupação e início do estabelecimento dos Portugueses no Congo, Angola, e Benguela* (Coimbra: Imprensa da Universidade, 1933), and *Angola: Apontamentos sobre a colonização dos planaltos e litoral do sul de Angola*, 3 vols. (Lisbon: Agência Geral das Colónias, 1940), and many others.

7. A certain amount of deliberate concealment in the reports of Portuguese traders on the scene back to Lisbon may have understated the true extent of their knowledge, thus limiting modern historians' access to what they may have known; for indications from upper Guinea, see George E. Brooks, "Kola Nuts, Senhores? What Kola Nuts?" (paper, Kaabu Conference, Dakar, Senegal, May 1980).

8. Specifically on demography, see John K. Thornton, "Demography and History in the Kingdom of the Kongo," *Journal of African History* 18, no. 4 (1977): 507–30. Two recent and important dissertations on early Kongo are Anne Wilson, "The Kongo Kingdom to the Mid-Seventeenth Century" (University of London, 1977), and John K. Thornton, "The Kingdom of the Kongo in the Era of the Civil Wars, 1641–1718" (University of California, Los Angeles, 1979). The latter has been revised as *The Kingdom of Kongo: Civil War and Transition, 1641–1718* (Madison: University of Wisconsin Press, 1983).

9. Joseph C. Miller, *Kings and Kinsmen: Early Mbundu States in Angola* (Oxford: Clarendon, 1976), especially pp. 37–42. Also on the early Mbundu: Beatrix Heintze, "Unbekanntes Angola: Der Staat Ndongo im 16. Jahrhundert," *Anthropos* 72 (1977): 749–805.

10. The lengthy bibliography on Bantu languages is conveniently summarized in Jan Vansina, "Bantu in the Crystal Ball, I," *History in Africa* 6 (1979): 287–333, and "Bantu in the Crystal Ball, II," *History in Africa* 7 (1980): 293–325. A recent general interpretation appears in Christopher Ehret, "Linguistic Inferences about Early Bantu History," in Ehret and Merrick Posnansky, eds., *The Archaeological and Linguistic Reconstruction of African History* (Berkeley and Los Angeles: University of California Press, 1982), pp. 57–65.

11. E.g., Luc de Heusch, *Le roi ivre, ou l'origine de l'état* (Paris: Gallimard, 1972) and much subsequent commentary. Some initial reactions by historians appear in Joseph C. Miller, ed., *The African Past Speaks* (Folkestone: Dawson, 1980), and in J. Jeffrey Hoover, "The Seduction of Ruwej: Reconstructing Ruund History (The Nuclear Lunda: Zaire, Angola, Zambia)" (Ph.D. dissertation, Yale University, 1978). The systematic critique of de Heusch's (and other

structuralist) method is Jan Vansina, "Is Elegance Proof? Structuralism and African History," *History in Africa* 10 (1983): 307–48.

12. Mario José Maestri Filho, *A agricultura africana nos séculos XVI e XVII no litoral angolano* (Porto Alegre: Instituto de Filosofia e Ciências Humanas, Universidade Federal do Rio Grande do Sul, 1978).

13. For dating on the basis of linguistics, see Hoover, "Seduction of Ruwej," and Robert J. Papstein, "The Upper Zambezi: A History of the Luvale People" (Ph.D. dissertation, University of California, Los Angeles, 1978).

14. An emphasis introduced by Jan Vansina, *Kingdoms of the Savanna* (Madison: University of Wisconsin Press, 1966), pp. 37–69.

15. Wilson, "Kongo Kingdom," and John K. Thornton, "Early Kongo-Portuguese Relations: A New Interpretation," *History in Africa* 8 (1981): 183–204, and *Kingdom of Kongo*, esp. pp. xv, 63–68. In addition, on Kongo religion and Christianity, see Anne Hilton, "Political and Social Change in the Kingdom of Kongo to the Late Nineteenth Century," in Franz-Wilhelm Heimer, ed., *The Formation of Angolan Society* (forthcoming); Wyatt MacGaffey, "Cultural Roots of Congo Prophetism" (paper read to Third International Congress of Africanists, Addis Ababa, 1973), and forthcoming work; and Susan Broadhead, "Beyond Decline: The Kingdom of the Kongo in the Eighteenth and Nineteenth Centuries," *International Journal of African Historical Studies* 12, no. 4 (1979): 615–50. See also António Custódio Gonçalves, *La symbolisation politique: le 'prophétisme' Kongo au XVIIIème siècle* (Munich: Weltforum Verlag, 1980).

16. Beatrix Heintze, "Das alte 'Königreich Angola' und der Beginn des portugiesischen Engagements, 1500–1580," *Internationales Afrikaforum* 12, no. 1 (1976): 67–74, and "Die portugiesische Besiedlungs- und Wirtschaftspolitik in Angola 1570–1607," *Aufsatze zur portugiesischen Kulturgeschichte* 17 (1981–82): 200–219.

17. Joseph C. Miller, "The Significance of Drought, Disease, and Famine in the Agriculturally Marginal Zones of Western Central Africa," *Journal of African History* 23, no. 1 (1982): 17–61, with some conclusions in "The Paradoxes of Impoverishment in the Atlantic Zone," in David Birmingham and Phyllis Martin, eds., *History of Central Africa* (London: Longmans, 1983), 1: 118–59.

18. Miller, *Kings and Kinsmen*, esp. pp. 176–223.

19. For the earlier interpretations, see Miller, "Requiem for the 'Jaga'," *Cahiers d'études africaines* 13, 1 (no. 49) (1973): 121–49. Subsequent exchanges: John K. Thornton, "A Resurrection for the Jaga," *Cahiers d'études africaines* 18, 1–2 (nos. 69–70) (1979): 223–27, and "Thanatopsis," ibid., pp. 229–31. My own position has developed in Miller, "The Formation and Transformation of the Mbundu States from the Sixteenth to the Eighteenth Centuries," in Heimer, ed., *The Formation of Angolan Society*, and in "The Paradoxes of Impoverishment."

20. E.g., the heroic style in which António de Oliveira de Cadornega

composed his *História geral das guerras angolanas,* ed. Matias Delgado and Alves da Cunha, 3 vols. (Lisbon: Agência Geral das Colônias, 1940–42).

21. David B. Birmingham, "Early African Trade in Angola and Its Hinterland," in Richard Gray and David Birmingham, eds., *Pre-Colonial African Trade* (London: Oxford University Press, 1970), pp. 163–73, and Wilson, "Kongo Kingdom."

22. For the later consequences of these early practices in upper Guinea, see George Brooks, "The Signares of Saint-Louis and Gorée: Women Entrepeneurs in Eighteenth Century Senegal," in Nancy J. Hafkin and Edna G. Bay, eds., *Women in Africa: Studies in Social and Economic Change* (Stanford: Stanford University Press, 1976), pp. 19–44. Thornton, "Early Kongo-Portuguese Relations," is suggestive for Kongo and São Tomé in the sixteenth century, and Joseph C. Miller, *Way of Death: The Angolan Slave Trade, 1730–1830* (in preparation), presents evidence for eighteenth-century Angola.

23. Thomas T. Spear, *Kenya's Past* (London: Longmans, 1981), pp. 88–96.

24. Thornton, "Early Kongo-Portuguese Relations."

25. Jill R. Dias, "Changing Patterns of Power in the Luanda Hinterland: The Impact of Trade and Colonisation on the Mbundu, c. 1845– 1920," in Heimer, ed., *The Formation of Angolan Society,* and other work in preparation. Also Miller, *Way of Death,* and "Central and Southern Angola," in Heimer, ed., *The Formation of Angolan Society.*

26. Mário António Fernandes de Oliveira, *Luanda: 'Ilha Crioula'* (Lisbon: Agência Geral do Ultramar 1961), and many other studies. For later Kongo Christianity, see works cited in note 15.

27. Dias, work cited in note 25.

IV

Camões: A Man for All Centuries

Camões perante o Portugal do seu Tempo

José Sebastião da Silva Dias

Quando o Poeta abriu os olhos para a vida (c. 1525), o feito da expansão portuguesa no mundo estava no zénite da fama e atingira o máximo do deslumbramento nacional em face dele. Na sua adolescência e verde mocidade, Gil Vicente, João de Barros, André de Resende, Damião de Góis, Diogo de Teive e toda a fina flor do Humanismo, tratavam-no como epopeia e como cruzada. Mas ouviam-se já então vozes (raras) dissonantes, sendo a mais autorizada de todas—se bem que por uma óptica passadista—a de Sá de Miranda. É com a voz dissonante do moralista do Neiva (passadismo à parte) que se encontra, dezenas de anos depois, a voz já menos dissonante, mas potentíssima, de Diogo do Couto. Entre o nascimento e a experiência asiática de Camões, deu-se a primeira descolonização portuguesa, com o abandono das praças de África, nos anos 40; e deu-se o crescimento da actividade dos corsários ingleses e franceses contra a frota portuguesa que rumava da Índia para Portugal ou da costa lusitana para os portos da Europa. Deu-se, igualmente, o colapso financeiro do estado e a perda do controle nacional sobre a comercialização dos produtos orientais.

Ao fecharem os anos 20, a opinião pública nacional poderia dizer-se ainda unanimente triunfalista em relação à empresa ultramarina da nossa Pátria. Pouco a pouco, porém, vieram à luz do dia sintomas, cada vez mais alarmantes, de quebras dos sentimentos de unanimidade e de triunfalismo. Nos anos 30, a divisão dos espíritos, em termos de classe política e de elites económicas, teve as primeiras extroversões e as primeiras lutas, ainda que circunscritas, umas e outras, ao foro sectorial da política africana—por causa entretanto (o que não quer dizer só) das suas coordenadas indianas.

Admitiu-se já nesses anos, e admitiu-se mais afoitamente nos anos 40, que se impunha um repensar da política oriental dos portugueses. Este repensar—agudizado e, em termos de público e de conflitos políticos, alargado desde os meados do século XVI—colocava-se dentro dos parâmetros da concepção de Portugal como nação pluricontinental, e nem por sombras punha em dúvida a continuidade da nossa presença na Índia. O problema consistia unicamente na busca de fórmulas de moralização e de eficácia da gestão ultramarina, incluindo nesta a segurança espacial na Ásia e a segurança policial nos mares. É neste contexto que ele se nos oferece ainda em Diogo do Couto. Como é a sua existência e o anseio dessa dupla segurança (sem esquecer a comercialização dos géneros industânicos), que explica, em boa parte, a esperança com que muitos dos nossos compatriotas olharam para a união das coroas de Portugal e de Castela, num esquema de monarquia dualista, em 1580.

Constituiu tudo isto um complexo de acontecimentos de grande ressonância no País. Os burocratas, os homens de negócio, dividiram-se em dois partidos, que se distinguiam, não por oposições irreconciliáveis sobre o ser do Império, mas por diferenças no caminho adequado para ajustar o seu modo de ser às realidades supervenientes à sua descoberta ou conquista. Um desses partidos, na fase de 30–40, favorito de personalidades como Gil Vicente (cfr. a *Exortação da guerra* e a farsa chamada *Auto da Índia*) e Sá de Miranda (cfr. a *Écloga Célia* e a *Carta ao Senhor de Basto*), privilegiava a expansão no Norte de África. Era o partido da alta nobreza, do alto clero dos ideólogos da cruzada, dos saudosistas de várias matizes, e das mentalidades arcaicas. O outro partido era o triunfalista; tinha por si toda a casta de aventueiros, a nobreza pobre ou cobiçosa de maior fortuna, a burguesia comercial em massa, o clero missionário, o funcionalismo civil e militar ao serviço das coisas asiáticas, os intelectuais profissionalmente identificados com os fumos da Índia, como Barros e Góis, ou com uma perspectiva histórica classicista, em que a gesta ou feito heróico tem o primeiro plano, como Resende e Teive. Um terceiro partido havia ainda, menos poderoso e com menor implantação: era o dos que, sem retirarem uma letra à proeza ultramarina como factor básico da identidade nacional, sem deixarem de analisar a Expansão em termos de cruzada, pugnavam pela reforma moral e administrativa das coisas da Índia. Tais se nos apresentam um D. João de Castro ou um Diogo do Couto.

A agudização da crise do expansionismo português no Norte de África coincide de perto com o auge deste no Oriente. Mas quando em 1542, após alguns anos de perplexidade da coroa e de controvérsias partidárias, venceu a falange da descolonização norte-africana, desencadeou-se um movimento de repulsa por essa política, com eco para lá da corte e das camadas dirigentes. E essa repulsa aprofundou-se e ganhou adeptos à medida que se manifestaram e agravaram as dificuldades do nosso domínio asiático. Pelos anos 60, quando Camões se encontrava no Oriente, esboça-se a ameaça de um colapso desse domínio. Não há ainda a sensação de que também ali teríamos de descolonizar, mas começa a aparecer o espectro dos custos elevadíssimos da contenção do mouro e do indu lá, dos corsários e comercializadores das drogas e especiarias cá. E avulta de maneira extraordinária a corrupção dos colonos, dos militares e dos funcionários civis, em acção nas paragens orientais. De momento, considerou-se esse inimigo interior muito mais responsável pelos indícios de decadência do que o inimigo do exterior. Foi para lhe fazer face que se colocaram nas chefias políticas e administrativas figuras enérgicas e incorruptíveis (de que nos ficou o protótipo em D. João de Castro), e apóstolos infatigáveis e intransigentes, como os jesuítas. A moral, porém, não produziu a moralização e acabou por revelar que esta—no mínimo, esta por si só—não detinha o progresso da decadência. Daí, nos fins do terceiro quartel do século XVI, a reprimordialização do político.

A reprimordialização do político, nas suas tangências imperiais, não resultou, entretanto, disso apenas. Resultou também—não quero dizer que resultasse sobretudo—do sentimento generalizado da impotência de Portugal, por si mesmo, isolado e com as suas próprias forças, para enfrentar vitoriosamente as pressões desagregadoras vindas do inimigo exterior. Estava em causa a preservação do império descoberto ou conquistado, e já não havia ilusões de que a simples moral não o salvaria. A salvação mostrava-se um conato da moral, sim, mas da moral associada à política. Se inteligências, como a de Couto, teimavam em privilegiar a moral, o grande número, na proximidade dos anos 80, privilegiava a política. Simplesmente, para estes, depois de Alcácer Kibir, a política era a aliança peninsular ou, dito de outro modo, a monarquia dualista, e não aventuras no Norte de África. No africanismo, só a arraia-miúda, e pouco mais, então acreditava. O projecto de D. Constantino de Bragança na Índia, anos atrás, ainda consistiu, fundamentalmente, em actos de força militar—actos, porém, que se mostraram ineficazes, que não tínhamos capacidade para cometer contra os corsários e que não resultariam contra a finança e o comércio de além-Pirenéus.

Ensaiaram-se entre nós, pelo fim dos anos 20, os primeiros voos de uma política cultural que, superando as dominâncias castelhanistas, acertasse a marcha da nação lusitana pela da Europa evoluída, na esfera dos saberes e dos pensares. O humanismo—não digo o classicismo—está ausente dos produtos culturais que por esse tempo circulavam no país. De um modo geral, ao nível da inteligência vulgar e, mesmo, até, da alta inteligência, vivia-se ainda em Idade Média. São os signos do classicismo medievo, em simbiose com as inovações literárias dos retóricos marginais à corrente humanista, que afloram no *Cancioneiro Geral*, compilado por Garcia de Resende e por este publicado em 1516. São esses mesmos signos, embora já retocados com influências estéticas e temáticas de origem italiana, que, no essencial, se deparam em Cataldo Áquila Sículo e seus discípulos.

Só arrancou nos anos 30 do século XVI a renovação da cultura portuguesa. Situam-se nessa década as grandes reformas escolares de D. João III e a obra italianizante de Sá de Miranda no campo da literatura. Situa-se também na década de 30-40 a chegada das primeiras levas de intelectuais pátrios formados em França a expensas do estado. Cite-se, por todos, o nome de André de Resende, poeta latino, antiquário e hagiógrafo, de altos voos.

No século XVI camoniano, podem distinguir-se duas hegemonias culturais: a escolástica e a humanística. A segunda teve maior projecção no reinado de D. João III; a outra ficou só em campo depois dos meados do século. A corrente escolástica caminhava pelos trilhos rasgados na Idade Média e reajustados na polémica com o humanismo cristão e com o luteranismo "lato sensu." A cultura dessa corrente alimentava-se do ensinamento das Faculdades de Teologia de Paris e de Lovaina, assim como do magistério emanado do Concílio de Trento. E alimentava-se, igualmente, da literatura doutrinal com que o integrismo cristão se opunha à doutrina do evangelismo fabroerasmiano e dos porta-vozes da Reforma. Entre os seus intelectuais de maior envergadura—que os tinha e em número apreciável—destacam-se, de maneira particular, Jerónimo de Azambuja—o inquisitorial que proibiu a circulação de um arranjo, moderador, dos *Colóquios* de Erasmo[1]—e Simão Rodrigues, o denunciante de Damião de Góis no Santo Ofício e introdutor da Companhia de Jesus em Portugal.

A corrente progressista foi a da inteligência que procurou, descobriu e defendeu novos rumos culturais para a Pátria. Inspirava-se no pensamento de Erasmo e Lefèvre d'Étaples e respectivas escolas. Queria um catolicismo aberto, despojado da ganga medieval, que assumisse os novos rumos da cultura e as directrizes de uma prática religiosa interiorista e liberta, ao menos, dos excessos do formalismo cultual. Sem cortar sempre com Aristóteles, cortava frontalmente com a peripatética escolástica. Era uma réplica, à portuguesa, do humanismo cristão e do saber renascentista.

O humanismo era a latinidade e, em menor grau, a helenidade clássicas, a emancipação das letras profanas, a recusa da escolástica, da arte de pensar, da metodologia e problematização do saber, legados pela Idade Média; era, numa palavra, a busca de uma cultura laica para uma sociedade em vias de laicização. Na sua vertente de humanismo cristão, estava também empenhado a fundo no repensamento da mensagem cristã, das suas pastoral e moldura institucional, das suas conotações ou consociações políticas.

As primeiras escaramuças entre as duas correntes travaram-se por cerca de 1542. É duvidoso que faça parte delas a proibição do *Fides religio moresque Aethiopum,* de Damião de Góis, em 1541. Integra-as, todavia, a colheita de elementos para a instrução dos processos instaurados mais tarde, pelo Tribunal da Fé, contra o polígrafo e autor da *Arte da guerra no mar,* Fernão de Oliveira, em 1547, e contra o guarda-mor da Torre do Tombo, Fernão de Pina, em 1548.

Na década que vai de 1545 a 1555, a falange escolástica tridentinista empenhou-se a fundo por ganhar posições no governo, na Inquisição e no ensino. No último daqueles anos, com a militância estimulada pela segunda fase do Concílio de Trento (1551–1552), estava solidamente vencedora em qualquer desses campos. A repressão da ala progressista, vinda dos anos 40, intensificou-se enormemente desde essa hora. A aplicação de penas e uma censura literária bastante rígida deram as mãos a um magistério adverso às orientações do humanismo cristão e a equipas de governantes apostados em vedar a carreira na função pública aos suspeitos de não-afectos ao imobilismo ideológico e político. Em pouco tempo, a linha progressista desapareceu, como tal, e quase sem deixar vestígios da sua existência.

A Contra-Reforma (que não a simples Reforma Católica) detém o poder, tanto na sociedade política como na sociedade civil, a partir de 1560/1565. Chefiam o estado, coetaneamente, na menoridade de D. Sebastião, primeiro a rainha D. Catarina e logo seu cunhado, inquisidor-geral, arcebispo de Évora, cabeça do partido integrista e mais tarde rei, o cardeal-infante D. Henrique. Com a subida de D. Sebastião ao trono, em 1568, a Contra-Reforma consolidou duradoiramente a sua implantação vertical e horizontal em todo o país. À medida dessa implantação, produziu-se na terra lusa uma ambiência cultural e política hostil às expressões mentais de raiz progressista, sem margem sequer para uma tolerância estreita e precária.

Tinha chegado o tempo em que um primeiro-ministro do Rei Desejado advertia assim o reitor da Universidade: "Os Padres da Companhia se encarregaram do Colégio Real [das Artes] em tempo em que alguns dos principais mestres dele foram presos pela Inquisição e se arreceava que também nós o viéssemos a ser, como discípulos que éramos seus. Agora o sustentam em tempos muito mais perigosos, em que o demónio parece já tem descoberta toda a sua artilharia. E tanto, que os que atentam bem o que vai pelo mundo e por nós, com muita razão arreceiam que depressa chegue a nós este tão geral incêndio, se não tem já chegado, e se contentam com sermos cristãos e católicos, ainda que menos latinos [= cultos]".[2]

Com a política cultural incorporada no programa de governo de D. João III, institucionalizaram-se no ensino e ganharam corpo na militância dos intelectuais as directrizes do humanismo. O humanismo firmou-se no século XV em Itália e divulgou-se no século XVI aquém dos Alpes como uma contra-cultura laica e centrada nos valores e nos conhecimentos adequados a uma sociedade civil e, enquanto tal, emancipada das perspectivas e tutelas eclesiásticas. Foi a essa contra-cultura, amalgamada com as suscitações do Evangelho e da Patrística, que na Europa cisalpina se chamou humanismo cristão. É ela que André de Gouveia tem em mira, quando, em referência à traça do Colégio das Artes, escreve ao Rei Piedoso: "todos eles [= arquitectos da corte] entendem tão pouco em fazer colégio como o eu quero e deve de ser, como aqueles que nunca fizeram outro senão para frades."[3]

O humanismo cristão e a sua polémica com a escolástica, com o legado cultural da Idade Média, com a visão mundana e política da mensagem evangélica, com as estruturas da igreja hierárquica, correram largamente entre a inteligência portuguesa, de 1535 a 1555. Nos anos 60 e 70, já até um pouco antes, viram-se porém alvo de uma verdadeira montaria, a qual expeliu do interior e exterior da cultura lusitana a presença daquilo que no humanismo europeu excedia as dimensões do classicismo católico. Denomino classicismo ou humanismo católico a cerebração mais ou menos eruditarizada, que recebe de fora, isto é, do aparelho eclesiástico e político do estado, a problemática e as directrizes culturais, e que pede às letras antigas ou renascentistas a forma, alguns conteúdos científicos e, em escala mais restrita, alguns subsídios metodológicos. Foi assim que a Companhia de Jesus o consagrou na rede de colégios com que monopolizava no país o ensino preparatório não-conventual das humanidades, das ciências e da filosofia—ensino cujo cânone se encontra no *De arte rethorica* (1562), de Cipriano Soares, no *De institutione grammatica* (1572), de Manuel Álvares, e nos *Commentarii Collegii Conimbricensis* (1592– 1606). Assim o temos também na *Imagem da vida cristã* (1572), de Fr. Heitor Pinto, nos *Diálogos* de Fr. Amador de Arrais (1589) e de Pedro de Mariz (1594), na prática de Andrade Caminha, no teatro novilatino.

O humanismo frustrou-se rapidamente em Portugal depois da morte de D. João III (1556). Não só deixou de ser uma cultura de vanguarda, mas deixou, mesmo, de ser uma cultura. Do seu preceptorado, ficou o classicismo e pouco mais. A acção judiciária e censória do Santo Ofício, a acção pedagógica da Universidade e da Companhia de Jesus, foram decisivas para esse efeito. Decerto que a sua eficácia foi secundada pelos condicionalismos sociológicos da nossa terra—mas não resultou singelamente destes. Resultou também de condicionalismos políticos específicos.

Não foi em vão que se envolveram professores e estudantes em processos inquisitoriais em 1552; que se queimou Fr. Valentim da Luz, na Ribeira de Lisboa, em 1562; que se julgou Damião de Góis em 1574. Esses e muitos outros actos similares valorizaram as proibições, cada vez mais vastas, de leitura, posse, circulação ou publicação de livros em desacordo com a ortodoxia tridentinista. Os dois factores juntos deram uma pauta à produção cultural lusíada. Intimidaram ou desmobilizaram, simultaneamente, a generalidade dos intelectuais, levando o maior número a acomodar-se com a ordem ideológica contra-reformista, quer fosse silenciando-se ou refugiando-se na arte pura, quer fosse adaptando-se e deixando-se ir ao sabor da corrente.

A cultura do humanismo desenvolveu-se em Portugal, numa boa parte, em simbiose com a gesta dos Descobrimentos. Tal o que se passa com João de Barros, André de Resende, Diogo de Teive, Damião de Góis, entre muitos outros. É sob o estímulo dos Descobrimentos e ao revés da escolástica, que cientistas ou filósofos, como Duarte Pacheco Pereira, Pedro Nunes, Garcia da Orta, Gomes Pereira, Tomé Pires, Francisco Sanches, escrevem as suas obras. A sua aproximação da metodologia experimentalista ou cartesiana não foi, contudo, retida pelos compêndios e textos de apoio em voga nas instituições de ensino. Uma grande parte do que produziram ficou, mesmo, inédito durante séculos.

Coexistiram com as expressões culturais hegemónicas expressões culturais subalternas—o que não quer dizer, necessariamente, expressões culturais menores e, sobretudo, sem importância ou sem futuro.

Há provas de reverberações, quer do platonismo cristão, quer do platonismo da Renascença, no pensamento dos portugueses da era quinhentista. São porém insuficientes para se falar de uma linha platónica ou neoplatónica, mesmo menor, na filosofia lusíada. Os *Dialoghi d'Amore*, de Leão Hebreu, publicados em Itália, no exílio do autor, mal circularam entre nós nesse tempo. O platonismo de Fr. Heitor Pinto, como o de tantos espirituais peninsulares, anteriores e subsequentes, constitui um momemto acidental da sua "forma mentis" e coexiste com a peripatética nos seus escritos. E o platonismo aristotelisante de Álvaro Gomes, aliás confessor de D. João III e escritor contra-reformista, corporizou-se no *Tratado da Perfeição da Alma,* que entretanto ficou inédito quase até aos nossos dias. Quanto a Camões, o platonismo, além de duvidoso como atitude filosófica consciencializada e consequente, tem uma presença meramente circunstancial e secundária.

As aflorações do platonismo na cultura portuguesa do século XVI (que não se limitam ao enunciado) justificavam esta referência. Correspondem de facto a uma expressão cultural menor, quase poderia dizer-se mínima, da era de Quinhentos, se abstrairmos da tradicional presença da versão platónica agostiniana na literatura espiritual. São, todavia, mais importantes do que elas e tiveram repercussão no ensino inovador da época as manifestações do aristotelismo renascental.

O aristotelismo da Renascença veio da Itália para aquém dos Alpes e constitui, lá como cá, uma reacção deliberada contra a peripatética arábigo-escolástica, uma nova filosofia, pois sustentava como máxima inatacável que a chamada filosofia perene, elaborada na Idade Média, pouco ou nada tinha de comum com o pensamento do Aristóteles helénico. As suas formulação e reivindicação inserem-se na polémica geral dos humanismos italiano e cristão com as estruturas culturais e medievais e substituem, no sector filosófico, o método dialéctico e silogístico de análise e tematização pelo método histórico-filológico. Estão voltadas, ao mesmo tempo, para emancipar a filosofia em face da teologia, arrancando-a assim ao estatuto de menoridade em que tinha vivido nos últimos séculos.

Em cenário lusitanizante, pelos actores e pelos espectadores, o aristotelismo humanista teve uma primeira prova de força com a peripatética escolástica—ela própria uma trave-mestra da teologia escolástica e de toda a cultura eclesial dos séculos XIII a XV—na disputa famosa de António de Gouveia com Pierre de la Ramée, na Universidade de Paris. Gouveia, professor de jovens lusitanos nos Colégios de Santa Bárbara e da Guiena, esquematizou o seu pensamento na *Pro Aristotele responsio.*[4]

O aristotelismo humanista foi a filosofia dominante do Colégio das Artes, antes da sua entrega aos jesuítas em 1555. Os mestres mais representativos desta escola-piloto do sistema pedagógico secundário, ideado para Portugal nos anos quarenta, compartilhavam as teses de António de Gouveia. Fizeram-se, mesmo, publicações para uso didáctico, segundo esse modelo.

Formalmente, o aristotelismo humanista sobreviveu nas elucubrações dos nossos jesuítas, dentro e fora do ensino. Materialmente, porém, morreu. Não há em Pedro da Fonseca, nem nos lentes do Colégio das Artes e da Universidade de Évora, nem nos autores do Curso Filosófico Conimbricense, vestígios da polémica anti-escolástica do aristotelismo humanista e da sua luta pela autonomia e maioridade da filosofia. Pelo contrário, os novos conhecimentos históricos e filológicos são recuperados e instrumentalizados ao serviço da restauração da escolástica e da subalternização da filosofia à teologia, isto é às dominâncias culturais de inspiração tridentina.

A chegada dos portugueses ao Golfo da Guiné e, mais tarde, à Índia e ao Brasil lançou em crises invencíveis a ciência legada pela Idade Média ou depurada pela Renascença, bem como os métodos tradicionais de conhecimento e de pesquisa e a consciência secular dos limites do mundo. Adquiriu-se, em poucas décadas, a consciência do poder ilimitado do homem e do espaço ilimitado do orbe terráqueo. Teve-se a percepção do aceleramento do saber e da urgência de outras metodologias (que não as dialécticas e de autoridade) para o progresso das ciências.

As hegemonias culturais do século XVI, sobretudo a da primeira metade, foram sensíveis a certos destes aspectos, designadamente ao colapso da consciência dos limites do poder humano. Assimilaram também—o facto é sensível no próprio Curso Filosófico Conimbricense—os produtos líquidos do saber carreado pela navegação, senhorio e comércio de Portugal com o ultramar. Pelo que respeita porém aos métodos, à problemática e perspectiva culturais, ao sistema das ciências, muito pouco disso foi integrado no património intelectual dos portugueses, na época de D. João III, e quase tudo isso foi ignorado pela inteligência dominante, no período sebástico e filipino. Foi além dos Pirenéus que a riqueza destes elementos deu o máximo dos seus frutos. Entre nós, manifestou-se apenas—mas manifestou-se em todo o caso—como expressão cultural subalterna.[5] E é essa subalternidade que, em larga medida, explica a rarefação ou o ineditismo de textos fundamentalíssimos, como o *Esmeraldo de situ orbis,* de Duarte Pacheco Pereira, os roteiros e outras obras geográficas de D. João de Castro, a *Suma Oriental,* de Tomé Pires, os *Colóquios dos simples e das drogas,* de Garcia da Orta.

Que traziam de novo estes e outros livros similares? Muitos e variados conhecimentos materiais no campo da náutica, da geografia, da medicina, da farmacopeia, da história natural, das civilizações, das crenças religiosas, etc. Mas traziam sobretudo o cepticismo em face da ciência feita e do saber livresco. Contra as autoridades gregas ou latinas, arábigas ou escolásticas, medievais ou renascentistas, erguiam a voz da observação e da experiência—uma observação ainda não sistematizada, uma experiência ainda não elevada a experimentação. Mas que no entanto estavam no caminho da revolução metodológica que os cientistas do século XVII iam operar e por que o libertinismo erudito do mesmo século se bateu.

Paralelamente a este esforço dos ultramarinos com interesses no âmbito das ciências naturais e antropológicas, verifica-se um labor de filósofos expatriados, no sentido de romper com o horizonte da escolástica, sobretudo no plano do método. Nem Gomes Pereira na *Antoniana Margarita,* nem Francisco Sanches no *Quod Nihil Scitur* e outros estudos, são precursores de Descartes, como por vezes se diz. Mas estão no caminho que vai dar a Descartes. Para eles, é um axioma que o método escolástico e o progresso científico são incompatíveis. É na batalha metodológica que, Sanches sobretudo, põe o máximo do seu empenhamento de filósofo. Um empenhamento, todavia, com escassa ressonância no Portugal da segunda metade do século XVI, e com nenhuma no Curso Filosófico Conimbricense.

Quando Luís de Camões veio ao mundo, por cerca de 1525, a universidade portuguesa estava ainda em Lisboa, para onde viera no reinado de D. Fernando, em 1377. Havia falhado o projecto do Infante D. Pedro, nos meados do século, de estabelecer uma escola paralela em Coimbra, organizada à maneira das de Paris e Oxford. As instalações de que o Infante D. Henrique a dotara, em 1431, e os estatutos outorgados por D. Manuel em 1503, não tiraram, pedagógica e cientificamente, a instituição lisboeta da modéstia em que nascera. No âmbito da filosofia e das ciências, o seu ensino continuava estritamente medieval; e na esfera das humanidades, só desde 1501 se verifica um leve acenar para fora do legado da Idade Média. É então que—à revelia da autoridade universitária—se condimenta o medievalíssimo texto gramatical de João Pastrana com alguns elementos extraídos do renascentista Élio António Nebrija. Em 1525—já no reinado de D. João III—a Universidade permitiu que os mestres, quando o desejassem, poderiam optar, pura e simplesmente, pela obra de Nebrija, isto é, pela latinidade renascentista. No ano seguinte, possibilitou-se que Martim de Figueiredo, um jurista formado na Itália, regesse um curso de retórica—precariamente, com un vencimento irrisório e com a relutância da Universidade.[6]

O ensino da filosofia e das ciências continuou enquadrado nas molduras da lógica, da filosofia moral, da filosofia natural e da metafísica, durante dois anos. O estudo era feito pelo método dialéctico, tomando-se contacto com as doutrinas erróneas e refutando-as. Assim se entrou no conhecimento das teses dos filósofos e naturalistas judeus e árabes e no das doutrinas dos antigos e dos medievais. Bem o sabe quem alguma vez se gastou com as manualizações e comentários dos mestres de Paris, Alcalá e Salamanca.

Mau grado os esforços de D. João III, a instituição universitária mostrou-se impermeável à ideia de reforma—salvo em matéria de vencimentos e privilégios. Para fazer dela um estabelecimento de ensino superior de perspectiva e nível europeus, concluiu-se que só havia um caminho: fundá-la de novo e em condições de excluir das suas cátedras o corpo docente que tinha. Foi a esses dois princípios que obedeceu a transferência para Coimbra em 1536, deixando em Lisboa a quase totalidade do professorado, amarrada aos antigos interesses e aos que expressamente o rei de novo lhe concedeu. Para satisfazer as necessidades do ensino, recrutaram-se os valores, perdidos, existentes no país e trouxeram-se de fora, pagos a peso de ouro, nacionais e estrangeiros de alta envergadura intelectual.

Pelo lado do corpo docente, pelo seu plano de estudos, pela orientação e conteúdo do saber, a mudança da Universidade para a cidade do Mondego constitui um corte pedagógico e cultural com a escola portuguesa encanecida e desacreditada de Lisboa. Esse corte pode definir-se por uma palavra: europeização, ela própria correspondente a outra: humanismo. E o humanismo, na Europa, nos anos trinta do século XVI, era, primacialmente, na Cultura o humanismo cristão, no Direito os estudos que preparam a escola de Cujácio, e na Medicina a restauração dos ensinamentos dos gregos. Neste último campo, porém, já com prenúncios de promoção dos estudos anatómicos, isto é, da medicina científica moderna.

As incidências da crise religiosa de além-Pirenéus e do endurecimento teológico e pastoral triunfante nas primeiras fases do Concílio de Trento—geraram entorses e soluções de continuidade na linha de rumo da política universitária. No fim dos anos quarenta e nos primeiros da década seguinte, o pluralismo escolástico e a óptica escolástica ocuparam, em força, a praça da Faculdade de Teologia, em cujos lentes a Inquisição, num gesto excepcional de confiança doutrinária, delegou a responsabilidade da censura das dissertações dos candidatos aos graus posteriores ao bacharelato.

Nos Cânones como na Teologia, instalaram-se, ao longo dos anos cinquenta e sessenta, os quadros científicos e mentais da Contra-Reforma, o que não quer dizer que não subsistissem nessas Faculdades mestres ilustres pelo grau do seu saber, mas impermeáveis aos métodos, às inquietações intelectuais, aos horizontes gnoseológicos, ao espírito de busca e de crítica, instilados pelo humanismo na mente humana do século XVI. Era a escolástica—expurgada, cognitivamente

enriquecida, tonificada pela polémica antiluterana, já senhora dos
processos histórico-filológicos—que ali reinava, como absoluta e única
corrente de saber, de problemática, de sensibilidade. É por esse ân-
gulo que um Heitor Pinto, um Luís de Sotomaior, um Cristóvão João,
um Luís Correia, são nomes ilustres do magistério teológico-canónico
de Coimbra. A inquietaçao e a sensibilidade da Renascença, com reflexos em Francisco de Monzon, Martinho de Ledesma e Azpilcueta
Navarro, cedem por completo o lugar à ideologia e às preocupações
em triunfo com a Contra-Reforma.

A Medicina, a Filosofia e as Ciências seguiram um trajecto aná-
logo. A base anatómica extinguiu-se, pelos anos 70/80, do plano dos
estudos de Medicina, retomando o secular prestígio o ensino livresco
e retardatário. As novidades nesta área do saber eram vistas, pelas autoridades, de sobrolho carregado—não porque, de si, brigassem com
os horizontes saídos do Concílio de Trento, mas porque eram por-
tadoras de reflexos metodológicos explosivos.

Para erguer o ensino da Filosofia, das Ciências e das Humanidades à altura dos padrões formais e materiais da Europa evoluída,
desenvolveram-se esforços aturados nos anos trinta, com a afectação
ao respectivo ensino, sob o controlo dos próceres universitários, de
um conjunto de mestres nacionais e estrangeiros, vários deles muito
categorizados e todos de bom nível científico e pedagógico. A experiência, devido ao condicionalismo institucional, falhou porém. Per-
sistindo todavia no mesmo propósito, fundou D. João III em Coimbra,
em 1547, o famoso Colégio das Artes, dando-lhe no entanto um estatuto de independência em face da Universidade, bem como o de estabelecimento padronizador de toda a escolaridade voltada para o in-
gresso nas escolas maiores. Não levou contudo a sua avante, sem que
as forças integristas não tivessem procurado barrar-lhe esse caminho.

Pôs à frente do Colégio, como director e como braço direito deste,
uma notável equipa de educadores e professores, formada e exer-
citada em França por espaço de anos. Destacavam-se nela, pelo saber e
pelos ideais, André de Gouveia, director do Colégio, Diogo de Teive,
João da Costa, Arnault Fabrice, Georges Buchanan, Nicholas Grouchy,
Elie Vinet, Marcial de Gouveia, Diogo de Contreiras.

O objectivo próprio do Colégio das Artes—contrariamente ao dos
tradicionais colégios universitários—não era a formação de frades ou
de clérigos, mas sim a de leigos oriundos da nobreza ou da burguesia
e destinados à vida secular. Inseria-se nesse contexto o estudo das
línguas e literaturas clássicas, o da Filosofia e o das Ciências. Tudo à
luz dos métodos, dos conhecimentos e dos ideais culturais postos em
voga pelo humanismo em geral e pelo humanismo cristão em especial.

Robustecia-se já porém a força política e institucional da Contra-Reforma no nosso país. E os processos inquisitoriais instaurados em 1552, que envolveram Diogo de Teive, João da Costa, Buchanan, Marcial de Gouveia, fizeram debandar os estrangeiros, intimidaram os nacionais e desembocaram na entrega do Colégio à Companhia de Jesus em 1555. Encerrou-se, assim, o ciclo do humanismo cristão, do aristotelismo anti-escolástico e do cientismo renascentista, a nível escolar em Portugal.

Pelos anos 70/80 do século XVI, a Universidade de Coimbra, quanto aos ideais culturais e aos seus suportes filosóficos, científicos e metodológicos, já só muito pouco tinha de comum com o que fora, em facto ou em aspiração, trinta para quarenta anos atrás. Era, consumadamente e com mestres ainda de envergadura intelectual, a universidade da Contra-Reforma. Partilhava esse estatuto com a Universidade de Évora, fundada em 1559 pelo cardeal-inquisidor D. Henrique e por ele entregue aos jesuítas.

Não há o menor indício de que Luís de Camões tivesse frequentado o Colégio das Artes. E não tem a menor consistência, a tese recentemente sustentada por um académico, de que aprendeu no Colégio de S. Miguel. Na sua idade madura, a instituição universitária tinha deixado de ser em Portugal um veículo dos novos saberes e das novas rotas da cultura europeia; tornara-se uma coluna inabalável da ideologia tridentina na terra portuguesa.

Perante este Portugal do seu tempo, heróico e dramático, progressista e repressivo, com esperanças, projectos e frustrações, como reagiu o autor de *Os Lusíadas*? O eclipse cultural do humanismo cristão, os dramas de consciência ideológica, a dureza da repressão, a recusa sistemática do direito à dissidência, o recurso ao obscurantismo como instrumento de contenção política, o lançamento de um ensino de conteúdos monolíticos—nada disso tem o lugar para uma referência ou encontra sequer o eco de um protesto na sua epopeia, na sua lírica ou no seu teatro.

A obra literária camoniana nasceu num tempo histórico com definições políticas (pelo menos aparentes) e sérias indefinições ideológicas. A essas definições e indefinições, subjaz um quotidiano português, reflectido na especificidade do ser português, de que o Épico se não alheou inteiramente. Fazem parte dele o naturalismo ingénuo, a sentimentalidade recorrente, a miscegenação da esperança e do desalento, o estatuto económico débil de boa parte dos estratos dominantes, a miséria de amplas camadas populares, o arcaismo das estruturas agrícolas, a fuga do trabalho rural para o trabalho urbano. E é o reflexo de uma parte deste quotidiano na inteligência do Vate—

que foi estouvado e cortesão, inadaptdo na Europa e aventureiro na
Ásia, homem de largos gastos e escassos rendimentos—que retira
ao seu petrarquismo, por exemplo, o carácter de uma simples cultura adaptativa de padrões estrangeiros, para a tornar uma cultura
existencialmente inserida na realidade lusa e portadora de um real
lusíada.

Foi no transcurso da infância, adolescência e juventude de Camões,
que o humanismo, com a variedade de linhas e de gamas nele existentes, penetrou em Portugal e enformou a mentalidade de muitos
dos nossos compatriotas. Em Santa Cruz de Coimbra (mas não no Colégio de S. Miguel, como já se tem escrito), se acaso lá estudou, não
poderia pegar-se-lhe mais do que o gosto e o saber de raiz classicista e
a concomitante afeição pelo maravilhoso pagão. O humanismo formal, politicamente triunfante na nossa terra, com a Contra-Reforma,
desde o limiar dos anos 60 do século XVI, quadrava bem ao sumo-
sacerdote do verso maneirista português. A dialéctica e a polémica do
humanismo italiano dessacralizado e do humanismo cristão não res-
soam, em contrapartida, mesmo em simples surdina, na vida ou na
obra do Poeta. Como não ressoa a revolução filosófica e científica em
fermentação além dos Pirenéus e com ilustres representantes na Pe-
nínsula Ibérica e até, mesmo, em Portugal. Ressoa, porém, a hos-
tilidade a Lutero e a identidade com a escolástica ("Elegia" VI, ed.
Cidade— II. 223–29).

A última demão do Épico n'*Os Lusíadas* verificou-se quando a Contra-Reforma e a sua inspiração tridentinista iam em maré alta de força
e prestígio entre nós. Estávamos longe do espírito de abertura ao
irenismo, que caracterizara os anos 30 e, em grande parte, ainda os
anos 40. No entretempo, o pessoal do integrismo apoderara-se de
todo o aparelho político e cultural do estado e impusera, através de
uma repressão metódica e de uma doutrinação intensa, os signos
mentais reformulados no Concílio de Trento. Ora o Génio, ao cotejar
a realidade ideológica e política de Portugal com a das nações eu-
ropeias não-hispânicas, salienta o contraste da infidelidade destas com
a fidelidade lusitana à ortodoxia religiosa e à "cruzada" contra o isla-
mismo—ortodoxia e "cruzada" que são (como se verá) o "leit-motiv"
do poema, na linha, aliás quase unânime, da inteligência pátria na era
quinhentista.

Na verdade, ao começar o canto VII do livro imortal, o autor cele-
bra orgulhosamente a "geração de Luso . . . ,/a quem não somente algum perigo/estorva conquistar o povo imundo,/mas nem cobiça ou
pouca obediência/da madre que no céu está em essência" (VII, 2). E
comparando Portugal com o Sacro Romano Império (cujo supremo

imperante pertencia à Casa de Áustria), aponta o escândalo da con-
duta deste: sob a bandeira de Lutero, "do sucessor de Pedro rebelado,/
novo pastor e nova seita inventa" e "em feias guerras ocupado,/(que
inda co'o cego error se não contenta!),/não contra o superbíssimo
otomano,/mas por sair do jugo soberano [=católico]" (VII, 4). Quanto
ao povo inglês, "nova maneira faz de cristandade: /para os de Cristo
tem a espada nua,/não por tomar a Terra [Santa], que era sua" (VII,
5). Do "galo indigno," afirma "que o nome de cristianíssimo quiseste,
/não por defendê-lo nem guardá-lo,/mas por ser contra ele e derribá-
lo" (VII, 6). Os próprios italianos não são poupados, perdidos nas de-
lícias e divícias mundanais (VII, 8).

Contrasta com este cenário o de Portugal, por vivência e observação imediata e directamente conhecido de Camões. O Vate passou
pelo Norte de África, como soldado, no final dos anos quarenta, aí
perdendo uma das vistas (cfr. a esparsa ["A uma dama que lhe chamou
cara sem olhos"] e a elegia ["Aquela que de amor descomedido"]—ed.
Cidade, I, 135; II, 208), e depois (1553) começou a experiência de
uma vida amarga no Oriente. Não lhe faltaram os encarceramentos,
os degredos e a miséria (Os Lusíadas, VII, 79-81). O que os seus olhos
viram nas paragens do Índico não chegou para o persuadir de que o
império português sofria, simultaneamente, de moléstia política,
moral e administrativa. A corrupção trabalhava em comum com a
ofensiva otomana (se bem terçando armas militares e comerciais entre
si) contra a presença estável e pacífica de Portugal na Ásia. Contudo,
embora a primeira não escapasse à sua atenção, foi principalmente a
segunda que o sensibilizou e motivou como artista.

O Velho do Restelo não é um porta-voz do Épico. Nas suas palavras repercute, entretanto, o juízo (negativo) que o escritor fazia quer
do norte-africanismo puro, quer da nobreza e do clero parasitários e
sedentários da metrópole (VIII, 39-42), quer ainda dos costumes
(corrupção) em voga no Portugal de aquém e de além mar. Repercute, igualmente, a crítica à recusa da aventura e das mudanças sociais
por muitos portugueses, assim como aos sentimentos de inveja e ao
culto do passado, de tantos outros.

O episódio do Velho do Restelo é, porém, um acidente na globali-
dade do poema, sem ressonância na lírica ou no teatro. A linha de
força d'Os Lusíadas está, a bem dizer, na história política e religiosa-
mente imaculada de Portugal e na grandeza ímpar do nosso feito
("mais do que prometia a força humana"—I,1). A leitura épica do
feito lusíada emparceira com a sua visão como acto superador ("cesse
tudo o que a musa antiga canta"—I, 3) de tudo que até então a huma-
nidade realizara, admitira como possível, ou sequer sonhara (I, 3 e

11). E toda a História Pátria, dos primórdios da monarquia ao reinado de D. Sebastião, tem na sua pena as cores de uma cruzada interminável, na fidelidade ao catolicismo, contra o "torpe ismaelita cavaleiro" (I, 8; "Elegia" X, ed. Cidade, II, 229), o "povo imundo" (VII, 2), o "mouro imigo" (VIII, 11), a "maura túmida vaidade" (VIII, 37), o "maomético ódio" (VIII, 63), o "soberbo gládio mauritano" e os "reveis à madre igreja" ("Oitavas" III, ed. Cidade, II, 187 e 88).

O fenómeno da corrupção, no Portugal de Aquém e de Além, não escapou a perspicácia de Camões. Embora sem ruído de maior, perpassa nalgumas clareiras da sua obra. Denuncia, de facto, a injustiça com que a realeza premiava mais correntemente os intriguistas e oportunistas do que os sinceros e verdadeiros servidores (X, 23–24; "Canção IX", ed. Cidade, II, 289–93; ["Oitavas a D. António de Noronha sobre o desconcerto do mundo"], ed. Cidade, II, 168–78). A sua sensibilidade à perspectiva moral exprime-se, de maneira particular, n'*Os Lusíadas*. Equipara o rico e o pobre no "vil interesse e sede imigo/do dinheiro, que a tudo nos obriga" (VIII, 96). E acrescenta:

> Este [=dinheiro] rende munidas fortalezas;
> Faz tredores e falsos os amigos;
> Este a mais nobres faz fazer vilezas,
> E entrega capitães aos inimigos;
> Este corrompe virginais purezas,
> Sem temer de honra ou fama alguns perigos;
> Este deprava às vezes as ciências,
> Os juízos cegando e as consciências.
>
> Este interpreta mais que sotilmente
> Os textos; este faz e desfaz leis;
> Este causa os perjúrios entre a gente,
> E mil vezes tiranos torna os reis;
> Até os que só a Deus omnipotente
> Se dedicam, mil vezes ouvireis
> Que corrompe este encantador, e ilude,
> Mas não sem cor, contudo, de virtude.

O flagicídio da corrupção entra aqui como uma casuística ou ganga de marginalidades. Não entra—e nisso se distancia da óptica de D. João de Castro ou Diogo do Couto—como uma análise explicativa da decadência do império português do Oriente. Entra como uma marginalidade, não como uma normalidade que corrói as bases da nossa presença na Índia, bem como o equilíbrio das finanças públicas e da economia nacional.[7]

Num livrinho de fortuna,[8] o prof. Mendes dos Remédios procurou mostrar a conexão do texto e contexto ideológicos camonianos com a fé católica. A prova dessa conexão não pode ser aqui aprofundada (e várias pistas, nem sempre das menos importantes, foram apenas afloradas pelo mestre conimbricense), mas as conclusões da nossa análise confluem, em geral, com as daquele estudioso. Um dos exemplos mais acabados da identidade católica do Poeta é a "Elegia VI" (ed. Cidade, II, 223–29), verdadeira suma da sua teologia, até com a invocação final; "Jesus, Maria." Faz aí uma ardente profissão de fé no "altíssimo ser, puro e divino,/que tudo pode, manda, move e cria," logo seguida de uma clara exegese católica da origem do mundo:

Não, que aquele [é] Deus alto, incriado,
Senhor das cousas todas, que fundou
O céu, a terra, o fogo e o mar irado [=água],
Não do confuso caos, como cuidou
A falsa teologia e o povo escuro [=islâmico],
Que nesta só verdade tanto errou;[9]
Não dos átomos falsos de Epicuro;
Não do largo oceano, como Tales;
Mas só do pensamento casto e puro.

Chora, depois, a paixão de Cristo[10] e insurge-se contra "o falsíssimo herege [="luteranos"], que carece/da graça e com danado e falso espírito/perturba a santa igreja, que floresce" e contra "o povo pertinaz [=judeus] do antigo rito,/que só o desterro seu, que tanto dura,/ lhe diz que é pena igual ao seu delito."

Não desmente esta identidade católica do grande Vate o recurso ao maravilhoso pagão (que encontramos em poetas do *Cancioneiro Geral*, de Garcia de Resende, e em muitos dos novilatinos arquivados pelo P. António dos Reis no *Corpus illustrium Poetarum Lusitanorum*) e nem, mesmo, o episódio da Ilha dos Amores. Foi o próprio Épico que cortou toda a dúvida pelo pé, ao classificar de fabulosos os deuses pagãos, úteis só "para fazer versos deleitosos" (X, 82–85).

Assim como não poupa a nação maometana, não poupa também a nação judaica. Para lá das numerosas referências-aderências a Jesus e a Cristo, considera o Salvador como o verbo divino encarnado ("Deus-Homem"—I, 66):

A lei tenho daquele a cujo império
Obedece o visíbil e invisíbil,
Aquele que criou todo o Hemisfério,
Tudo o que sente e todo o insensíbil,

Que padeceu desonra e vitupério,
Sofrendo morte injusta e insofríbil,
E que do céu à terra enfim deceu,
Por subir os mortais da terra ao céu.

[I, 65]

O tópico da Encarnação ("Deus foi em carne ao mundo dado"—
IV, 87) vem à tona do poema várias vezes. Um dos passos mais expres-
sivos desta visão (anti-talmúdica) de Cristo como o Messias vindo, é o
que se refere à batalha de Ourique ("Quando na cruz o Filho de Maria,/amostrando-se a Afonso, o animava"—III, 45). E se o dogma da
Encarnação figura frequentemente voltado contra os muçulmanos,
não deixa de se reflectir na acção de Tito contra Jerusalém, evocada
pelo Gama:

E se tu tantas almas só pudeste
Mandar ao reino escuro de Cocito [= inferno],
Quando a santa Cidade desfizeste
Do povo pertinaz no antigo rito [= judeus],
Permissão e vingança foi celeste,
E não força de braço, ó nobre Tito,
Que assi dos vates [= profetas] foi profetizado
E depois por Jesus [= Messias] certificado.

[III, 117]

Os mistérios da encarnação e da redenção andam, aliás, frequentemente associados. O Lírico destaca, com efeito, por mais de uma vez
esses dois mistérios:

Esta causa das causas, revestida
Foi desta nossa carne miseranda,
Do amor e da justiça compelida,
Pelos erros da gente, em mãos da gente
(Como se Deus não fosse) perde a vida.[11]

O Poeta, clarificando e reforçando a sua identidade teológica com
o catolicismo, acentua ainda não só que Cristo "morreu pelo mundo"
("Elegia VI", ed. Cidade, II, 228) e que n'Ele se cumpriram "as profecias [= vinda do Messias]/pelos profetas santos declaradas" ("Elegia
X", ed. Cidade, II, 257), mas também que é o "Deus, na cruz subido"
(*idem*. 258).

É sintomático da ideologia e dos sentimentos do Génio em face das tensões conexas com os dissídios religiosos em processo na Europa do seu tempo e com a presença de Portugal no Ultramar a exortação que, numa hora crítica e de controvérsia, faz ao Rei Desejado. Não contém essa exortação uma escolha entre a prioridade da expansão norte-africana e a prioridade da expansão asiática, mas contém a ideia nítida de que a expansão perigará sem um golpe bélico mortal no "torpe ismaelita cavaleiro" (I, 8), ou seja, no mouro do Norte de África, e outro, não menos mortífero, no "turco oriental," aquele que, associado ao gentio, batalha contra nós para os lados do Ganges (*Idem*). É a esse duplo golpe militar que Camões incita o jovem rei, vendo neste o "jugo e vitupério" desses inimigos do nosso domínio índico. E depois de uma larga fundamentação histórica da tese, conclui: "Comecem a sentir o peso grosso/(que pelo mundo todo faça espanto)/de exércitos e feitos singulares,/de África as terras e do Oriente os mares" (I, 15). Em 1575, já em Lisboa, saúda D. Sebastião como a "esperança clara/que sereis braço forte e soberano/contra o soberbo gládio mauritano" ["Oitavas a D. Sebastião"], ed. Cidade, II, 186–89).

A complexa e aguda problemática extra-militar da expansão portuguesa só aflora na obra camoniana ao nível do divórcio existente entre a expansão e o português médio. É um afloramento que se projecta no pessimismo de certos passos d'*Os Lusíadas* (cp. I, 8–9, com VII, 80–81, e X, 145) e da própria lírica (Canção IX, ed Cidade, II, 289–93), mas que não foi assumido política e ideologicamente. Parafraseando o que Hegel escreveu da filosofia, quase pode dizer-se que o poético quinhentista atingiu os mais altos voos nos textos de um Génio que já mal cantava o presente e, em grande parte, se abstraía do drama já visível do futuro.

Quando se percorre a obra épica, lírica ou teatral de Camões, não se depara com a menor permeabilidade às inquietações metodológicas e científicas em avanço além dos Pirenéus. E não se depara, por outro lado, com vivências ou anseios redutíveis aos denominadores do progressismo ideológico, seja nas suas formas de irenismo religioso, seja nas de humanismo cristão. Do irenismo, segundo todas as aparências, nada se lhe pegou; e do humanismo, só calaram fundo no seu espírito a latinidade e a helenidade ou, por outras palavras, aquilo que constituiu o classicismo católico, assumido pela Companhia de Jesus em Portugal e pela Contra-Reforma em toda a Europa. A própria lição da cultura portuguesa subalterna, tanto quanto nos é dado compreender, não o sensibilizou mentalmente. E o drama dos mestres do Colégio das Artes, de Frei Valentim da Luz, de Damião de Góis, tal como a opressão dos judeus e dos dissidentes católicos, não se projectou no édito ou inédito da sua escrita.

As conflitividades pessoais e políticas de Camões têm, assim, aos meus olhos, o carácter de processos subjectivos, contaminados por assomos éticos. Não retira isto um ápice sequer à genialidade do Poeta ou à imortalidade da Obra. Coloca-os, sim, numa perspectiva cultural diferente da que serpeia na literatura ocasionada pelas comemorações do III Centenário da sua morte e que, com outra linguagem e outras roupagens intelectuais, se afigura persistir na literatura ocasionada pelas comemorações do IV Centenário. Trata-se, nestas literaturas, de esforços instrumentalizadores e recuperativos, com finalidades partidárias ou grupusculares. Pela minha parte, quis situar o artista no lugar que julgo ter sido o próprio, restituindo a sua produção e o seu pensamento, para lá das leituras de hoje, à leitura que, segundo a minha análise (e talvez me engane), foi objectivamente a sua e a do seu tempo.

Notas

1. Juan Fernández de Sevilha, *Coloquia Erasmi ad meliorem mentem revocata* (Coimbra, 1551 (?)).

2. Carta de Martim Gonçalves da Câmara para o reitor da Universidade de Coimbra, de 21 de Maio de 1570, apud *Deducção chronologica e analytica*, p^{te} 1ª, divisão V, §106.

3. Carta de André de Gouveira para D. João III, de 13 de Março de 1548, apud Mário Brandão, *Alguns documentos respeitantes à Universidade de Coimbra na época de D. João III* (Coimbra, 1937), pp. 130–31.

4. Cfr. Joaquim de Carvalho, *António de Gouveia e o aristotelismo da Renascença* (Coimbra, 1916); António de Gouveia, *Em prol de Aristóteles*, trad. de Aquilino Ribeiro (Lisboa, 1940).

5. Cf. J. S. da Silva Dias, *Os descobrimentos e a problemática cultural do século XVI* (Coimbra, 1973).

6. Cfr. J. S. da Silva Dias, *A política cultural da época de D. João III* (Coimbra, 1969), cap. 5º.

7. Cf. o estudo de A. Farinha de Carvalho, *Diogo do Couto—o Soldado Prático e a Índia* (Lisboa, 1979).

8. Mendes dos Remédios, *Camões, poeta da fé* (Coimbra, 1924).

9. A exegese filosófica deste passo está feita, eruditamente, por Joaquim de Carvalho, *Obra Completa*, t. I, pp. 301–15.

10. Cfr. "Elegia X," ed. Cidade, II, 257–58.

11. "Elegia VI," ed. Cidade, II, 224.

Cultura e Sociedade na Infância e Adolescência de Camões

Graça Silva Dias

COSTUMA CONSIDERAR-SE que o tempo social em que determinada pessoa vive é aquele que decorre do seu nascimento à sua morte. Todavia, ao vir ao mundo, ela encontra uma sociedade instalada e esta imprime-lhe a primeira, e muito profunda, marca. O mundo dos seus pais acompanha-o até à emancipação cultural, mais precoce ou mais tardia, mas que podemos situar no dealbar da juventude. O homem nasce, pois, culturalmente antes de nascer fisicamente.

Neste trabalho, privilegiamos aqueles sinais dos tempos, indicativos de mudanças na mentalidade sociocultural de uma época. Mudanças que, para além da "vulgata, do denominador comum da época" (na expressão de Philippe Ariès), revelam ou veleidades sem amanhã ou anúncios com frutificações. Mudanças que, já incidindo sobre as estruturas, se afiguram aos contemporâneos oscilações conjunturais que abalam um pouco o edifício, mas não o fazem ruir. São fumos da Índia, ambições vãs, heresias . . .

Ao escolher Gil Vicente como testemunha desta época de crise, tenho plena consciência da acusação de sociologismo (no sentido pejorativo) que a maioria dos estudiosos da literatura, que se apoderam dos escritores como objecto de dissecação, me irão assacar. Todavia corro o risco, plenamente consciente de que o artista pinta o real, nega o real e idealiza o real—mas o referente é o real.

Parece inegável que o teatro apresenta uma certa imagem da sociedade. Não se nega a originalidade da visão pessoal do dramaturgo, mas esta traduz uma representação do mundo inserida nos esquemas de cultura prevalecentes no seu tempo. O pensamento do artista só pode definir-se, portanto, em relação à ideologia dominante—mesmo quando (o que é vulgar) a contesta. Não há pois uma imagem objectiva

155

da sociedade (só possível graças ao distanciamento histórico), porque o artista vê os homens *sub specie artis*, não *sub specie aeternitatis*. A sua visão é colorida pelas suas convicções—fé religiosa, adesão política, interesses de classe. Depende também de um público, de um mecenas, embora procure preservar a sua independência, afirmar a autonomia da sua obra. Estas considerações permitem-nos compreender a tão decantada antinomia entre teatro como documento social e teatro como obra de arte, e fazer a sua superação. Porque o autor que atinge um determinado nível artístico é forçado a instaurar um debate entre vozes, paixões, vontades, opostas. Os personagens (que não títeres) escapam, por assim dizer, ao seu criador e, para serem autênticos, terão de ter possibilidade de se exprimir.

Ao fazer recair a minha escolha sobre um determinado auto de Gil Vicente, como local privilegiado de observação—o auto geralmente denominado de *Mofina Mendes*—, determino-me por um certo número de razões. Em primeiro lugar, porque nesse auto se encontram abordados três grandes temas da problemática sociocultural europeia da época: a voga dos prognósticos (*versus* profecias); a questão guerra justa—guerra injusta; a emancipação do campesinato assalariado. Esses sinais anunciadores de novos tempos eram lidos, no Portugal de princípios-meados do século XVI, em termos de apocalipse, por pôrem em causa toda uma estrutura social.

Em segundo lugar, porque grandes linhas de uma *forma mentis* em crise—a concepção da vida e da morte, da fé e da dúvida—estão presentes (mesmo *in absentia* neste auto exemplar, que é também, quanto a mim, o Auto da Subversão).

O auto da *Mofina* abre com uma fala, "a modo de pregação", feita por um frade "sandeu", o qual, usando um processo de distinções escolásticas, se enreda numa série de referências, citações, reservas, interrupções, numa argumentação absurda, só comparável à célebre arenga do mestre Janotus de Bragmardo rabelaiseano. Sem dúvida que nos encontramos perante uma paródia que tem em mira atingir uma escolástica decadente que teimava em sobreviver. Quer-me parecer, porém, que, para além desse alvo a atingir, Gil Vicente se aproveita do frade-bufão para veicular o seu ponto de vista em relação aos prognósticos.

Sabe-se que o terramoto de 1531 deu azo a especulações pseudocientíficas que produziram um certo impacto na sociedade portuguesa do tempo. O próprio mestre Gil, no famigerado sermão de Santarém (1531), tomou parte activa na contenda que contrapôs os falsos profetas aos homens sensatos. Todavia, para além do episódio catalisador, importa determo-nos na importância então assumida pelo fenómeno da generalização dos prognósticos. Estes eram objecto de proibições constantes, tanto da legislação civil como da eclesiástica, embora nada perdendo do seu atractivo. As adivinhações pelos augúrios, a crença nos presságios, a leitura pelos astros, eram praticadas pelos próprios clérigos que se escudavam no exemplo dos santos e invocavam mesmo as Escrituras.

Numa era de profunda crise política, social e religiosa, proliferava por toda a Europa uma literatura considerável dedicada a este tipo embrionário de futurologia. Parte dessas obras era, ou fazia-se passar por ser, paródica, como *La Grande Pronostication* e *L'énigme en prophétie*, a que andam associados os nomes de Rabelais e de Mellin de Saint-Gelais. Mas outra havia que se reclamava de "séria", da qual destacamos os numerosos almanaques (tipo borda-de-água), de que as *Prognostications des laboureurs* eram os de maior difusão. Dirigidos primordialmente à gente do campo, como o título indica, incluíam, evidentemente, predições sobre o tempo (meteorológico) e a agricultura (sementeiras). A atitude de um João da Murtinheira, da *Romagem dos Agravados,* que verbera um Deus que permite que "chove quando não quero / e faz um sol das estrelas / quando chuva alguma espero / ora alaga o semeado / ora seca quanto hi é / ora venta sem recado / ora neva e mata o gado / e ele [Deus] tanto se lhe dá", é sintomática de uma visão de um Deus dos almanaques que, segundo a feliz expressão de Geneviève Bollème, não é exactamente o Deus da religião. Mas os almanaques não se limitavam a atribuir ao Criador essa distribuição da chuva no campo e do sol na eira, mas veiculavam também toda uma maneira de interpretar a vida e a sociedade que, pela forma correntia de exposição, era acessível às camadas populares, embora não fosse a mais desejável, segundo a óptica das classes possidentes.

É até interessante notar que no mesmo auto em que Gil Vicente condena as predições, se ocupa—tomando posição, como veremos— com as lutas pela hegemonia europeia, travadas entre o imperador da Alemanha e o rei de França. Acontece que esse tema era objecto, um pouco por toda a Europa, de uma quantidade infinita de literatura futurológica, geralmente de carácter sombrio e escatológico, com referências muito concretas aos movimentos religiosos da época. Mas também outros tópicos, como o casamento, o nascimento, a virilidade, eram abordados. E—o que mais devia fazer tremer as autoridades— esses livros, folhetos e almanaques, pondo em dúvida a existência de astros especiais para reis, papas, grandes senhores e o comum dos mortais—*democratizando* os astros—apontavam, senão para o naufrágio total da hierarquia, pelo menos para uma transformação profunda da sociedade.

Estes dados e a sua correlação com a escrita vicentina levam-nos, desde já, a admitir o conhecimento que o dramaturgo teria do género de literatura de prognósticos, de difusão europeia. A Lisboa das primeiras décadas de Quinhentos era uma capital que fervilhava de estrangeiros e onde a censura livresca ainda não se tinha instalado.

Se Gil Vicente condena os prognósticos, enquanto falsas profecias, admite e reverencia as profecias autenticadas. Aliás, já no *Auto de Sibila Cassandra*, o poeta contrapõe a insensatez da interpretação do futuro, não inspirada pelo espírito divino, à que é avalizada por ele. No *Auto da Mofina Mendes*, o autor é mais explícito, pois as damas da Virgem—Prudência, Pobreza, Humildade e Fé—são as leitoras das visões antecipatórias das profetizas do Velho Testamento. Por outras palavras, constituem as virtudes que devem ornar o profeta autêntico. "Por os frutos os conhecereis . . .", diz o Evangelho.

Este ponto afigura-se-me de grande relevância para o estudo da mentalidade da época, abrindo pistas pouco exploradas entre nós. Mestre Gil, ao condenar os falsos profetas, insere-se dentro da mais estrita ortodoxia. Contudo, nesta Idade Média atardada a que ele ainda pertence, os valores religiosos dobram-se de valores sociais. Os *mercimonia inhonesta* não designavam apenas aquelas categorias profissionais ligadas ao sangue e à sujidade mas também às actividades dos negociantes, não só por o dinheiro se poder incluir na sujidade, mas porque vendiam o tempo (estabelecendo prazos, por exemplo). Ora os arautos e divulgadores dos prognósticos incorrem no mesmo pecado: transacionam com o tempo e, mais, utilizam, sem para isso terem delegação divina, a ciência. *Tempo* e *Ciência* eram, no esquema teológico medievo, dois atributos ou monopólios do Criador. Isto explica a desconfiança, e até uma certa marginalização, de homens de lei e professores laicos. Ambos vendiam a palavra, porque os segundos, fora das escolas monásticas e sem as prebendas canónicas, só poderiam subsistir com as gratificações dos alunos. O assalto dos intelectuais aos direitos de cidade é já renascentista.

Chegamos agora ao ponto fulcral—ao episódio-chave—dos *Mistérios da Virgem*, baptizados pelo povo, com uma intuição feliz, de *Auto da Mofina Mendes*. A fábula, ou conto popularizado, em que assenta a anedota da nossa Mofina Mendes era pré-existente ao repertório vicentino, como todos o sabem. Tem ascendência latina e adopção castelhana, pois no *Conde Lucanor*, de D. Juan Manuel, aparece uma Doña Truhana, parenta muito próxima da nossa pegureira. Primeiro ponto a reter: "truhana" é feminino de truão.

Na sequência das cenas do auto, à cena da Anunciação, em que a mãe de Cristo vem assessorada pela Prudência, a Pobreza, a Humildade e a Fé, segue-se anúncio da entrada no proscénio daquela que, pela boca do amo, é a "Virgem louca" do catecismo cristão. De pegureira sem sentido das responsabilidades, passa a personificação da própria desgraça: onde ela estiver, está o mal. E um dos sinais "maléficos" da época era o conflito armado entre dois príncipes cristãos, dos quais um ousava profanar a Cidade Santa dos Católicos (Carlos V) e o outro aliar-se ao turco, inimigo tradicional da Cristandade (Francisco I). Mofina é aqui a alegoria da subversão dos valores morais que deveriam reger os monarcas cristãos.

Toda a "inteligência" europeia estava empenhada e mobilizada nesta campanha de opinião. Punham-se os grandes problemas de princípio: guerra justa—guerra injusta, determinação do agressor, em cuja polémica se vão evidenciar Erasmo, Alfonso de Valdés, Guilhaume du Bellay, Pietro Aretino, Garcilaso, e tantos outros. Mellin de Saint-Gelais, já citado, compõe um poema, de registo satírico, em que a luta pela posse de Itália é descrita como um jogo de cartas, aplicando à situação política, à repartição de forças, às vantagens e fracassos dos intervenientes, a terminologia do jogo. Rabelais, na sua "guerra picrocholine", põe em causa o expansionismo agressivo de Carlos V e seus aliados. Tomás Moro, por seu lado, atribuiu a Francisco I pretensões de hegemonia mundial. No autor gaulês, o fenómeno histórico fixa-se em formas carnavalescas, próprias da "festa", no sentido autêntico de riso popular. Em Moro, a projecção na utopia é o processo escolhido. Gil Vicente recorre à alegoria e nela incarna não só a atitude oficial do nosso país—uma não-beligerância—mas uma evidente sensibilização às repercussões dos ventos novos que sopravam no resto do mundo. Para Gil Vicente, como para Rabelais, os cataclismos políticos e sociais estavam numa tal associação com os fenómenos cósmicos (tremores de terra, inundações) que os leva a uma tomada de consciência, traduzida embora em esquemas de pensamento não coincidentes. Na visão horizontal de Rabelais, depois da tempestade virá a bonança, depois da derrocada de um mundo, o aparecimento de um novo.

Para mestre Gil, há ainda a relutância na aceitação de um novo mundo que vê em termos de subversão hierárquica e de abandono dos moldes do viver patriarcal. Todavia, começa a acusar-se a fadiga do velho lutador que, defrontado com uma sociedade em mutação, se mostra já perplexo.

Façamos um pequeno resumo do episódio da prestação de contas. Mofina Mendes, empregada do maioral Paio Vaz, é por este interrogada sobre o paradeiro da boiada e a sua reposta (a sua primeira fala) é: "Mas que cuidado vós tendes / de me pagar a soldada / que há tanto que me retendes?". Portanto, o contra-ataque da assalariada é uma acusação muito concreta: há ordenados em atraso. Questão que Paio Vaz não contesta, prosseguindo a inquirição—que se revela infrutífera, porque a Mofina só lhe apresenta um rol de mortandades, concluindo: "Meu amo, já tenho dada / a conta do vosso gado / muito bem, com bom recado; / pagai-me minha soldada, / como tendes concertado".

A leitura que se tem feito desta cena põe a acentuação no cinismo (e no cómico) da "má pastora" que não olhou pelo rebanho e ainda tem a desfaçatez de exigir a sua paga. Seria assim que o público de então leria este passo? Não esqueçamos que é com os olhos do passado que devemos ler o passado, para dele podermos extrair o significado, com projecção no presente. Vamos desmontar a cena: cotejar o reflexo do real (os dados estéticos) com os dados históricos que pudemos obter.

Lê-se num texto, pouco posterior a esta época, que o pastor-partiarca, estilo Paio Vaz, "não se deixava enganar pelos pastores que roubam suas ovelhas; se necessário, ele retém-lhes do soldo o valor dos animais que eles, falsamente, declaram ter perdido; se um deles se mostra exageradamente desonesto, ele ameaça-o com o seu cajado". Historiadores da craveira do Prof. Oliveira Marques registam, a par da elevação das tabelas salariais no campo, a partir dos fins do século XIV, a dificuldade sentida pelo patronato rural em satisfazer o pagamento aos seus jornaleiros. O próprio Gil Vicente reproduz num outro dos seus autos, o *Auto da Fé*, uma canção que poderemos apelidar de protesto, embora, aparentemente, só a transcreva para extrair dela um efeito folclórico. É como uma litania, monótona na sua forma, mas dramática no seu grito: "No, no, no, no, no, no / no, no, no / que no, que no / que no quiero estar en casa / no me pagan mi soldada / no, no, no, que no, que no. / No me pagan mi soldada / no tengo sayo ni saya / no, no, no, que no, que no". Era uma canção popular do século XVI; é um documento social do século XVI.

Mas voltemos atrás, à Mofina e à sua "conta de negregura". Segundo Costa Lobo, o Portugal dos séculos XV-XVI era ainda uma "brenha selvática" em que as alcateias de lobos eram tão numerosas que "até nas costas do mar os concelhos se viam obrigados a fazer-lhes montaria todos os sábados". Acrescente-se a isto a falta de cobertos ou currais, para defender o gado das intempéries e das investidas dos animais ferozes, e ter-se-á uma ideia das condições não muito favoráveis (e usamos uma litotes) para a manutenção de um rebanho. Além do que, fiando-nos no processo de prestação de contas (que é da responsabilidade de mestre Gil), a Mofina tinha à sua conta um número excessivo de cabeças de gado, o que nos coloca perante um outro problema: a escassez de mão de obra rural.

Embusteira ou desleixada, ou ambas as coisas, a pegureira recebe do amo um pote de azeite, paga à primeira vista muito generosa, mas não tão valiosa como parece, dado que o nosso país, nesse tempo, se encontrava coberto de extensos olivais, pelo que o azeite era um produto agrícola de escasso valor. Todavia, Mofina Mendes embarca num sonho, ao qual Gil Vicente empresta cores manifestamente exageradas. Mesmo sem entrarmos em estudos aprofundados sobre o valor da moeda e o poder de compra, lembramos um pormenor de outro auto vicentino: quando o marido de Constança (*Auto da Índia*) refere à mulher a possibilidade de ter regressado rico, cita a quantia de um milhão de cruzados. A Mofina, na sua venda hipotética do pote de azeite, chega ao milhão e meio. Até o traje de casamento que ela idealiza—brial de escarlata—a aponta como alguém que não possui o sentido dos limites, pois a escarlata era o tecido principesco por excelência, e o brial tinha já, aliás, caído em desuso. Porém, o desatino (infracção às pragmáticas) não atingia só esta Mofina, mas outra "gente mean e meúda", pois "até os de baixa sorte vestem panos de seda e de fina lã, como outrora os fidalgos usavam". Como se sabe, a presumível noiva não chega a envergar o brial, porque o pote cai e ela não atinge o seu "pays de Cocagne".

Mestre Gil tinha de condenar a má pastora às trevas exteriores. Desaparece da cena antes de ver a Luz, só reservada aos bons pastores: os que têm a fé (mas a ignorância dos simples), a humildade (e a submissão), a pobreza ("pão, cebolas e alhos" era a alimentação do dia) e a prudência (de não porem em causa a sua situação). Mofina cai no pecado da *avaritia* (que não é a avareza, o desejo de acumular ou a repugnância em gastar, conforme o conceito actual), mas o amor apaixonado da vida, das coisas materiais. É, numa palavra, o apego excessivo dado aos *temporalia,* às coisas exteriores e perecíveis: ao "humano deleite. . . que há-de dar consigo em terra". Já S. Bernardo falava de uma distinção essencial: havia duas categorias de homens— os *vani* (ou *avari*) e os *simplices* (ou *devoti*).

Torna-se evidente que Gil Vicente, no *Auto da Mofina Mendes,* se ergue contra toda a tentativa de subversão, contra tudo o que possa pôr em causa a ordem e a hierarquia—os valores tradicionais. A sua posição enraiza-se na sua vivência cristã e na sua inserção social.

Como cristão, ele situa-se na corrente denominada da Restauração Católica, corrente essa que desabrocha na Europa durante o cisma do Ocidente. É uma corrente de bases, de militantes, sem cobertura, a princípio, da hierarquia eclesiástica; mais ou menos combatida por esta, tem a sua primeira afirmação no Concílio de Constança (1412), através do chanceler Gerson e de Nicolau de Clemanges, formalizando-se depois no Concílio de Basileia (1432–38). Este movimento foi, durante a maior parte do século XV, visto, como se disse, com maus olhos pela hierarquia eclesiástica, por variados motivos, entre os quais avulta o conflito em que o Concílio de Basileia se envolveu com o Papa Eugénio IV. Apesar disso, foi ganhando sempre maior influência dentro da Igreja e acabou por ter uma certa oficialização no 5° Concílio de Latrão (1513–17). Este movimento pretendia o congelamento das especulações teológico-filosóficas e o voltar do apostolado cristão para a vida cristã. Daí a crítica ao intelectualismo escolástico e aos seus representantes, preconizando o regresso às origens do cristianismo e a reconversão das congregações religiosas ao espírito da época da sua fundação.

Mas este sobressalto evangélico, que tão evoluído foi, já nesta época não respondia aos problemas e às implicações dos homens de uma economia com tendência para se tornar de mercado. Estes, inseridos em corporações ou em associações urbanas, empenhavam-se numa comunidade horizontal que, através da iniciativa e da livre opção, conduzisse a uma autêntica tomada de consciência. A este anseio vem responder um erasmismo, vem responder um humanismo cristão, para os quais "la ville rend libre".

Mas Gil Vicente, neste auto, não responde apenas como cristão a problemas candentes do seu tempo. Se o fluxo migratório para a cidade, se o movimento emancipatório do rural tinha de ser detido, não era apenas porque a ambição é o mal, e cada um deve permanecer no lugar que Deus lhe destinou. É porque o "fazedor dos autos d'El-Rey", ocupando essas funções palacianas durante 34 anos consecutivos, acabou por assumir valores e interesses de um dos grupos sociais das classes hegemónicas.

No nosso país, nessa época, existiam, nos estratos superiores, duas correntes que se afrontavam numa luta surda de manobras de bastidores, com vista ao domínio do aparelho de estado. Uma é a alta aristocracia, a nobreza cavaleiresca, à qual interessava a fixação no norte de África. É uma nobreza agrária, imobilista e conservadora. A outra é a nobreza secundária, aquela cuja base social e económica de apoio é o mundo mercantilista, é a expansão no Oriente.

Dois fenómenos se vão dar que, em planos diferentes, concorrem para um mesmo fim, e aos quais Gil Vicente assiste, não como espectador, mas como parte interessada. A sua nobreza, a dos feitos de África (da *Exortação da Guerra*, dos cavaleiros da *Barca do Inferno*), se ainda conservava esperanças de hegemonia, vai-as perdendo com o fim do reinado de D. Manuel. No dealbar dos anos 30 (e até mesmo antes) era manifesto que a manutenção das praças do norte de África era insustentável. Por outro lado, o êxodo dos trabalhadores rurais para a cidade, ou para além-mar, afectava uma lavoura deficitária, em fase de reconversão de terras baldias em terrenos de cultivo. Estes dois factores perturbaram todo o equilíbrio económico, político e social da velha aristocracia agrária. Ora nostálgico dos bons velhos tempos em que ainda "s'enxergava uma alegria que agora não tem caminho", ora apresentando, maliciosa mas impiedosamente, os diabos-mercadores, mestre Gil é o porta-voz de um mundo cujos alicerces estão em perigo. A *Mofina Mendes* é o último grito de alarme do velho artista.

Conclusão

Muito havia ainda a ·dizer, pelo que esta conclusão melhor se apelidaria de fim da 1ª jornada. Pela década de 40, Luís Vaz de Camões vai deixar a adolescência. O mundo que encontrou ao vir à luz e nos primeiros anos, e que o marcou na sua problemática e na sua mentalidade está a transformar-se. Para esses problemas, novas respostas e novas propostas surgem.

Foquemos só, muito rapidamente, dois tópicos: o sentido da morte e o ideal da vida. A morte, para Gil Vicente (ela está metaforicamente presente na *Mofina Mendes*), é uma preparação para o Julgamento: uma prestação de contas a Deus, e não aos homens. Para Camões, há já uma volúpia pré-barroca, um consórcio Eros-Thanatos (lembrar sonetos e elegias em que a Morte aparece como o rival que goza o belo corpo da amada).

E a vida, como ideal? Gil Vicente e Camões vêem no campo o oásis de paz e simplicidade (apetecido mas não procurado . . .). Mas mestre Gil lê o campo em termos de passado: de retorno aos bons velhos tempos. Luís Vaz, renascentista, projecta nele o milenarismo laico: é a Idade de Oiro, de uma pastorícia clássica, que o desencanto da curialização traz consigo.

On the Title of *The Lusiads*

Harold V. Livermore

SOME MIGHT consider that the history of the word "Lusiad" is too well known to require further comment. It was traced at the beginning of this century by J. M. Rodrigues, and Dona Carolina Michaelis added her views with her usual acumen. Their contributions are summarized by B. X. Costa Coutinho in his *As Lusíadas e os Lusíadas*, published in 1938, a learned and well-organized study of the emergence of the neologism. Its conclusions are judicious, and if there is something to add it is because the word itself has a certain ambiguity, and because its appearance as a classical neologism does not in itself explain its transition to the vernacular, thirty or forty years later.

The word "Lusíadas" does not occur anywhere in the poem, only in the title and in the authorization to print, dated September 1571. It does not occur anywhere else in the poet's works, lyrics, plays, or letters. It apparently does not occur in contemporaneous Portuguese writers, that is, in writers of Portuguese poetry or prose. Moreover, "os Lusíadas" is only one of four forms that are found. On the title page it is masculine plural, the form generally adopted. In the manuscript *Cancioneiro* of Luís Franco Correia (begun in 1557 and finished in 1589), the first canto is copied out as "Elusiadas de Luiz de Camões a El-Rei D. Sebastião" and concludes, "não continuo porque se imprimiu" ("I do not continue because it has been published"). But Diogo do Couto (who was with Camões in Moçambique in 1569 and noted that the poet was working on the epic) made it feminine plural, *As Lusíadas*. Although he knew Camões before the publication, he wrote in 1611–14. The feminine plural was also used by another of Camões's friends, Fernando Álvares do Oriente, in his *Lusitânia transformada*, in which Camões is one of the characters: it was published posthumously in 1607. These two friends were the first writers to accord the poet the title "Prince of Poets." Luis de Tapia's Castilian translation, published at Salamanca in the year of the poet's death, 1580, also made it feminine but singular. Others have followed Tapia. In particular, Fanshawe called his translation *The Lusiad*. Owing to the hermaphroditic nature of English, the gender remains obscure. As the word was unknown, Fanshawe added "Portugal's historical poem" by way of explanation, showing that he was in fact thinking of *Lusiad* as feminine. In languages that make the distinction, the masculine form means "the sons of Lusus," or their descendants, and their deeds. If, however, the feminine singular is used, it would recall such titles as *La Austriada* (published in 1584) or *La Franciade* (1572) and mean a work about the house of Austria or the land of France or, in this case, "Portugal's historical poem." However, if the word is feminine plural, as Couto and Álvares supposed, the meaning is again different.

There is no doubt that the word first appeared in Latin, that it was a creation of the Grecizing tendency that reached Portugal in the decade of 1530, and that it was devised to mean the sons of Lusus, the equivalent of Lusitani. It was printed by the humanist André de Resende (1500–1573) in his Latin poem on St. Vincent, *Vincentius levita et martyr*, published in 1545. In his *De Antiquitatibus Lusitaniae*, Resende noted its formation: "From Lusus whence Lusitania gets its name, we called the Lusitanians Lusíadas, and from Lysa Lysíadas, just as Virgil derived *Aeneid* from Aeneas." He went on to say that the neologism had proved successful and had been taken up by others, notably Jorge Coelho, whose Latin style he praises. But Resende's explanation is already close to ambiguity. The *Aeneid* is now thought of as the poem of the foundation of Rome, or of the deeds of Aeneas, not the sons and descendants of Aeneas.

Although *Vincentius* gave rise to the note, it is clear from the reference to Coelho that the word was in circulation before 1545. And indeed the poem *Vincentius* had been written fifteen years earlier. Resende was born at Évora, lost his father as a child, and was sent as a boy to study at Salamanca, whence he moved on to Paris and Louvain in 1529. He there composed a Latin *Epitome* of the deeds of the Portuguese in India based on a letter written from Cannanor by Nuno da Cunha, governor of India from 1529 to 1538. The translation was made at the request of Conrad Goclenius. It was printed at Louvain in July 1531, together with verses by Resende. The word "Lusíadas" does not appear in either prose or verse. But it was used in another work printed in the same year, the *Erasmi encomion*. In February 1531, Resende asked Goclenius to submit this to the sage, who was then at Fribourg. Erasmus expressed his approval, and the work was printed at

Basle in September. In the same year Resende was working on his poem on St. Vincent, so that the word "Lusíadas" was launched in 1531, when Camões was, according to the usually accepted biography, seven years old.

But this was outside Portugal itself. Resende returned to Portugal, summoned by the king to act as tutor to the royal brothers at Évora. In 1534 he was asked to deliver the inaugural address for the opening of the academic year at the university, then still situated in the Alfama in Lisbon. He seized the opportunity to denounce traditional methods of teaching and to condemn the stultification of bright young minds by academic hacks. The speech was at once printed by Galharde of Lisbon, in a little book that bears the date October 1534. It uses the word "Lusiad" in a piece of verse appended to the discourse. The speech played its part in the decision to close the university, which was done in December 1536. (It reopened as the University of Coimbra the following March, in the monastery of Santa Cruz, which had been reformed by Frei Brás de Barros, or de Braga, who had preceded Resende in studying at Louvain.) This use of the word "Lusíada," if not the earliest in Portugal, was the one that had the greatest impact owing to the importance of the occasion. The word, evidently a Grecism, emerged when the fashion for Greek was reaching Portugal. A Portuguese, Aires Barbosa, taught Greek at Salamanca, but Resende brought from Salamanca a Fleming, Nicholas Cleynarts, to help to educate Prince Henry, later cardinal and king. At the time Resende delivered his oration before the university, no Greek typefaces were available in Lisbon, and his Greek quotations were inserted in ink. The first translator of the Greek drama in Castilian, Hernán Pérez de Oliva, died in 1531. His *Agamemnon* was translated and adapted into Portuguese *quintilhas* at Oporto in May 1536 by Aires Henrique de Vitória, who informs us that his object was to change the minds of those who thought that the performance of plays by pagan poets was bad for Christian audiences. Camões later adapted Pérez de Oliva's translation of Plautus's *Amphitruo* into Portuguese quintilhas.

Resende's example was soon followed by Jorge Coelho, who, though a pupil of Resende's, could not have been much his junior. He was the son of Nicolau Coelho, the captain of Vasco da Gama's third ship. His brother Francisco became *estribeiro-mór* to Queen Catherine. He himself went to study and teach at Salamanca, where he spent eleven years before being recalled to Portugal. He became Latin secretary to Prince Henry. But Henry was preceded in the church by his brother Afonso, created cardinal as a boy. One of Coelho's Latin poems is supposed to have been written for this occasion, in 1526, when Coelho was still at Salamanca. It contains the word "Lusíada." However, the poem was not printed until later and may have been revised. What is certain is that Coelho took up the neologism with enthusiasm. His Latin poem *Victoria adversus Turcas* uses the term no less than ten times. It is not a long poem, less than a single canto. But Resende praised Jorge Coelho's quality as a Latin poet and thought he might be destined to compose the Portuguese epic. Coelho's poems commemorate the success of the Portuguese Prince Luis at Tunis and the achievements in India. Cardinal Afonso, to whom he dedicated one of his poems, died in 1540, and Coelho composed an elegy calling him the "glory of the Lusiads." In the same year Coelho published his poems as *De patientia Christiana,* from which Camões probably derived his version of Prince Antioch in *El-Rei Seleuco.* But there is little to suggest that Camões heard from Coelho any stories of Gama's great voyage. He called Nicolau Coelho "grande soffredor" in the *Lusiads* but gave no indication of having known his son. As to Coelho, he seems to have been kept busy composing the constitution of the diocese of Évora, of which his employer, Prince Henry, was the first archbishhop.

But from this time the word "Lusiad" passed into fairly regular use by Portuguese Latinists. Costa Coutinho mentions its use by Manuel da Costa—*o subtil*—who studied at Salamanca and was recalled to teach at the new University of Coimbra in the year of its opening, 1537. In April, the month after its inauguration, another prince, Duarte, was married to Isabel, daughter of the Duke of Bragança. Costa wrote a poem for the occasion in which he used the new word twelve times. He also used it in his poem on the resumption of the university at Coimbra and later in his funeral oration for John III. Miguel Cabedo de Vasconcelos, born in 1525 (a nephew of Dom Gonçalo Pinheiro, who negotiated Camões's release from prison), used it in celebrating the wedding of Prince John in 1552, just before Camões left for India. Diogo Mendes de Vasconcelos (1523–99), another nephew of Bishop Pinheiro and Resende's literary executor, also used it.

All these writers are Latinists and poets. The word had not yet made its appearance in the vernacular, or, so far as I am aware, in Latin prose. As I have pointed out, it does not occur anywhere in Camões's works except as the title of his epic, and yet it later became so general that it eclipsed Camões himself. At least, when the Carmelite bishop of Targa, Tomás de Faria, turned *The Lusiads* into Latin, he introduced the word generally into the body of the poem but did not think it necessary to mention the name of Camões at all.

The reason for this is probably simple. The word "Lusitanus" is admirable in Portuguese. But it does not scan properly and is unsuitable for Latin verse. Writers of Latin verse who wished to strike a high classical note seized upon "Lusíada" because they needed it. Writers of Latin prose and of Portuguese did not require it. It remained the property of poets who wished to cultivate a lofty style, appealing to members of the royal family or dealing with heroic events, which we may broaden to include the foundation of a university.

The word "Lusíada," though a classical neologism, did have an existence in classical times but as a feminine word. It occurs in Athenaios of Naucratis for the bathing nymphs who entertained the youth of Sybaris. In this case the name comes from the root *lous*, to wash or bathe, and thus ought to be rendered "Lousiada." This may recall Camões's use of the phrase "fresh-water nymphs" in the letters. Classical compendia explained the word "Lusíadas" in this sense, and it may have been known to Camões, though he does not appear to have made use of it. Costa Coutinho traces this use to the *Antiquarum lectionum Commentarios* of Luigi Ricchieri Rhodigiano, first printed at Venice in 1516, with several other editions in the course of the century. But Camões had at his disposal the word "Tagides," and the revival of the feminine would clearly only have caused confusion once the usual modern meaning of "Lusiads" had been adopted.

Camões was quite familiar with the famous passage in Pliny's *Natural History* in which the legendary Lusus makes his appearance. In Canto III, 21, Camões declares:

Esta foy Lusitania dirivada
De Luso, ou Lyso: que de Bacho antigo,
Filhos forão parece, ou companheiros,
E nella antam os Incolas primeiros.

The "parece" suggests that he was not fully convinced of the legend. Similarly in VIII, 3 and 4, he introduces Luso:

Foi filho & companheiro do Thebano,
Que tam diversas partes conquistou
Parece vindo ter ao ninho Hispano,
Seguindo as armas que contino usou,
Do Douro, Guadiana o campo ufano,
Ja dito Elisio, tanto o contentou
Que ali quis dar, aos ja cansados ossos
Eterna sepultura, & nome aos nossos.

O ramo que lhe ves pera divisa,
O verde Tyrso foi de Baco usado,
O qual aa nossa idade amostra & avisa
Que foi seu companheiro & filho amado.

This Elisio may account for the exceptional Elisiadas mentioned in the manuscript of Luís Franco Correia, now fortunately available in facsimile, owing to the work of D. Maria Lourdes Belchior Pontes. It seems not to occur elsewhere.

It is strange that the word "Lusíada" should have remained in the domain of Latin poetry for more than thirty years. Yet so it did. It was only in 1571 and 1572 that the sons of Lusus cast off their classical limitations and appeared in the vernacular. When Luis Gómez de Tapia made his Castilian translation, published at Salamanca in 1580, he called it *La Lusíada*, in the singular, perhaps unaware of its origins. Also unaware, it appears, were Diogo do Couto and Fernando Álvares do Oriente, despite their intimacy with the poet. The form *La Lusíada* would seem to be justified by the *Iliad* and by *La Austriada* and *La Cristiada*. But Juan Rufo, the author of the *Austriada*, published his poem only in 1584, and his subject was suggested by the victory of Lepanto, at which he had been present. Camões had by then written most of his *Lusíadas*. Tapia obviously did not understand the reference to the sons of Lusus. The cases of Couto and Fernando Álvares do Oriente show the form had not penetrated the vernacular.

The belief that the word "Lusíadas" was confined to the Latinists and to poetry is confirmed by reference to another friend of Camões, André Falcão de Resende, the nephew of Garcia de Resende and second cousin of his namesake, Lúcio André. He did not use the word in his poems in Portuguese, which remained unpublished until about 1860 (the edition is not dated), but it did appear in some Latin verses by Pedro Gomes in his honor, where he is described as "the glory of all the people of the Lusiads"—*Lysiadum totius gloria gentis.*

Gil Vicente's Vision of India and Its Ironic Echo in Camões's "Velho do Restelo"

Jack E. Tomlins

G IL VICENTE has likely given to the modern world the first literary reflection of India outside the Portuguese chronicles themselves, which—owing to their very nature—came to light after the poet-playwright's death, generally conceded to have occurred in the year 1536. The specific mention of the conquest of India and of its effects on the *metrópole* is to be found in two farces, so denominated by the goldsmith's son, Luís Vicente, in his cavalier categorization of his father's theatrical pieces in the *Copilaçam de todalas obras de Gil Vicente* of 1562.[1] The farces bore the titles *Farsa chamada Auto da Índia* and *Farsa chamada Auto da Fama*. The first title has the distinction of being Gil Vicente's earliest preserved farce (1509), and the second holds special interest in that it is, in reality, a farce-allegory and dates from 1520 (and not 1510, as Luís Vicente erroneously surmised).[2] The eleven-year separation of dates of composition and presentation at court stands for the maturation of the playwright's conception of the meaning of the Portuguese discovery of the Orient.

Basically, the earlier playlet—the *Auto da Índia* of 1509—gives us a glimpse into a humble Lisbonese household, from whose hearth the husband is absent because he has enlisted in the fleet that departed for India under the Capitão-Mor Tristão da Cunha in 1506. Thus the presentation of the *auto* before the dowager queen Dona Leonor, sister of the reigning monarch, Manuel I, provided the court playwright his first opportunity to face the sad situation of Portuguese manhood in the service of God and country, along with the glad situation of the return of the same—which, as a matter of fact, did indeed coincide

170

with the bounteous return of the Capitão-Mor's fleet in 1509. Gil Vicente turned to a plot at least as old as that of Aesop's urban and rustic
rodents to prove once again that while the cat is away, the mouse will
play. The bereaved wife is named Constance, and her grief is only
doubled when she learns that there has been an unexpected delay in
the armada's departure. Gloom changes to exultation, however, when
she learns that the caravels have at last sailed down the Tagus and out
to sea. Her housemaid slyly suggests that Constance will have to resort
to some manner of work, since her adventuring husband has left her
so ill-provided. Constance requires no instruction:

> Est'era bem graciosa,
> quem se ve moça e fermosa
> esperar pola ira má.
> Hi se vai elle a pescar
> Meia legoa polo mar,
> isto bem o sabes tu;
> quanto mais a Calecu:
> quem ha tanto d'esperar? [. . .]

> Partem em Maio daqui,
> quando o sangue novo atiça:
> parece-te que he justiça?
> Melhor vivas tu amen,
> e eu comtigo tambem.—
> Quem sobe por essa escada?[3]

[V, 93–94]

The newcomer on the staircase is the braggart and boorish Castilian who has come to court the abandoned Constance, soon to be
joined by the loutish but love-sick squire Lemos serenading from the
street below and promising to provide a sumptuous feast. The servant
girl is amazed at her mistress's talents:

> Quantas artes, quantas manhas,
> que sabe fazer minha ama!
> Hum na rua, outro na cama!

[V, 107]

Time passes fast in farce and dalliance, and the servant announces
that it has been three years since the departure of Tristão da Cunha.

In other words, it is now 1509. Constance reacts with notable lack of enthusiasm:

Mas que graça, que seria
se este negro meu marido
tornasse a Lisboa vivo
pera a minha companhia!
Mas isto nao pode ser
qu'elle havia de morrer
sómente de ver o mar.
Quero fiar e cantar,
segura de o nunca ver.

[V, 109]

But he is even then on the staircase, home from India. When he enters. Constance lies expertly about her solitude and sadness and immediately inquires of the riches he has brought from the Orient. The cuckold answers that had the *capitão* not taken his lion's share first, he would have brought home at least a million *cruzados*. And the pious Constance:

Pois que vós vivo viestes,
que quero eu de mais riqueza?
Louvada seja a grandeza
de vós, Senhor, que m'o trouxestes.

[V, 115]

Her next line gives her the lie and virtually closes the farce: "A nao vem bem carregada?" [V, 116].

In this first farce, then, the outcome of the Indian conquest and its concomitant commerce is reduced by the comic playwright to marital infidelity, bedchamber slapstick as one suitor is played off against the other, parody of the Castilian swain, and the vaguest hint that the promise of great riches holds at least the possibility of inducing the populace to venality. This was, of course, an early play; Vasco da Gama had not been too long back from his second voyage to India. We are witnessing here a kind of farcical dawn.

The same is not true of the second Indian piece, the *Auto da Fama* of 1520,[4] where boudoir hijinks are transformed into whimsical allegory. Portugal by then was beginning to feel the full import of commercial and political power. The monumental outcome of years of pioneering maritime feats swelled the nation with pride.[5] Little Portugal and its once meager Fame, now represented by a simple farm girl from the province of Beira herding her ducks in the company of a village simpleton named Joane, is courted by the great powers of the West, allegorically represented by three amorous suitors: a Frenchman, an Italian, and a Castilian, the first two speaking in a rough approximation of French and Italian. All are rebuffed by the country maid, who feels no need for their empty show of affection now that *beiroa* has become Fama Portuguesa. She recognizes the covetous nature of her admirers, refuses their gifts since Portugal's empire is so much more splendid, sends them on their way, and is finally awarded by the appearance of the virtues Faith and Fortitude, who crown the peasant girl with the laurel and carry her away on a triumphal cart to the sound of music. Faith entones three strophes, in *arte maior*, elevating Portuguese Fame above Trojan and Roman, for the Christian faith has not only spread the doctrine of Christ but has routed the heathen and brought prestige and amplitude to Lusitania. This is farce of a more serious nature in 1520, the year generally conceded to correspond to the apogee of Portuguese power.[6] So exhilaratingly successful was it that it immediately enjoyed three presentations before various branches of the court.[7] Barely fifty years later, the new-found India that inspired both a burlesque of the institution of Christian marriage and an allegory of an empire of hitherto inconceivable power and breadth will strike a strange and ironic chord in the words of Camões's old man on the Restelo strand. Gil Vicente both burlesqued and exalted the Indian venture at the beginning of the sixteenth century; by the end of the century Camões had written what must be viewed as that venture's valedictory.

The Manueline Age presaged doom and degeneration, all historians agree; and it was precisely in that transitional period between magnificence and deterioration that Luís Vaz de Camões came of age. In 1553 he sailed for an India and a Goa already famed as pestholes of corruption. From John III onward, reports abound of depravity at home and abroad, but that tragedy of lingering destruction is far too intricate to analyze here. It is sufficient to suggest that the idea of constructing an epic to honor Portuguese conquests abroad and Portuguese history at home probably occurred to Camões in his youth, some nine years before the death of John III, although it appears nearly impossible to place a date on the poet's genial notion of linking the deeds of the Lusitanians to the voyage of Vasco da Gama. As a consequence, scholars are in accord, also, that likely most of Cantos III and IV were composed before the sojourn in the Orient, excepting the opening of the third—which, like the closure of the second, involves Gama's recounting of Portuguese history to the king of Melinde, and the climactic finale of the fourth, which contains the rebuke of the "velho do Restelo." Similarly, there can be little doubt that the initial dedication to Sebastian in Canto I and the closing solemn counsel to the king regarding the stewardship of monarchy in Canto X were composed after Camões returned to Lisbon in 1570.

Because it is so closely tied to the voyage of Vasco da Gama, it is almost impossible to assume that the incident of the old man and his bitter outrage on Restelo beach was not, likewise, composed after the poet's return from India. The opening dedication, the rebuke of the "velho do Restelo," and the disillusioned *envoi* of the epic itself must be viewed as the afterthoughts of an epicist who returned from Babylon to Zion, only to learn that Zion was a chimera.

The mystifying episode of the old man of Restelo closes, as was mentioned, Canto IV (strophe 94 to the end, comprising only eleven strophes). It is an eloquent diatribe *contra Famam* angrily flung against the sparse fleet of Vasco da Gama immediately prior to its departure from Restelo beach at Belém, traditional embarkation point called by João de Barros "praia das lágrimas." These eleven stanzas comprise a condemnation of Lusitanian pride and lust for power even before those ills perniciously infected the *res publica*. Of course, they were composed by an aging and bitter soldier-poet of the Crown after seventeen years of incredible vexations in the Orient. Camões spoke through the other old man, borrowed from all the croaking sages and seers of Antiquity. Gil Vicente's delightfully haughty maid from Beira is damned here for vile covetousness. Fama Portuguesa, heedlessly courted by a foolish populace, will produce only disquietude of soul, abandonments, and adulteries. The pranks of Gil Vicente's Constance were no longer a joke in 1570. The ages of man, from the Golden to the Iron, have but brought Adam's generation to arms and warfare; and *homo lusitanus* is the vilest of Adam's sons. Why cast the flower of Portugal's manhood to distant shores when the Ishmaelite attacks the back door? The malediction damns princely pride—apparently Manuel's but effectively Sebastian's—in history foretold:

> Porque a fama te exalte e te lisonje,
> Chamando-te senhor, com larga cópia,
> Da Índia, Pérsia, Arábia e de Ethiópia?

[*Lus.* IV, 101, 6–8]

These are the very words of Barros himself when they were published in Década I in 1552; Manuel has taken to himself new titles through the brilliant victories of Vasco da Gama: "el rey acreicĕtou a sua coróa os titulos q̃ óra tem, de senhor da conquista nauegaçam & cõmercio da Ethiopia, Arabia, Pérsia & Jndia."[8]

Then follows the ancient *topos* of the condemnation of the first builder of ships: "Ó, maldito o primeiro, que no mundo / Nas ondas velas pôs em seco lenho!" Mankind would have fared well without the mad dash for the prize of Fame. Mankind is a babbling fool who will pass through fire, iron, water, doldrums, and ice to secure the vanity of impermanent Fame. The final, chilling denunciation of Man ends the canto: "Mísera sorte! Estranha condição!" [IV, 104, 8].

Before the *Lusiads* was published in 1572, then, the old Camões saw the Oriental conquest—with India the brightest diamond in the crown—as mere vanity and total ruin. The creative literature of Portugal's sixteenth century opened with laughter and pride in that adventure. The so-called Renaissance epic of the modern world, through its dedication and finale directed to the monarch, and through its prognostication of doom in the words of the "velho do Restelo," brings us to the frontier of the Baroque Age. This strangest of epics, written to glorify all the sons of Lusus, flies apart at three junctures: beginning, middle, and end, all sections composed after the poet's passage to India. These junctures undo the very business of the epic and indicate to us that the vaunted Camonian *desconcerto do mundo* may well have roots that lie far deeper than the bedrock of mere Platonic doctrine.[9]

Notes

1. Luís Vicente divided his father's plays into *obras de devaçam, comédias, tragicomédias, farsas,* and *obras miúdas.* An enlightening study on the use of the terms *comédia* and *tragicomédia,* vis-à-vis Gil Vicente's contemporary, the Spaniard Bartolomé de Torres Naharro, may be read in the late I.-S. Révah, "La *comédia* dans l'œuvre de Gil Vicente," in *Études Portugaises* (Paris: Fundação Calouste Gulbenkian, Centro Cultural Português, 1975), pp. 15−36. The problem of Vicentine taxonomy in general, viewed in the light of the playwright's prose *Carta* directed to João III in 1531, is analyzed in Jack E. Tomlins, "Una nota sobre la clasificación de los dramas de Gil Vicente," *Duquesne Hispanic Review* 3 (Winter 1964):115−31 and 4 (Spring 1965):1−16.

2. Révah discusses this distinction in the article mentioned in note 1. Here he also subdivides the *comédia* into romanesque comedy and allegorical comedy, the latter derived from the fifteenth-century *momo.*

3. All quotations from Gil Vicente are taken from the six-volume edition of the *Obras completas de Gil Vicente,* ed. Marques Braga (Lisbon: Livraria Sá da Costa, 1942–44).

4. Ibid., 5:117–40.

5. These years are admirably and succinctly chronicled in Bailey W. Diffie, *Prelude to Empire: Portugal Overseas before Henry the Navigator* (Lincoln: University of Nebraska Press, 1960).

6. The crucial matter of the apogee of Portuguese power in the Orient and its relationship to the composition of *Os Lusíadas* may be briefly studied in J. D. M. Ford, ed., *Os Lusíadas* (Cambridge: Harvard University Press, 1946), pp. 8–9; Leonard Bacon, trans., *The Lusiads of Luiz de Camões* (New York: The Hispanic Society of America, 1950), pp. xxiii–xxv; H. V. Livermore, *A New History of Portugal* (Cambridge, England: The University Press, 1967), pp. 150–51. A more extensive—if romanticized—rendition of the degeneration of Portuguese power may be read in the chapters "O Império e a Fé" and "Holocausto Africano" of João Ameal, *História de Portugal,* 7th ed. (Porto: Livraria Tavares Martins, 1974), pp. 271–329.

7. According to the rubric of 1562, these locales were Lisbon before the dowager Dona Leonor and at Santos O Velho before the monarch Manuel I. Oscar de Pratt believes that there was a third presentation at a slightly later date and at an unnamed place, in *Gil Vicente: Notas e Comentários* (Lisbon, 1931), pp. 153–56. At any rate, the date of presentation of the rubric (1510) is clearly in error and is, no doubt, better placed around 1520.

8. *Ásia de Joam de Barros, Primeira Década,* ed. António Baião (Coimbra: Imprensa da Universidade, 1932), p. 164.

9. A highly original article now allows us to view the Camonian *lírica* in the light of the epic, and vice versa: Sônia Maria Viegas Andrade, "Fundamentos filosóficos da obra de Camões," *Suplemento Literário Minas Gerais* 14, no. 715 (14 June 1980):8–10.

The Theme of Amphitryon in Luís de Camões and Hernán Pérez de Oliva

René Concepción

A MONG Camões's works are three plays—the *Auto dos Enfatriões,* the *Auto de El-Rei Seleuco,* and the *Auto de Filodemo*—all of which were published posthumously. The *Auto dos Enfatriões* and the *Auto do Filodemo* appeared in 1587; the *Auto de El-Rei Seleuco* was not published until 1645.[1] I shall limit myself to a discussion of the first play, the *Auto dos Enfatriões.*

The theme of Amphitryon in literature relates to the birth of Hercules. Jupiter, the god, impregnates a mortal, Alcmene, already pregnant, by assuming the likeness of her husband, the Theban soldier Amphitryon, who is away at war. As Hernâni Cidade stated, the *Auto dos Enfatriões* "é imitação da comédia do Plauto, escritor latino (por 250–184 A.C.) intitulada *Amphitruo,* que percorreu o teatro europeu de Quinhentos, na imitação do espanhol Villalobos e do italiano Ludovico Dace."[2]

José Maria Rodrigues wrote that "o nosso poeta por vezes aproveitou o trabalho pessoal de" Hernán Pérez de Oliva (1494?–1533), a Spanish humanist and professor at Salamanca.[3] Pérez de Oliva's version of the *Amphitruo,* entitled *Muestra dela Lengua Castellana enel Nascimiento de Hercules o Comedia de Amphitrion,* appeared "without date or place sometime before 1525."[4] The earliest version of *Amphitruo* in the peninsula, however, appeared in 1515 and is a translation attributed to Francisco López Villalobos, who wrote in his introduction to the play that "la transladación es fielmente hecha, sin añadir ni quitar, salvo el prólogo."[5] Rodrigues indicated further that "a literatura cas-

177

telhana do primeiro quartel do século XVI oferece-nos, além da tradução literal do *Amphitruo,* devida a López de Villalobos, outra com várias modificações e acrescentamentos: é a do professor de Salamanca, Pérez de Oliva."[6]

It is my intention to compare the plays by Camões and Pérez de Oliva with the *Amphitruo* of Plautus in order to emphasize the similarities in the two peninsular authors, demonstrating that Camões's borrowings from Pérez de Oliva were indeed numerous but not profound, especially with regard to characterization and dramatic technique. The first element to be discussed is the characterization of Alcmene, Jupiter-Amphitryon, and Sosia-Mercury.[7]

Alcmene

As the play opens, both Camões and Pérez de Oliva present Alcmene lamenting Amphytrion's absence. In Pérez de Oliva's version she says:

> Quando Amphitrion estaua en Thebas todas las cosas me parescian llenas de alegria mas agora en su absencia todo el mundo me paresce desierto de aquella gracia con que me solia contentar. Velando estoy siempre en tristeza y pensamiento, y mi sueño no es sino representación de guerra y sangre. Consigo se lleuo todo mi contentamiento; no me quedo otra alegria sino esperar de verlo.
>
> [529–30]

In Camões, she laments her state in this manner:

> Ah! Senhor Anfatrião,
> Onde está todo meu bem!
> Pois meus olhos vos não vêem,
> Falarei co coração,
> Que dentro n'alma vos tem,
> Ausentes duas vontades,
> Qual corre mores perigos,
> Qual sofre mais crueldades;
> Se vós entre os enemigos,
> Se eu entre as saudades?
>
> [1]

I find in these two speeches a certain similarity in spirit, but what becomes immediately evident is a difference in attitude. The Alcumena in Pérez de Oliva does not sound as convincing in her loneliness as Almena does in Camões. His rendering of Almena's feelings shows a greater psychological insight, and in the verses I find the esthetic perception that is associated with Camões.

Jupiter then appears with Mercury in the forms of Amphitryon and his servant Sosia, respectively. In Pérez de Oliva, when Jupiter sees Alcumena, he says:

Júpiter:
> Es el que de tu salud ha mas plazer que dela suya.

Alcumena:
> O tu, tanto tiempo desseado de tu Alcumena, echado
> has con tu presencia cient mill cuydados de mi.

Júpiter:
> ¿Has tenido siempre salud?

Alcumena:
> ¿Que salud quieres que pudiesse yo alcançar,
> temiendo no ouiesse peligro enla tuya?

[530]

In Camões, Jupiter says:

Jupiter:
> Pois esta hora de vos ver
> Alcançar, Senhora, pude
> Pera mais contente ser,
> Conformem co este prazer
> Novas de vossa saúde.

Almena:
> A vida foi pesada e crua
> A saúde que a sustinha,
> Que enquanto, Senhor, a tinha
> Temer perigo na sua,
> Me fez descuidar da minha.

[27]

The similarity here between Pérez de Oliva and Camões is complete in structure, action, and character delineation. In Plautus, however, it is

Amphitryon who inquires about Alcmene's health, when he finally
meets her later in the play. Pérez de Oliva's divergence from the original is reproduced in Camões. It is also interesting to note the striking
similarity in Alcmene's reply in Camões and Pérez de Oliva.

After Jupiter leaves Alcmene at the end of the play, she once
again laments her loneliness. In Pérez de Oliva she rationalizes her
feelings by saying:

> Todos los plazeres desta vida no son sino aparejo que se faze
> para el dolor de ser pasados. Breue es qualquier deleyte, y
> luengo el pesar que de auerlo perdido se sigue. Agora assi
> me acontesce, que del breue plazer que con la presencia de
> mi marido vue me ha quedado luenga tristeza de su absen-
> cia. Pero pues es menester que nuestro descanso y nuestro
> contentamiento den ventaja ala virtud, y Amphitrion por
> ella y el bien de nuestra cibdad me es absente, mejor es
> gozarlo con el animo que con los ojos, considerando quan
> magnanimo se muestra, quanto honor y gracias ha ganado
> para si y para los suyos, pues contra tanto peligro como esta
> cibdad tenia puso su vida y su persona por escudo, y con su
> trabajo gano descanso a nuestra tierra.

[550]

Alcumena is a stoic, a woman resigned to her lot. Not so Almena in
Camões, who says:

> Que fado, que nascimento
> De gente humana nascida,
> Que, de escasso e avarento,
> Nunca consentiu na vida
> Perfeito contentamento!
>
> Anfatrião, que mostrou
> Um prazer tão desejado
> A quem tanto o desejou,
> Na noite que foi chegado,
> Nessa mesma se tornou!
>
> De se tornar tão asinha
> Sinto tanto entristecer
> O sentido e alma minha

Que certo que me adivinha
Algum novo desprazer.

(pp. 45–46)

Jupiter / Amphitryon

The Jupiter in Pérez de Oliva is amorous but more bellicose, as befits his position as a god and in his incarnate form of Amphitryon:

Júpiter:

Todos los peligros he quitado a nuestra gente y
nuestra fama con tan prospera victoria como
desseauamos; y vencida la guerra delos enemigos, soy
venido a vencer la que tu me hazes con desseo desta
tu gentileza, discrecion y honestidad.

Alcumena:

Si gentileza llamas amarte, discrecion seruirte,
honestidad dessearte, todo ay en mi lo que dizes. Pero
ruegote me hartes mas deste plazer que me diste a
gustar. ¿Dizes que venciste los enemigos?

Júpiter:

¿Crees que me faltassen industria y fuerças para la
victoria, acordandome que era cosa que tu tanto
desseauas? No ay animo para la batalla mas fuerte que
el encendido de amor.

[p. 531]

In Camões, Júpiter says:

Oh! grande e alto destino!
Oh! potência tão profana!
Que a seta de um minino
Faça que meu ser divino
Se perca por cousa humana!
Que me aproveitam Céus
Onde minha essência mora
Com tanto poder, se agora,
A quem me adora por Deus,
Sirvo como senhora?
Oh! que estranha afeição
Quem em baixa cousa vai por

A vontade e o coração,
Sabe tão pouco de Amor,
Quão pouco Amor da rezão.
Mas que remédio hei-de-ter
Contra mulher tão terrível,
Que se não pode vencer?

[12]

The Júpiter here is "portuguesamente amoroso,"[8] inquiring as to the nature of love in the best platonic fashion.

Jupiter gives Alcmene news of the real Amphitryon's role in battle. He also gives her the cup that the real Amphitryon had taken as booty and which he, Jupiter, had stolen.

Júpiter:

Soy contento. El rey Ptherela es vencido y muerto de mi mano. Su taça con que el beuia vino te traygo aqui, con que tu siempre beuas plazer en memoria de mi fortuna.

[pp. 531–32]

In Camões, Júpiter says:

De tudo quanto passei,
Por vos dar contentamento,
Em suma vos contarei.
Trago, Senhora, a vitória
Daquele rei tão temido,
Com fama crara e notória.
Porém, maior foi a glória.
De me ver de vos vencido.

Sem me terem resistência,
Os grandes me obedeceram,
Como El-Rei morto tiveram,
Esta copa me trouxeram.
El-Rei por ela bebia:
(Ela, e tudo o mais é nosso)
Por onde craro se via,

Que tudo me obedecia,
Pois tinha nome de vosso.

[27]

In Plautus, Jupiter gives Alcmene the cup as a consolation when he is
ready to leave her. Pérez de Oliva changed the action from the end of
the scene to the beginning, a change that Camões adopted.

In Camões, Júpiter, upon parting from Almena, is much more
tender to her:

Toda a pessoa discreta
Terá, Senhora, assentado
Que um bem muito desejado
Se há-de alcançar por dieta
Para ser sempre estimado.
E quem alcançado tem
Tamanho contentamento,
Por conservá-lo convém
Que tome por mantimento
A fome de tanto bem.
Por isso hei-de tomar
Este tempo tão ditoso
Para a frota visitar;
E depois quando tornar,
Tornarei mais desejoso.

[41]

A similarity in character portrayal occurs when, after Jupiter has left,
the real Amphitryon and Sosia, returning from the war, come upon
the scene. Amphitryon says:

¿Con que muestras de plazer, Alcumena, o con que palabras
podria saludarte que satisfiese ami voluntad? Cierta mente
con ningunas. Porque el amor que te tengo es muncho, y tu
gracia merece mas. Plazeme de verte alegre y sana, y huelgo
me muncho de ver lleno tu vientre de nuestra esperança. Si
lo que enel esta asu madre paresciere, muncho sera amado y
loado de todos. Dime, ¿has estado siempre buena? ¿Tenias
por ventura muncho desseo de verme?

[551]

In Camões, Anfatrião says in like manner:

> Com que palavras, Senhora
> Poderei engrandecer
> Tão sublimado prazer,
> Como é ver chegada a hora,
> Em que vos pudesse ver?
>
> Certo grão contentamento
> Tive de meu vencimento;
> Mas maior o hei de mim,
> De me ver posto no fim
> De tão longo apartamento.

[46]

We see here a similarity in the vocabulary used by the two Amphitryons. This speech does not occur in Plautus.

After the scene in which Alcmene accuses Amphitryon of lying and defends herself from Amphitryon's implication of infidelity, Jupiter decides to return and intervene. He appears to Alcmene and apologizes for his behavior. Alcumena does not accept his frivolous excuse that the whole discussion was just a joke, whereupon Jupiter says:

> Pues te ha plazido, Alcumena, condenar mi vida a tanta
> pena que perder la sea mejor, quiero buscar donde acabar
> la. A mis enemigos quiero tornar, do solia yr a traer victoria
> y fama, agora a buscar la muerte.

[563]

In Camões there is the same attempt to find an excuse when Jupiter uses the words "leve zombaria," and the same apologetic sentiment is expressed:

Júpiter:
> Ora pois assi tratais
> Que em tanto risco pôs
> O amor que vós negais,
> Eu me ausentarei de vós,
> Onde mais me não vejais.[. . .]
> E despois que a desventura

Puser este coração
Debaixo da sepultura,
As letras na pedra dura
Vossa dureza dirão.

[56–57]

Sosia / Mercury

In Camões and in Pérez de Oliva, both Sosias admit to being cowards. In Pérez de Oliva, Sosia says, "pues tengo de contar muchas cosas por vistas, delas quales ninguna vi; porque cosas de guerra y peligro segun mi natura yo no podria ver, sino touiese ojos enel colodrillo" (533). In Camões, Sosia, speaking in Spanish, says:

Cuando yo vengo a pensar
Que uno matarme quisiera,
No hago sino temblar,
Porque creo si muriera
No pudiera mas cantar.
Porque estando a un rincon
De la casa adó quedé
Sentí muy grande ronrón
Y mirando, que miré?
Vi que era un gran ratón.

[31]

The cowardice that Sosia displays is one of the characteristics of the *gracioso* of the Spanish theater. The Sosias of Camões and Pérez de Oliva are both characterized by buffoonery and glib tongues. In Pérez de Oliva:

Merc.:
    ¿Avn dizes que eres Sosia?
Sos.:
    Pues sino soy Sosia, ¿quien so? yo te pregunto.
Merc.:
    Tu mesmo no lo sabes, y quieres que lo sepa yo.
    Responde, dime quien eres.
Sos.:
    Soy este que habla contigo.

Merc.:

    ¿Assi me desprecias?

Sos.:

    ¿En que mas precio esperas que te tenga?

Merc.:

    Agora lo veras..

Sos.:

    A traydor! descuydado me tomaste con ventaja. Dexa
las narizes; sino sacar te he este ojo.

Merc.:

    ¿Ojo, o que?

Sos.:

    ¡O! ¡Ay! Rodillada enel vientre.

Merc.:

    Espera, villano, que peor auras.

[538]

In Camões:

Mercúrio:

    La carne de algun humano
    me seria muy sabrosa.

Sósia:

    Oh! que voz tan temerosa!
    Hombres comes, ó mi hermano?
    No és mejor otra cosa?
    Carne humana és muy mezquiña.
    Oh! no comas deso, no!
    Antes carne de gallina.
    Pero, se más se avecina,
    Que más gallina que yo?

Mercúrio:

    Una voz de hombre ahora
    A la oreja me boló.

Sósia:

    Pésate quien me parió!
    La voz traigo boladora?
    Ella quisiera ser yo.
    Pues mi voz pudo bolar
    Do la pudieses oyr,

Por contigo no reñir,
Me debiera de prestar
Las alas para huir.

[34]

The similarity in character portrayal of the two Sosias is not necessarily attributable to Pérez de Oliva's influence on Camões. When
Camões wrote his play, the character of the gracioso was already
present in the Spanish theater, and the bilingualism of Mercury /
Sosia was traditional in the Portuguese theater of his time.

An analysis of the structuring of various scenes in the two plays
reveals some interesting similarities. For example, the scene in which
Sosia tells Blepharo, the ship captain, that he has seen another Sosia
and that there is another Amphitryon is found in Plautus and was expanded by Pérez de Oliva and subsequently adopted by Camões, although the rendering is totally different in Camões in that, instead of
reprimanding Sósia, he celebrates his wit. In Pérez de Oliva, Blefaron
states:

Y ruego te, Sosia, que de aqui adelante mires mejor lo que
dizes, no pierdas la fe de tus palabras; que sin ella ni ternas
honrra ni amigos; porque la honrra sigue siempre la verdad,
y la confiança ata las amistades, y confiança no puede auer
do se sospecha mentira.

[570]

In Camões, Belferrão says:

Ora ninguém presumira
Que tinhas tão pouco siso;
Pois vais achar de improviso
Tão bem forjada mentira,
Que me faz cair de riso.
Um moço, que alevantou
Tal graça, nunca nasceu
Porque vos jura que achou
Que ou ele em dous se perdeu
Ou de um dous se tornou.

[63]

Blefaron later on sees two Amphitryons and, once he has overcome his shock, steps in as mediator between the two:

> No renoueys, yo os ruego, nuestra renzilla con injurias. Oyd me. El arma mas vsada del hombre discreto ha de ser la razon, porque las otras armas no son sino para quando ella no valiere.

[576]

In Camões, Belferrão takes the same position:

> O homem que for sesudo,
> Nũa tão grande questão
> Há-de tomar por escudo
> A justiça e a rezão,
> Que estas armas vencem tudo.

[68]

Blepharo proceeds to question Jupiter and Amphitryon in order to establish the identity of the real one. In both Pérez de Oliva and Camões, but not in Plautus, Blepharo finally chooses to go into the house to dine, but with Jupiter. The real Amphitryon, alone outside, complains bitterly and threatens vengeance by setting fire to the house:

> El fuego que en mi arde no se puede apagar sino con sangre. Quiero conuocar todos mis amigos, que me ayuden a quemar mi casa, do todos perezcan los que enella estan, de crueles heridas derrocados enlas llamas, do no aure piedad de Alcumena, avn que mi hijo en sus braços me muestre; do hartare yo mi coraçon de vengança.

[578]

In Camões, he says:

> Oh! ira p'ra se não crer,
> Em que minha alma se abrasa,
> Que me faz endoudecer,
> E não me ajuda a romper
> As paredes desta casa!

E porque não tenho eu
Forças, que tudo destrua
Pois que tanto a salvo seu,
Outrem acho que possua
A milhor parte do meu?

Eu irei hoje buscar
Quem me ajude a vir queimar
Toda esta casa sem pena,
Donde veja arder Almena
Com quem a vejo enganar.

[71]

In the two cases the vocabulary is different, but the real Amphitryon's intention to wreak vengeance is the same in Camões and Pérez de Oliva.

In Pérez de Oliva, the character Naucrates, Alcumena's cousin, is sent for and finally appears, promising to help the real Amphitryon, but he also errs and goes inside with Jupiter. In Camões it is Aurélio, Almena's cousin, who also goes inside with Jupiter. The borrowing here is quite evident. We have identical character delineation traceable only to Pérez de Oliva, for in Plautus, Naucrates never appears, although he is mentioned as a *cognatum* of Alcmene. The role of mediator that Pérez de Oliva conceived for Naucrates is repeated in Camões. It is the cousin who comes out of the house and informs the real Amphitryon of the miraculous happenings at the time of the birth of Hercules.

It is also in this scene where we find the greatest divergence between Camões and Pérez de Oliva. In Camões, Aurélio tells Amphitryon that wondrous events had occurred inside the house—that as soon as Aurélio had appeared the other Amphitryon, Júpiter, had disappeared with much noise and light. As Aurélio is speaking, the voice of Júpiter is heard:

Anfatrião, que em teus dias
Vês tamanhas estranhezas,
Não te espantem fantesias,
Que às vezes grandes tristezas
Parem grandes alegrias.
Júpiter sam manifesto
Nas obras de admiração,

Que por mi causadas são.
Quis-me vestir em teu gesto,
Por honrar tua geração.

[pp. 75–76]

Anfatrião is left speechless and Camões's play ends.

But in Pérez de Oliva, after hearing from Naucrates that Alcumena had borne him twin sons, that the first born, Hercules, was heard to announce that he is the son of Jupiter, and that the child himself had killed a snake in his cradle, Amphitryon replies:

Ciertamente, Naucrates, yo creo que aquellos hombres
adoraron a Jupiter que quisieron tener enlos dioses exemplo
de sus vicios con que se escusassen; que entre los buenos con
tales hechos por tirano sera auido, pues se vsa de su poderio
para seruir a sus viles deleytes. Pesame que no somos de
ygual suerte, para poderlo combatir, pero algun dios sancto
y bueno destos malos nos dara vengança. Vamos agora a dar
consuelo a Alcumena, que bien se que lo ha muncho men-
ester, segun su honestidad; la qual tengo por engañada, mas
no por corrompida.

[582]

In the final scene of Pérez de Oliva's play there is a declaration of his faith in Christianity, as a kind of disavowal, thereby renouncing the pagan ideals he found in Plautus. He injects a strong moralistic tone here and elsewhere in his work. The play, then, was destined primarily to edify the reader by pragmatic examples. As William Atkinson tells us, Pérez de Oliva "is a product of his age and environment— his mind, saturated with the works of Aristotle, could hardly do otherwise than sprinkle a few moral precepts across his pages."[9] The play had a secondary purpose, as can be seen in the title, which was to serve as a linguistic exercise in prose. Pérez de Oliva himself stated in the dedication, which is addressed to his nephew:

Hete pues escrito el nascimiento de Hercules, que primero
escriuieron Griegos, y despues Plauto en Latin; y he lo
hecho no solamente a imitación de aquellos auctores, pero a
conferencia de su inuencion y sus lenguas, porque tengo yo
en nuestra castellana confiança que no se dexara vencer.

[526]

The result of this dual purpose on the part of Pérez de Oliva is an overt moral tone in his play and a style so rhetorical that it detracts from the dramatic action. For example, in the parting scene between Jupiter and Alcumena, Jupiter delivers a long, official speech:

A todas aquellas cosas que a nuestro seruicio pertenescen ponemos buenos nombres, como osadia, lealtad, sufri- miento, trabajo, diligencia, menosprecio dela vida y los de- leytes. A ninguno solemos loar con otros nombres. Y a los que solemos vituperar dezimos couardes, traydores, impa- cientes de sed y de hambre y de pobreza, temerosos del tra- bajo, negligentes, amadores de su vida, hombres viles, indignos de honor; coneste sonido henchimos la red de hombres vanagloriosos, de crueles, de ociosos, de locos, de perdidos. Assi que para limpiar la republica delos hombres dañosos fue bien instituyda la guerra, que no es otra cosa sino justicia vniversal que dellos se faze.

[544]

Camões, on the other hand, was an epic and lyrical poet, a man deeply immersed in the current emanating from Petrarch and the neoplatonic elements of the Renaissance. His intentions in the play are not pragmatic or overtly Christian. In his version of the *Amphitruo* he is moral without being moralistic and philosophical without sound- ing rhetorical.

We can appreciate the difference in approach to parallel situa- tions that we find in Camões and in Pérez de Oliva. In Camões there is evidence of psychological depth and aesthetic perception, while in Pérez de Oliva we have a very formal rendering of the theme, almost devoid of human emotion. This is not to say that Pérez de Oliva is never effective in his dramatic presentation. On the contrary, the speeches between Alcumena and Amphitrion in which he accuses her of infidelity are exceptions. Equally effective is the bantering scene be- tween Sosia and Mercury, which conveys the comic elements already found in Plautus.

In Camões's play, language conveys beauty as well as meaning. He is essentially dramatic and much more emotional, while displaying a profound feeling for the national traditions of the Portuguese the- ater, particularly the farcical elements, which can be traced back to Gil Vicente. Certainly the recreation of a character such as Brómia, a ser- vant, and the introduction of Feliseu and Calisto, also servants, and Aurélio, the cousin, should be explained in this context. The popular and sometimes vulgar but always witty and comic exchanges between these characters are also reminiscent of Gil Vicente. Camões's use of verse in the play, no doubt a personal preference, the bilingualism of Mercury / Sosia, and the lack of theatrical divisions into acts and scenes, can also be interpreted as stemming from popular, medieval traditions.

The plot taken from Plautus is kept intact by both authors, but there are changes which lend originality to the two plays. Neither Pérez de Oliva nor Camões felt the need to adhere faithfully to the Latin original, and they adapted the *Amphitruo* as best suited their particular styles. Camões, as I have tried to show, has certain elements related to the structure, character portrayal, and vocabulary in his play that are different from those in Plautus and are found only in Pérez de Oliva.

The influence that Pérez de Oliva exerted on Camões might be judged as considerable in view of the number of similarities in their adaptations of Plautus. But, as we have seen, Camões's borrowings from Pérez de Oliva are related solely to external elements, such as the inclusion of certain scenes and situations and some facets of characterization. These elements, although important for the total effect achieved in the play, did not affect in any profound way the style that is so characteristic of Camões. The poet of *Os Lusíadas* is not known for his work as a dramatist. He wrote only three plays, but in this *auto* he shows a definite feeling for the dramatic. In his theater as in his poetry Camões remains the lyrical poet, the interpreter of the sensibilities of love, in the best Renaissance tradition. It is in this context that he excels and becomes original. He improved on Plautus and Pérez de Oliva in many instances, particularly in the monologues and the love verses between Almena and Anfatrião and between Almena and Júpiter. These verses, written in the traditional *redondilha*, if removed from the dramatic dialogue, would stand up well in comparison with his lyric poetry.

Notes

1. Hernâni Cidade, *Luís de Camões: Os autos e o teatro de seu tempo* (Lisbon: Livraria Bertrand, 1956), p. 76.

2. Hernâni Cidade, ed., *Luís de Camões: Obras completas,* 2d ed. (Lisbon: Sá da Costa, 1956), 3:viii. All quotations from Camões are from this edition.

3. José Maria Rodrigues, "Introdução ao Auto Camoniano *Os Enfatriões,*" *Boletim da Segunda Classe da Academia das Ciências* n.s. 1(1929):18. In this article

Rodrigues cites three examples to prove that it was Pérez de Oliva and not Villalobos who exerted an influence on Camões.

4. William Atkinson, ed., "*Teatro*, by Hernán Pérez de Oliva," *Revue Hispanique* 69(1927):522. All citations from Pérez de Oliva are to this edition.

5. Francisco López Villalobos, "Anfitrión, Comedia de Plauto," *Biblioteca de Autores Españoles,* vol. 36: *Curiosidades Bibliográficas* (Madrid: Atlas, 1969), p. 461.

6. Rodrigues, p. 18.

7. To differentiate between the characters introduced by Plautus, I shall use the following standards of spelling of their names: (1) when referring to the characters in general: Amphitryon, Alcmene, Jupiter, Mercury, Sosia, Blepharo; (2) when referring to Pérez de Oliva: Amphitrion, Alcumena, Jupiter, Mercurio, Sosia, Blefarón; (3) when referring to Camões: Anfatrião, Almena, Júpiter, Mercúrio, Sósia, Belferrão.

8. Cidade, *Obras,* 3:12.

9. William Atkinson, "Hernán Pérez de Oliva, a Biographical and Critical Study," *Revue Hispanique* 71(1927):309–484.

The Place of Camões in the
European Cultural Conscience

William Melczer

T HE TITLE of this paper, in which we will look at a few aspects of
the European fortune of Camões and of the *Lusíadas,* requires
some further clarification.[1] What follows is intended primarily as a
contribution to the study of the prodigious rise of Camões in the fir-
mament of nineteenth-century Europe. I limit myself to that period
in the belief that the subsequent and even present-day unquestioned
eminence on which Camões stands in Europe has its roots in that
nineteenth-century revival.

In the sea of studies dealing with the great Portuguese poet, three
works stand out that pertain, in a peculiar way—and with no undue
disconsideration of numerous other contributions of importance—to
our subject: Richard Burton's two-volume *Camoens: His Life and His
Lusiads,*[2] in which the nineteenth-century English translations are reviewed (next to Burton's own translation of the work); J.-J.-A. Bertrand's
"Camoëns en Allemagne," published in the *Revue de littérature com-
parée* in 1925,[3] which superseded the earlier studies of J. de Vasconcellos[4] and of W. Storck;[5] and G. C. Rossi's "As traduções italianas de
Os Lusíadas," published in the *Acts* of the 1972 International Congress
of Camonistas.[6] Bertrand spoke for all three of them, and actually for
many more, when he wrote:

> L'Allemagne, surtout l'Allemagne romantique, a fait le rêve
> de s'approprier les cultures les plus lointaines et d'en ex-
> primer tous les apports. Ce n'est pas la réalité historique, et
> c'est à peine un mince filet des courants économiques qui
> entraîne, en particulier, les écrivains allemands sur les routes
> de Portugal et de sa littérature. Et pourtant ne voyons-nous

pas ces deux peuples communiquer avec prédilection, tout
au moins dans les choses de la vie intellectuelle, et se trans-
mettre des influences généralement fécondes? C'est Ca-
moéns, qui a été le porteur de ces influences portugaises,
comme le fils adoptif du Romantisme allemand.[7]

According to this view, Camões captured the imagination of German romantic culture, for reasons precisely intrinsic to the culturally
expansionist, outgoing, and intensively *interested* outlook of Romanticism (hence, exotic motifs, the discovery of the East, of the Middle
Ages, etc.). In appropriating distant cultural realms—not unlike the
affective appropriations of Saint-Exupéry's *Le petit prince*—Bertrand
tells us, German, and, by extension, European romanticism, made of
Camões its predilect adoptive son. On the other hand, and this is even
more remarkable, the possible influence of distinct historic realities,
the commensurability of historic evolutions understood as congenial
and germane to each other, is expressly denied, even on the level of
symbolic forms. "Ce n'est pas la réalité historique," Bertrand tells us.[8]

The study of the interest elicited by Camões's *Lusíadas* (leaving
aside for the moment the rest of the poet's works) will illuminate our
own investigation. We propose to trace such interest, in the briefest
fashion, in four Western European countries only, with no more than
a few side glances at other European developments. The cultural domains that these countries represent—France, Italy, Germany, England—for all their evident nineteenth-century momentum, should
not mislead us into thinking that other cultural realms were of lesser
importance. By no means. Simply, logistic considerations have imposed upon us such restrictions.

On the French scene, apart from two very rare anonymous versions dating to the beginning of the seventeenth century,[9] the eighteenth century saw an important surge in the study of Camões. No
fewer than seven or eight French translations are registered, a few of
which are only fragments or partial translations (usually the Inês de
Castro and sometimes the Adamastor episodes). Duperron de Cas-
tera's version is of 1735,[10] followed by a number of later editions.[11]
Jean François de la Harpe's version of 1776[12] had a number of later
editions.[13] Vacquette d'Hermilly's contribution, a prose rendering revised by de la Harpe, was also of 1776.[14] No doubt, such an eighteenth-
century French interest in Camões studies must be accredited to the
Enlightenment's general cultural and scientific impact. One of the
translations (undated) is called, appropriately, "voyage imaginaire."[15]

The nineteenth century saw no fewer than a dozen French ver-

sions of Camões's masterpiece. Shortly after Napoleon's retreat from
Russia, the Duke of Palmella issued a translation up to Canto VI.[16]
The second and third decades of the century saw a total of five translations (most of them fragments), of which the one by J. B. J. Millié,
a very popular prose version of 1825,[17] was reissued at least seven
times.[18] The greatest number, however, came in the forties: Ortaire-
Fournier-Descoules's collective translation of 1841;[19] François Ragon's
verse translation, of 1842;[20] Charles Aubert's verse rendering of 1844.[21]
Meanwhile, some of the later Millié editions were also being issued
(1841, 1844).[22] There were still more in the fifties (Émile Albert's version, 1859)[23] and the sixties (Escondeca de Boisse, 1865; episodes
only),[24] and a new vigorous wave in the seventies and the eighties: Fer-
nand d'Azevedo (1870)[25] and the same with a prologue by Pinheiro
Chagas (1878–80),[26] both editions containing original *and* translation,
then the commemorative issue of Henri de Courtois (1887),[27] and
Hyacinthe Garin's translation (1889),[28] both issued in Lisbon. On the
whole, then (and I did not intend to provide a complete list), it may be
said that the nineteenth-century French interest in the *Lusíadas* was
uniformly strong throughout the entire century, reaching its peak in
the early forties.

The situation in Italy differed from the one in France in one important respect: the larger number of probable early translations—
probable, because we know of some of them by reference only. There
were two sixteenth-century versions, both anonymous, and two seventeenth-century ones, the first of these also anonymous.[29] The second
seventeenth-century translation, from 1658, was by Carlo Antonio
Paggi,[30] the proconsul of his native Genoa in Lisbon. His translation,
in *ottava rima*, considerably faithful to the original though without
being very poetic, is quite meritorious. Subsequently, we register three
eighteenth-century translations (two of them anonymous, and one a
partial version)[31] before we arrive at the great nineteenth-century
renderings.

The intensity of such early Italian interest in Camões's *Lusíadas*
must be accounted for in terms of the particular relationship between
the two momentous Renaissance poems, the *Lusíadas* and the *Gerusa-
lemme Liberata* of Tasso,[32] that appeared within three years of each
other, the Italian following the Portuguese poem. Tasso's personal
contribution to the consolidation of the Portuguese poet's fame should
not be minimized. The Italian poet, in two famous sonnets, one
glorifying Vasco da Gama and the other exalting Camões himself,
constituted the earliest witness for a major international, and hence

European, recognition of Camões. Both sonnets were published in the 1597 edition of Camões's *Rimas*.

In Italy, nineteenth-century interest in Camões began with an anonymous translation that appeared in Rome in 1804–5;[33] it was followed by Antonio Nervi's 1814 version,[34] "good poetry and poor translation," as Richard Burton put it, which attained no fewer than eleven more editions, the last in the year 1891.[35] The century saw at least three more complete versions of the Portuguese poem (Bricolani, 1826; Bellotti, 1862; Bonaretti, 1880)[36] and possibly a fourth one, which we know of by reference only (Bertolotti, in the 1860s),[37] as well as two partial versions (Carrer, 1850; Ravara, 1853).[38]

In Germany, interest in Camões soared; within less than fifty years, his works rose from little more than total obscurity to a position of the greatest eminence. Schörer spoke of Camões, presumably the first to do so, in 1710, in his *Atlas Novus seu Geographia Universalis*, as "insignis poetis" and further as "the Vergil of Portugal."[39] Johann Burkhard Mencken's *Compendiöses Gelehrtenlexicon* (1715) gives a summary biography of the poet. The year 1762 saw the first attempt at a German translation in prose, by J. N. Meinhardt. The episodes selected were, as expected, those of Inês and Adamastor. German awareness of Camões continued to evolve slowly. Junk's *Portugiesische Grammatik* was published in 1778 and the first verse translation (of Canto I only) by the Baron von Seckendorff in 1780–82. Another baron, von Soden, wrote a tragedy in five acts: *Inês de Castro* (1784). *Die Aufklärung*, the German version of the Enlightenment, soon produced its fruits. The count of Hoffmansegg and the scientist Link undertook a scientific journey to Portugal (*Bemerkungen auf einer Reise durch Frankreich, Spanien u. vorzüglich Portugal*, 1801–4).[40] Suddenly Portugal lost its status of *terra incognita*. Herder set Camões next to Dante and Tasso, but he was still almost alone in doing so. The *Literärgeschichte* of Eichhorn took two steps backwards. The *Handbuch* of Buchholz placed Camões, curiously, in Spanish literature.

It is with the Schlegel brothers that, as in so many other respects, the definite turn took place. Friedrich Schlegel discovered the poet in Paris, a discovery full of insight and enthusiasm crystallizing in the *Beiträge zur Kenntniss der romantischen Dichtkunst . . . nebst einer Charakteristik des Camoens u. der portugiesischen Dichtkunst* (1803).[41] Schlegel went beyond Herder in both scope and evaluation: the epic of the *Lusíadas* was the only one that may stand next to the Homeric poems, he declared. Even more interesting for us is what he said in the fatal Napoleonic year 1812, in the frame of his famous literature confer-

ences in Vienna (*Geschichte der alten und neuen Litteratur*):[42] Camões's
poem became here a sublime expression of patriotism and national-
ism. "No poet since Homer became [as Camões] the idol of his nation.
Portuguese patriotism is crystallized around the poet." In a *Kunst-
sonnet,* dedicated to the poet, Friedrich Schlegel wrote: "Be, then,
Camões, my model. Tell me to dare lift from the currents the relics of
German glory, trusting in salvation."[43] Wilhelm Schlegel continued in
the wake of his brother. In the *Vorlesungen* of Jena, he called the
Lusíadas a supra-terrestrial poem. In the *Berliner Vorlesungen über
schöne Litteratur und Kunst* (1801–4),[44] Wilhelm Schlegel spoke of the
"heroic spirit" of the *Lusíadas*[45] and characterized Camões and Shakespeare as the best "national historians."[46]

It is this cultural-critical vein that produced the most mature and
beautiful fruits. Tieck wrote in his notes, published posthumously:
"In no epic poem of modern times does one find united naïve poetry
and history with so much art."[47] More significantly, Tieck made
Camões the hero of one of his *Novelle: Der Tod des Dichters.*[48]

We cannot follow here the details of the cultural evolution of such
veritable critical *ideas* concerning Camões. Some of the literary consequences would only be those expected. Heise translated the *Lusíadas*
in *ottava rima* in the year 1806.[49] A new translation, by Kuhn and
Winkler, appeared in 1807.[50] In 1808 an anonymous version appeared in Hamburg.[51] Fichte himself translated a section of the poem
in iambic verse. Subsequent versions abound: in 1833, the *meisterhafte
Übersetzung* of a Tübingen professor, C. Donner;[52] in 1852, the sonnets
of Camões, by Arentschildt; in 1854, again the sonnets, by W. Storck;
and at least three more versions of various works of the poet before
the end of the century.[53]

In England a similar evolution occurred. Richard Fanshawe's classic translation of 1655[54] was followed in the next century by that of
William J. Mickle (1776),[55] which had over a dozen editions in the ensuing two centuries.[56] The nineteenth century's own versions of the
Lusíadas begin with Thomas Moore Musgrave's version (1826),[57] followed by Thomas L. Mitchell's (1854),[58] John J. Aubertin's (1878),[59] and
that of Robert Ffrench Duff into Spenserian verse (1880).[60] That same
year saw a further English translation of significance, that of Richard
Francis Burton, mentioned earlier.[61] There were some six more translators in the century associated with this British effort to make
Camões known in the islands and overseas.[62]

In Spain, there were four sixteenth-century versions (some known
by reference only),[63] one seventeenth-century,[64] and four complete
nineteenth-century translations.[65] The rest of Europe followed in the

wake of the significant Western European models: there is a Greek version (known by reference);[66] two Dutch ones (Pietersyoon, 1777,[67] and Bilderdyk, 1808);[68] one Polish translation of 1790[69] and two more of the nineteenth century;[70] one Czech (Bog-Peckla, 1836);[71] one Hungarian (Greguss Gyula, 1865);[72] two Danish (Lundbye, 1828;[73] and Guldberg, somewhat later);[74] two Swedish (Lanstrom, 1838,[75] and Lovén, the following year);[76] and two Russian versions, one by Dmitrief and one by Merzliakoff, the latter in 1833.[77] Most of these translations of the *Lusíadas* appeared in the 1830s and the 1860s.

This account of the literary fortunes of the *Lusíadas* in Europe, particularly in the nineteenth century, has been long, all of it a tribute to Camões's popularity. The conclusion may now be brief.

The German contribution to the European discovery, reception, and interpretation of Camões must be appreciated in its proper magnitude and importance. After the very early Italian and the eighteenth-century French interpreters of the great Portuguese poet, the German cultural intelligentsia was the first to fully recognize Camões as a national *and* nationalistic poet, actually a *Kulturträger* of a very particular moment of Portuguese, and hence of European, historic evolution: the moment of consolidation and of national expansion. And it was this concept of national consolidation and expansion that must have fired the imagination and conditioned the intellectual attitude of the European minds that discovered, read, studied, and translated the *Lusíadas*.

It seems not unduly hazardous to try to find the historical motivations for such an overwhelmingly widespread and deeply felt attitude. Between the First Empire (1804–14) and the Third Republic (1870–1914), the larger European realm had known many upheavals. Napoleon's Janus-faced shadow—the liberator of the oppressed and, at the same time, the embodiment of French continental dominance—had for long been cast on Europe. Once this hope or nightmare, depending on the point of view, was set to rest at Waterloo, Europe prepared herself, not without considerable inner strife, for a long winter of reaction and repression. Barricades went up from time to time: in 1830 in Paris; in 1848 in Pest, Milan, Lyon, Berlin—all over Europe. But the Hapsburg, czarist, and French monarchic establishments tenaciously held their grip of power. After Metternich, each revolution had its ensuing restoration. It was only slowly, and not before the Second Empire (Napoleon III) and the euphemistically called Liberal Empire (1860–70), that liberalization, and with it national self-affirmation, reached some measure of progress in Europe. The Italian and German national unifications were achieved only in the seventies.

Hungary was evolving toward national independence through a continuous string of advances and retreats. The Hapsburgs and the czarist empires, resilient as old bears at bay, did not disintegrate before World War I.

Within such bleak and unpromising historical parameters, Camões helped to uphold the torch of national consolidation and national independence. The countless intellectuals—whether translators, scholars, or readers—who came in contact with the sobering fresh wind swelling the sails of Vasco da Gama's ships found in the great Portuguese epic both a paradigm and a spark of hope. It is not by chance that the period between 1840 and 1848, which saw the emergence in France of the utopian movements, was also the period of so many new translations of the *Lusíadas*. For similar reasons, it is equally not by chance that so many of the translations appeared in the decade immediately subsequent to the revolutions of 1830 and 1848. Who knows, in the last analysis, what the great European national revolutions of the 1830s, 1840s, and 1870s owe to the spirit, and the letter, of Camões's epic?

Hence—and this, if any, is the *Hic Rhodus, hic salta* of the present contribution to Camonian studies—it is true but insufficient to say that nineteenth-century Europe, romantic Europe, rediscovered Camões. Certainly, it happened as many others were rediscovered. But, in the case of Camões, it is the nature of the rediscovery that is unique, a rediscovery rooted in the national emancipation and independence of the European political conscience of the nineteenth century.

Notes

1. The present text is a slightly modified version of the paper delivered at the 30th Annual Conference of the Center for Latin American Studies of the University of Florida, Gainesville, Florida, in September 1980. The notes were added subsequently.

2. 2 vols.. edited by Isabel Burton. London: B. Quaritch, 1880–81.

3. Pp. 246–63.

4. *Camoens em Allemanha* (Oporto, 1880); and *Bibliographia Camoniana* (Oporto, 1880).

5. *Camoens in Deutschland,* Klausenburg, 1880; also, in the appendix to his version of the lyrical poems (Paderborn, 1881).

6. Lisbon, 1973, pp. 317 ff.

7. P. 246.

8. Ibid.

9. Both around 1612 (?).

10. In Amsterdam, by Honoré, and the same year in Paris, by Huart.

11. Amsterdam: J.-F. Bernard, 1736; Paris: Babuty, 1768; Paris: Briasson, 1768; Paris: Nion, 1768.

12. London (no printer given).

13. Paris: Laurent-Beaupré, 1813; in *Oeuvres*, vol. 8, Paris: 1820; Paris: Verdière, 1820.

14. Paris: Nyon aîné.

15. Fragments published in Amsterdam; after Burton, *Camoens* (hereafter cited as Burton), p. 692 (see note 2).

16. 1813; no place given.

17. Paris: F. Didot père.

18. Paris: Charpentier, 1841, 1844, 1862; Paris: Bureaux de la publication, 1867, 1869.

19. Paris: Librairie de Charles Gosselin.

20. Paris: Gosselin & Hachette. There was a second edition from Hachette in 1850.

21. Paris: G.-A. Dentu.

22. See note 18.

23. Paris: Cosse et Marchal.

24. After Burton, p. 693. I could not find a further reference to this work.

25. Paris: Librairie Ve. J.-P. Aillaud, Guillard.

26. Lisbon: Imprensa Nacional.

27. Lisbon: Imprensa Nacional.

28. Lisbon: Typ. da Companhia Nacional Editora.

29. The appropriate references are in Burton, p. 693. The sixteenth-century editions are quoted in the epitaph of Martin Gonçalves de Câmara by the editor of the *Lusiads* in 1609 and by Frei Bernardo de Brito before 1617, respectively. The seventeenth-century edition is quoted by M. de F. y Sousa. The probable publishing year given is 1632, when the Commendator was in Rome, but the grounds for the dating are not specified.

30. Lisbon: H. Valente de Oliveira; second edition in the same place and by the same printer in 1659.

31. All these are, curiously, from the year 1772. The first is "tradotta in italiano da N. N. piemontese . . . ," Turin: Fratelli Reycends librai. The second is not really an anonymous translation: erroneously attributed to Count Lauriani, the translator seems to have been M. A. Gazzano. The third, the partial version (only Canto I), is by the Count B. Robbio di S. Rafaelle.

32. 1575.

33. V. Poggiolo.

34. Genoa: Stamperia della marina e della gazzetta.

35. Milan: Società tipog. dei classici italiani, 1821; a second edition in the same year and the same place; Milan: N. Bettoni, 1828; Naples: Stamperia Francese, 1828; a second edition in the same year and the same place; Naples: "A spese dell'editore del piccolo Parnaso italiano," 1829; Genoa: A. Pendola,

1830; Turin: Fontana, 1847; Milan: Società tipog. dei classici italiani, 1871; Milan: E. Sonzogno, 1882, 1891.

36. Paris: F. Didot; Milan: C. Branca; and Leghorn: P. Vannini e F. Editori [*sic*], respectively,

37. Mentioned by Cristoforo Negri; following Burton, p. 694.

38. Quoted in Burton, p. 694.

39. For the German contributions, I am following the already quoted "Camoens en Allemagne" by J.-J.-A. Bertrand, hereafter cited as Bertrand.

40. Kiel: Helmstädt, Braunschweig.

41. In *Werke*, 8: 38 ff.

42. Only subsequently gathered and published.

43. *Werke* (Vienna, 1846), p. 33, under the general title of *Kunstgedichte*.

44. Published in 1884.

45. 2: 203.

46. 3: 242.

47. Kopke, *L. Tieck, Erinnerungen* (Leipzig: 1855), 2: 214.

48. Appeared in the *Novellenkranz* of 1834.

49. Hamburg and Altona: G. Vollmer, 1806–7

50. Leipzig: Weidmann. Subsequently reissued: Vienna: A. Pichler, 1816; Vienna, C. F. Schade, 1828; Stuttgart: J. G. Cotta, 1886.

51. Cf. Burton, p. 695. I could not find any further reference to this work.

52. Stuttgart: C. S. Löflund. Later editions: Stuttgart and Sigmaringen: H. W. Beck, 1854; Leipzig: Fues's [*sic*] Verlag, 1869; Stuttgart: W. Spemann, 1883.

53. Of these, the *Lusíadas* translated by F. Booch-Árkossy (Leipzig: Arnold, 1854; 2d ed., 1857); by Karl Eitner (Hildburghausen: Verlag des Bibliographischen Institute, 1869, 1879, 1886); and by A. E. Wollheim da Fonseca (Leipzig: P. Reclam jun., 1879).

54. London: "Printed for Humphrey Moseley, at the Prince's Arms in St. Pauls church-yard, M.DC.LV."

55. Oxford: Jackson and Lister.

56. Oxford: Jackson and Lister, 1777, 1778; Dublin: J. Archer, 1791; London: 1793; London: T. Cadell jun. and W. Davies, 1798; London: J. Harding, 1807; London: Lackington, Allen, and Co., 1809; London, W. Suttaby, 1809. There are more editions. The American (Philadelphia) editions do not figure here.

57. London: J. Murray.

58. London: T. & W. Boone.

59. London: C. K. Paul & Co. A second edition: London: K. Paul, Trench & Co., 1884.

60. Lisbon: M. Lewtas; Philadelphia: J. B. Lippincott & Co.

61. *Os Lusiadas (The Lusiads)*, 2 vols., edited by Isabel Burton (London: B. Quaritch, 1880). [Editor's note: Regarding Burton's and other English translations, see Alfred Hower, "Camões's Proudest Lines Translated and Mistrans-

lated," paper delivered at the University of Toronto's conference on Camões in April 1980, to be published in a forthcoming volume of proceedings of that conference.]

62. Strangford, Hemans, Cockle, Hayley, Quillinan, and Harris.

63. By Benito Caldera (in *ottava rima*), Alcalá de Henares, Iuã Gracián, 1580; by Luys Gomez de Tapia, Salamanca: I. Perier, 1580; and by Henrique Garces, Madrid: Guillermo Drouy, 1591. A translation by Francisco de Aguilar, quoted by Manoel de Faria y Sousa, is known by reference only.

64. By M. C. Montenegro, known by reference only (M. de Faria y Sousa). Cf. Burton, p. 690.

65. By Lamberto Gil, Madrid: Impr. de M. de Burgos, 1818; by the Count of Cheste, Madrid: Impr. de A. Perez Dubrull, 1872; by Don Carlos Soler y Arques, Badajoz: José Santamaria, 1873; and by Manuel Aranda y Sanjuan, Barcelona: La Ilustración, 1874.

66. By Timotheo L. Verdier, executed sometime in the nineteenth century. Cf. Burton, p. 690.

67. The full name of the translator is Lambartus Stoppendaal Pieters zoon [*sic*], Middelburg: W. Abrahams.

68. Of the year 1808. Episodes only. Cf. Burton, p. 696.

69. By Jacka Przybylskiego (Cracow: A. Grebla).

70. By Dyonizego Piotzowskiego, Boulogne s/mer: H. Delahodde, 1876(?); another translation was issued in Warsaw: S. Lewental, 1890.

71. In the Casopio Coskcho Museum of Bohemia, Prague, Jur. vi. 475 (after Burton, p. 696).

72. Pest: Emich [*sic*] Gusztáv. A second edition: Budapest: Athenaeum, 1874.

73. Copenhagen: N. G. F. Christensens Enke, 1828–30.

74. Cf. Burton, p. 696.

75. A partial translation. See Burton, p. 696.

76. Stockholm: L. J. Hjerta, 1839; and again, Lund: C. W. K. Gleerup, 1852.

77. See Burton, p. 696. The information provided by Burton, as he himself acknowledges (p. 697, note 3), is often unreliable.

Camões and Some of His Readers in American Imprints of Lord Strangford's Translation in the Nineteenth Century

Norwood Andrews, Jr.

A NOTION held with some frequency by Lusophiles in the United States and abroad is that we Americans of descent other than Portuguese have customarily ignored Luís Vaz de Camões from lack of interest on those rare occasions when we have not disregarded him out of ignorance. The modest handful of exceptions traditionally accorded us is either defined, a priori, as too small to merit serious consideration, or its constituents are labeled in one of two ways: "specialists," a term which includes professional writers and critics, on the one hand, members of an elite even more minuscule than selective, on the other. Whichever the case, the continued definition of the general reading public as uninterested or ignorant—if not, by unveiled extension, both—is conveniently undisturbed.[1] With the help of some of the Lord Viscount Strangford's American readers, all of them drawn from the general reading public, I shall here advance arguments in support of the view that, as far as most of the nineteenth century is concerned, this notion is false.

I shall not address myself to Camões in twentieth-century America, to *The Lusiads* at all, or to any translations from the lyrics other than Lord Strangford's in book form.[2] In dealing with these, I shall limit myself to the three American imprints, one of which, as I shall point out, has a variant title page but is not a fourth imprint. I shall underline the fact that there were nevertheless three. Despite the influx of British imprints, there was obviously a healthy market for domestic publishers.[3] Who constituted that market?

It seemed—and seems—logical to me to assume that Americans

bought American imprints of Lord Strangford's *Poems from the Portuguese of Luis de Camoens* and that they did so with enthusiasm, for, while it might otherwise be possible to explain the existence of the first imprint, it would be difficult to account for that of the second and the third. It seemed—and seems—equally logical to assume that, if a reasonable group of American buyers could be identified, there would emerge a partial picture of Camões's readership in this country, beginning in 1805 with the Philadelphia imprint, the first in book form.[4]

I have found twenty-four libraries and two private collections known in fact to hold forty-four copies of the three American imprints: twelve by H. Maxwell (Philadelphia, 1805), seventeen by Kid & Thomas, with that title page (Baltimore, 1808), three by Coale & Thomas (also Baltimore, 1808, only the title page changed after Coale bought out Kid in the year indicated), and twelve by West and Greenleaf (Boston, 1809).[5] Using these forty-four copies, I have established a "nineteenth-century control group" of adequately identified owners. I here thank the many people who helped me.

Single copies often, and interestingly, reveal two or more owners. Twenty-two owners fall into the fully identified category. Others, about whom somewhat less is known, are on their way toward possible or probable full identification. Others still, who would remain unidentified by their signatures alone, kindly added a date, a place, or both to those signatures. There is also one convenient if still slightly mysterious toponym which, although it has no person attached, is dated.

It did not take long to discover that there are bibliophiles among the owners, but I detected no one of that breed of collector who bought books by the yard. I shall by no means exclude bibliophiles as a class, but I shall exclude those who, although they were old enough in the nineteenth century to have done so then, may have bought their imprints in the twentieth. I shall also exclude American writers— poets, novelists, essayists, others—for two reasons: they may legitimately be termed specialists, and they are the subjects of other studies.

Employing, then, appropriate members of my control group, I shall present a geographical, chronological, and societal spread of readers of Lord Strangford's Camões that will come as something of a shock to those who cherish the notion specified above. Most of the names I cite will be prominent, at least within their own bailiwicks, but not all of them began that way. I shall proceed geographically, adding chronological and social data, for I believe it important to establish the boundaries of that part of our country where we can know that Camões was read. As a point of departure, I have chosen, at random, a city that will not have been universally anticipated, Cleveland.

Daniel Wilbert Manchester was born in 1839, in the township of

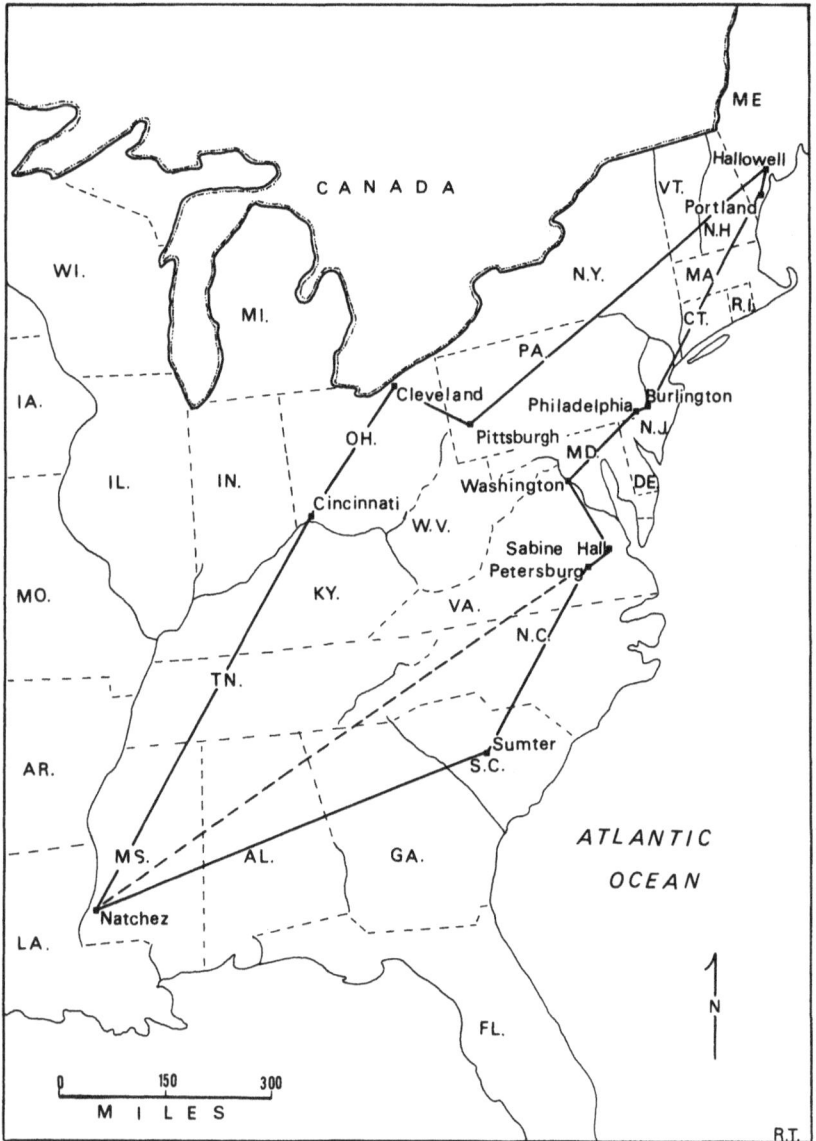

Colebrook, Litchfield County, in northwestern Connecticut, near the Massachusetts border.[6] While the first twenty-nine years of his life are still a mystery to me, he surfaced as an "insurance solicitor" in Cleveland, Ohio, in 1868.[7] He made his mark as a businessman, becoming, by the time of his death in 1905, treasurer of the important American Trust Company.[8] Manchester signed his name and his city, "Cleveland, O," on the title page of his H. Maxwell.[9] His characteristic signature there, "D. W. Manchester," is that of a younger man than is the variant on his application for membership in the Society of the Sons of the American Revolution, dated August 1, 1892. Manchester was an incorporator and an officer of the Western Reserve Historical Society (Rose, pp. 534, 343), whose *Historical Sketch* he authored.[10] Whatever his beginnings, he was a literate and cultured man who probably acquired his Camões in the 1870s and certainly did so in Cleveland.

Susan Gibson Lea Jaudon, an aunt and, though she never lived to know it, mother-in-law of Henry Charles Lea, the important Philadelphia publisher and medieval scholar, was born in 1799 in Wilmington, Delaware.[11] Between 1810 and 1822, she was living with her family in Pittsburgh (*Ancestry and Posterity*, loc. cit.), where a "sincere friend," in a bold, masculine hand, inscribed to her a Kid & Thomas on February 14, 1820. He signed himself with three initials, the first of which is uncertain, but the last of which is an "M," not a "J." In 1822, Susan Gibson Lea, not yet Mrs. Jaudon, moved with her family to Cincinnati (ibid.), leaving a male admirer behind but taking her Camões with her, down the Ohio. "Sôbolos rios. . . ."

Louisiana State University's Department of Manuscripts and Archives holds the papers of Henry David Mandeville (1787–1878).[12] The university's Rare Book Room holds his signed Kid & Thomas.[13] Mandeville's early years, like Daniel Manchester's, are still unclear to me, but by 1815 he was established in Philadelphia.[14] There, he both profited as a supercargo in the China trade and married into an important banking family.[15] There, too, he probably acquired Strangford's *Poems*. In 1835, thanks to his family connections, he assumed the position of cashier of the Planters' Bank in Natchez, Mississippi, a city one of whose "nabobs" he rapidly became (James, p. 139). When he moved, he did so lock, stock, expensive Philadelphia furniture, barrel, and Camões.[16]

H. Maxwell is in the Rare Book Room of the University of South Carolina in Columbia. This copy has the conveniently dated toponym—"Sumter/1882." S-U-M-T-E-R, Sumter, South Carolina, is only forty-some miles east of Columbia. Given the fact that the University of Virginia has four copies of Strangford's *Poems*, all of which belonged to Virginians and one of which was acquired as recently as 1980, and given the lack of evidence to the contrary, it seems reasonable for the nonce to apply the "doctrine of relative propinquity" and assume that the "Sumter copy" was acquired in Sumter, South Carolina, in 1882. There are several—though not many—other Sumters in nineteenth-century atlases, but the one in South Carolina appears a more realistic choice than, for example, the one in Nebraska.

The University of Virginia's four copies are of Kid & Thomas. Three have fully identified owners. The fourth has an unidentified signature—James T. Rahily—but a specific place, Petersburg. There is not time to discuss all the other owners, even though, collectively, they leave no doubt that Camões was read, for generations, in "the stately homes of Virginia." One of those stately homes, still standing and overlooking the Rappahannock River, is Sabine Hall, built by Robert "King" Carter, reputed to be the richest man in the colonies, for his son, Colonel Landon Carter, in 1730.[17] I learned on 2 June 1980 that Sabine Hall's library had recently been bequeathed to the University of Virginia.[18] It contains what is now the university's fourth Kid & Thomas. The Virginian who owned it was Beverly R. Wellford, M.D.

Dr. Wellford was a direct descendant of Landon Carter's granddaughter and therefore of "King" Carter himself (Farrar and Hines, loc. cit.). Born in Fredericksburg in 1797, he died in Richmond in 1870. "He was Professor of Materia Medica in Medical College of Virginia [i.e., part of William and Mary] . . . [and] president of the . . . [American] Medical Association in 1852."[19]

"James Cox died in Philadelphia in March, 1834, at the advanced age of eighty-three. His great passion was book collecting. . . . He was long the fashionable drawing-master of our wealthiest citizens. . . . Robert Morris and George Washington were his patrons."[20] Mr. Cox of course collected a copy of H. Maxwell, one which had previously belonged to James S. Smith, in all probability another Philadelphian, who acquired it in 1806. The copy is now held by the Library Company of Philadelphia.

Yet another collector in the same city who owned a Kid & Thomas, was General Augustus James Pleasonton (1808–94), a Baltimore-born graduate of the U.S. Military Academy who took up residence in Philadelphia.[21] The volume is held by the Free Library of Philadelphia, which bought it at the sale of Pleasonton's library in 1895.[22] Pleasonton was admitted to the Pennsylvania Bar and began the practice of law in 1832. He was a president of a railroad for a year (1839–40), the "brigadier general in charge of organizing the defense of Philadelphia, 1861–65," and the originator, in 1876, of the "'Blue-glass' theory of [the] beneficial effects of [the] sun's rays" (*Who Was Who,* loc. cit.). A man of parts, this reader of Camões, I dare say.

Those very traditional, very American-upper-class surnames, typified in Virginia by Beverly Wellford's, also appear in Philadelphia among Camões's readers. One of them is Biddle. William Shepard Biddle (1781–1835), a lawyer, owned a West & Greenleaf now held by the Library Company. William was the oldest and least known—but by no means the least learned—of several brothers, the best known of whom was Nicholas Biddle (1786–1844), president of the Second Bank of the United States (1823–1836).[23]

After William's death, his widow, Elizabeth B. Biddle, kept his West & Greenleaf, affixing to it, probably in 1860, her bookplate indicating her address at 1500 Locust Street. She was forty-one.[24] Did her brother-in-law, Nicholas himself, also know Strangford's Camões? There is no doubt. The proof, unfortunately, does not lie within my control group, and I cannot present it now.[25]

Not far from Philadelphia, but on the New Jersey side of the Delaware River, is Burlington. Nearby is Princeton, where in 1809, a Burlingtonian named Elias E. Boudinot took his baccalaureate. He took his master's degree there in 1812.[26]. His characteristic signature, "E. E. Boudinot," is in his West & Greenleaf. In 1783, his uncle, Elias Boudinot, had become president of the United States in Congress Assembled.[27] The Boudinot family, of French Huguenot stock, had enjoyed periods of prosperity. However, although Elias *E.*'s uncle, the famous Elias, unquestionably rose to lofty station, to wealth as well, he began life as the son of a relatively obscure American silversmith also named Elias (Boyd, passim).

A Maine "Downeaster," one who graduated from Dartmouth the year the next reader of the *Poems* was born and whose signature is in his Kid & Thomas, is Albion Keith Parris (1788–1857), a cousin of Alexander Parris, the architect. Parris enjoyed a long and personally successful although otherwise undistinguished career in politics. He was a congressman (1815–19), a probate judge (1820–21), five times governor of Maine (1821–26), a U.S. senator (1826–27), again a member of the Maine judiciary (1828–36), and comptroller of the U.S. Treasury, appointed initially by Andrew Jackson (1836–49). Parris's signature is unaccompanied by either date or place, and one can only speculate as to when and where he acquired his copy of the *Poems,* although the geographical limitations, at least, are reasonably well specified. Perhaps he learned of Camões at Dartmouth—where, coincidentally, he was only a year ahead of George Ticknor—and bought the best-selling translations after graduation, while he was still in Maine reading for the bar. On the other hand, once he had established himself in politics, his career centered on Portland, the state capital until 1830, and Washington. He had ample opportunity to buy a Baltimore imprint in the latter city. Whatever the case, Camões may fairly be associated with both cities through his readership.[28]

Far north from Philadelphia and Burlington on the Delaware, farther still from Sabine Hall on the Rappahannock, even farther north than Portland on Casco Bay, and a long way indeed from Natchez on the Mississippi, is the hamlet of Hallowell, Maine, on the Kennebec. There, in 1828, at age twenty-two, a printer's devil with no formal schooling to speak of and the son of sharecroppers bought his West & Greenleaf. His name was Henry Knox Baker (1806–1902). By dint of native intelligence, hard work, and Yankee ingenuity, he became a prosperous and important jurist in his state.[29] Poor as a child and a youth, Baker nevertheless read omnivorously, acquiring a habit he never lost (ibid.). In 1896, he and his family presented a gift of books to the Hubbard Free Library in Hallowell. The books were housed in an expensive case, with Knox's marble bust on top (*My Story—Part II*, p. 1). Camões was not in that case. Either the printer's devil, who became, as Parris did for a time, a probate judge, saw fit to keep him for himself, or a member of his family did. Ultimately, his great-granddaughter gave the volume to Bowdoin College.[30]

It becomes useful now to consult the map and to follow the solid lines from Hallowell southwest to Pittsburgh, northwest to Cleveland, southwest again to Cincinnati, far south to Natchez, northeast to Sumter, through Petersburg to Sabine Hall, northwest to Washington, then, in a northerly and easterly direction, to Philadelphia and Burlington, and finally, continuing through Portland, back to Hallowell. Those to whom my "Sumter theory" is unacceptable should feel free to follow the dotted line from Natchez straight to Petersburg. In either case, the border garrisons in which Lord Strangford's Camões is now on record as having been stationed are widespread, and the vast territory they guard extends far beyond what was, in the nineteenth century, the nation's heartland.

At this juncture, of course, it will have been noted that absent from the map are Boston and Baltimore, both of which cities, as will be remembered, produced imprints. I could include Boston easily, if I had not excluded writers from consideration, by citing Henry Wadsworth Longfellow's H. Maxwell.[31] I could also make as strong a case for another whole group of well-known Bostonians—John Quincy Adams and his family—as I can for Nicholas Biddle in Philadelphia, but I would again have to depart from my control group.[32] As it concerns Baltimore, or at least Maryland, I do not know that the Mary E. Hicks who dated her signature in her West & Greenleaf "June 8th [?]/48" was the daughter of Governor Thomas Holliday Hicks (1798–1865), but neither do I know that she was not.[33] The governor had a daughter named Mary Elizabeth Porter Hicks, born in 1831.[34] She would have been seventeen in 1848 (ibid.), a good age at which to read the High Romantic into which Strangford converted Camões, man and poet.[35] Whoever she turns out to be, Ms. Hicks is already important because of the date she inscribed in her copy.

Let me now turn specifically to a summary of dates. James S. Smith acquired his H. Maxwell in 1806. So did John Cliffton [sic], Jnr., unidentified, on the sixth of June.[36] Elias E. Boudinot *could* have acquired his West & Greenleaf in 1809, perhaps as a graduation present.[37] Myra Montgomery, unidentified, owned hers about 1811.[38] James Cox, who acquired James S. Smith's H. Maxwell, did so sometime between 1806 and 1834, possibly as late as the twenties or thirties, more probably in the teens, or before them, unless Smith kept the book longer.[39] Susan Gibson Lea received her Kid & Thomas in 1820. A. Cutter, also unidentified, dated his *Coale* & Thomas either 1821 or 1831.[40] Henry Knox Baker wrote "1828" in his West & Greenleaf, Mary E. Hicks "1848" in hers; Elizabeth B. Biddle's bookplate points toward 1860 in hers. I have suggested that Daniel W. Manchester probably acquired his H. Maxwell in the 1870s. In 1871, Myra Montgomery's unidentified niece, Isabella Gaines, did make a gift of her aunt's West & Greenleaf to Mrs. Myra Greely, likewise unidentified. *Someone* boldly inscribed the Sumter H. Maxwell "1882." There are other mid- and late-nineteenth-century owners who can be adduced.[41]

In virtually every, if not in every, decade of the nineteenth century, Americans made their ownership of Lord Strangford's Camões—in American imprints—known, or it was made known for them. This I have demonstrated from a grand total of forty-four books, not all of which I have used, to be sure, but not all of which have I needed to use. It is, furthermore, an almost iron-clad rule that nineteenth-century Americans who owned volumes of poetry read the poetry in those volumes. I take the rule as axiom in the case of the owners I have cited, not one of whom was a professional writer or, for that matter, a "specialist" of any other kind.[42] The professions I have brought forth among members of my control group include printer's devil, politician, drawing master, military officer, businessman, banker, lawyer, physician, and housewife. There is at times as great a distance in terms of social class as there is in terms of profession and geography. The middle and upper classes, the elite, predominate, of course. It would be hard to argue, however, that their doing so in the nineteenth century was limited to the reading of poetry, or, indeed, that any other classes read poetry as thoroughly as they did. It would be even harder to argue that a highly literate, poetry-reading elite was peculiar to America, or that, in fact, it was not proportionately larger and less exclusive here in the 1800s than it was, for example, in Camões's native land. A better name for the notion I set out to render suspect at the beginning of this study is myth.

Notes

1. Herman Melville, for example, so obviously knew Camões that he cannot be overlooked. See George Monteiro, "Poetry and Madness: Melville's Rediscovery of Camões in 1867," *New England Quarterly* 51 (December 1978): 561n.1, for a very good partial bibliography of the relationship between Camões and Melville. Monteiro's bibliography is improved by the addition of his own article. Melville, however, was a professional writer, those who have published about him are critics, and all, therefore, are "specialists." So, too, of course, were Charles Brockden Brown, Joseph Dennie, Henry Wadsworth Longfellow, and George Ticknor, whom I have discussed elsewhere. See my article, "Toward an Understanding of Camões's Presence as a Lyric Poet in the Nineteenth Century American Press," *Luso-Brazilian Review* 17 (Winter 1980):171–85.

A very real danger inheres in the relegation of knowledge of Camões even to literary specialists, because not all of them specialize in the same thing. George Ticknor, for example, saw in Camões, when the latter chose to write in Spanish, one of the great poets of that language (*History of Spanish Literature*, 1849), and good American histories of Spanish literature have repeated the message to students of that literature ever since. Newton Arvin (Monteiro, "Poetry and Madness") was a professor of English and his message was intended primarily for students of American literature. And so it goes. When all the separate fields of literarily related specialization are viewed as a whole, the collective membership is impressively large.

2. That Lord Strangford "rewrote" Camões to suit his own purposes is duly recognized; see Monica Letzring, "Strangford's *Poems from the Portuguese of Luis de Camoens*," *Comparative Literature* 23 (Fall 1971). There were, particularly in Joseph Dennie's *Port Folio*, numerous reprints of the *Poems*, beginning in 1803, before the first American-bound volume appeared ("Strangford's *Poems*"). The first edition, *Poems from the Portuguese of Luis de Camoens, with Remarks on His Life and Writings, Notes, &c. &c. by Lord Viscount Strangford*, was published by J. Carpenter, London, 1803.

3. As Letzring has pointed out, "Strangford's *Poems from the Portuguese*

was on the whole very successful. In the seven years after its publication in 1803, it was reprinted six times in England, three in America, with a new [British] edition in 1824 and a French translation in 1828" (Letzring, "Strang-ford's *Poems,*" p. 302). The work's popularity in Britain assured it a substan-tially equal popularity in the United States, where, beginning in 1803, two years before the first American imprint, it was also welcomed effusively by the periodical press (Andrews, "Toward an Understanding," pp. 171–73). Ameri-can publishers, beginning in 1805, were obviously riding the coattails of an already established market. Copies of the various British imprints are readily available in university libraries in this country today, and a study of their American owners in the nineteenth century is under way.

    4. The title of all of the American imprints is identical with that of the first British edition (note 2 above). The publishers are given in my text and in n. 5 below.

    5. I have called attention elsewhere to the theory, advanced by Hester Rich, librarian of the Maryland Historical Society, that once Coale had bought out Kid, the new firm kept on using the former's stock, changing to the new title page only when the supply of the old one ran out (Andrews, "Toward an Understanding," p. 176). My initial sources for this study were, of course, the *National Union Catalog of Pre-1956 Imprints* 91(1960):697 (hereafter *NUCP-561*), and Shaw and Shoemaker, *American Bibliography,* 1805 (1958), 1808 (1961), and 1809 (1961) (New York: Scarecrow Press, Inc.). Neither source is entirely accurate and both are outdated. However, through correspondence with the libraries listed, I have been able to eliminate some errors and to update some holdings as follows: (HMx—Philadelphia: H. Maxwell, 1805; K&T—Bal-timore: Kid & Thomas, 1808; C&T—Baltimore: Coale & Thomas, 1808; W&G—Boston: West & Greenleaf, 1809; libraries listed after *NUCP-561*):

Library	Editions	Library	Editions
1. *CSt*	HMx		K&T
2. *CUSf*	W&G		W&G
3. *CtY*	HMx	10. *MStow*	W&G
	K&T	11. *MWA*	C&T
	W&G		HMx
4. *DGU*	K&T		W&G
	K&T	12. *MdBE*	K&T
5. *DLC*	HMx	13. *MdBJ*	C&T
	K&T		K&T
	W&G	14. *MdHi*	K&T
6. *InU*	HMx	15. *MeB*	W&G
7. *LU*	K&T	16. *NN*	W&G
8. *MB*	K&T	17. *NcD*	**C&T**
	W&G	18. *OClW*	HMx
9. *MH*	HMx	19. *PP*	K&T
	K&T	20. *PPL*	HMx

Library	Editions	Library	Editions
	W&G	24. ViU	K&T
21. PU	HMx		K&T
	K&T		K&T
22. RPB	HMx		**K&T**
	W&G	Private	**HMx**
23. ScU	HMx	Private	**W&G**

6. I am indebted to Col. R. H. Goodell, Jr., executive secretary, National Society of the Sons of the American Revolution, for the photocopy of Manchester's application for membership in the SSAR, dated 1 August 1892, which reveals this information.

7. *Cleveland Leader City Directory, 1868–1869*, p. 224. I am indebted to James B. Casey, head reference librarian, Western Reserve Historical Society, for providing me with this and much other valuable information, including part of that in note 8.

8. *A Cleveland City Directory for 1905* (n.p., n.p.), p. 893. See also William Ganson Rose, *Cleveland, The Making of a City* (Cleveland: The World Publishing Co., 1950), p. 439; the American Trust Company was merged into the Citizens Savings & Trust Company in 1902. Manchester's last business address, as it appears in the *City Directory* here cited, is "treas 708 Amer Trust bldg."

9. This volume is housed at the Freiberger Library, Case–Western Reserve University.

10. Daniel Wilbert Manchester, *Historical Sketch of the Western Reserve Historical Society, Cleveland, O., by D. W. Manchester. Secretary, May, 1888* (Cleveland: The Williams Publishing Co., 1888); later published by the society in its series of *Tracts:* 3(74), 1892. See *NUCP-561*, 358, 279.

11. Susan Gibson Lea Jaudon, later Lamb (after William Latta Jaudon's death in 1832), died in Cincinnati in 1834 (James Henry Lea and George Henry Lea, *The Ancestry and Posterity of John Lea* [Philadelphia: Lea Brothers & Co., 1906], p. 97). See also Edward Sculley Bradley, *Henry Charles Lea, A Biography* (Philadelphia: University of Pennsylvania Press, 1931), p. 79: Henry Charles Lea married his first cousin, Anna Caroline Jaudon (i.e., Susan Gibson Lea Jaudon's older daughter) on 27 May 1850 in Cincinnati. I am indebted to Lyman W. Riley, assistant director for Special Collections, the Charles W. Van Pelt Library, University of Pennsylvania, for initially suggesting to me that "Susan Lea may have been an aunt or a great-aunt [of Henry Charles]" (letter to author, 28 March 1980). Ms. Lea's Kid & Thomas is at the Van Pelt Library.

12. For Mandeville's dates, see Inventory of the Henry David Mandeville Papers (Baton Rouge: Department of Manuscripts and Archives, Louisiana State University Library), [p. 1]. These papers are cited in D. Clayton James, *Antebellum Natchez* (Baton Rouge: Louisiana State University Press, 1968), p. 139. I am grateful to Michelle Hudson, historian, Archives and Library Division, State of Mississippi Department of Archives and History, for calling this

useful volume to my attention, and for much other indispensable information about Mandeville.

13. I am grateful to Michelle L. Fagan, register of manuscripts, Department of Archives and Manuscripts, Louisiana State University Library, for forwarding to me a copy of the Inventory of the Mandeville Papers, for comparing several variants of Henry D. Mandeville's signature on manuscript letters with the signature in his Kid and Thomas, and for sending me copies of the former so that I might make my own comparison. His signature on a letter dated 25 January 1833, while that of a more mature man, patently matches that in his copy of Strangford's *Poems*.

14. See Inventory of Mandeville Papers: "Cashier of the Planters' Bank, Natchez, Mississippi; formerly resident of Philadelphia, Pennsylvania. Family letters and other papers, 1815–1925. . . . The earliest letters deal primarily with Mandeville's early career as a supercargo in the China trade; the education of his son, Henry D. Mandeville, Jr., at Princeton University, and the family's move to Natchez in 1835" ([p. 1]).

15. Mrs. Richard W. Graham, Gladwyne, Pa., telephone conversation with author, 21 August 1980. Mrs. Graham is engaged in preparing a formal study of Mandeville's now rare and valuable Philadelphia-made furniture, which, via a bequest, found its way in the twentieth century back to its native city and is housed in the Philadelphia Art Museum. She has located documentation of the fact that Mandeville's brother-in-law, J. Schott, was an important officer in Stephen Girard's bank.

16. Ibid. Mrs. Graham holds that Mandeville moved not only his family but also his household.

17. E. F. Farrar and E. Hines, *Old Virginia Houses: The Northern Peninsula* (New York: Hastings House, 1972), pp. 49–50. I am indebted for this information, and for much other concerning Virginia owners, to my friend and colleague David Haberly of the Department of Spanish, Italian, and Portuguese, and to Mildred K. Abraham, general services librarian, Rare Book Department, Alderman Library, both of the University of Virginia.

18. David Haberly, letter to author, 2 June 1980.

19. R. A. Brock, *Virginia and Virginians*, 2 vols. (Richmond: H. H. Hardesty, 1888), 2:808. Brock states that Dr. Wellford was president of the "National [sic] Medical Association," but, writing in 1888, he means the American Medical Association, founded in 1847. The *National* Medical Association was founded for black physicians, chiefly in the South, in 1895. See *National Cyclopaedia of American Biography*, 12:201.

20. Henry Simpson, *The Lives of Eminent Philadelphians* (Philadelphia: William Brotherhead, 1859), p. 257. I am indebted to Anne P. Hennessey of the Library Company of Philadelphia for a great deal of assistance in the case of Cox and other Philadelphia owners. My thanks also to Marie Korey, curator of printed books.

21. *Who Was Who in America. Historical Volume*, p. 415.

22. J. Randall Rosensteel, administrative assistant to the director, The

Free Library of Philadelphia, letter to the author, 24 March 1980. I am indebted to him for this and much other valuable information.

23. *Autobiography of Charles Biddle, Vice-President of the Supreme Executive Council of Pennsylvania. 1745–1821,* privately printed (Philadelphia: E. Claxton and Co., 1833), p. 370.

24. See *McElroy's Philadelphia City Directory for 1860,* 23d ed. (Philadelphia: E. C. and J. Biddle & Co., 1860), p. 64. Elizabeth B. Biddle does not appear in the 1859 edition but is listed at various other addresses in previous ones. For her age see Report of the United States Census Office, 8th Census, 1860, Philadelphia, Ward 8, p. 139. I wish to thank my graduate research assistant at the University of Pennsylvania, Maryjane Dunn-Wood, for her help in this and other instances.

25. Part of another study, this case is based on Biddle's known passion for literature and his association with Joseph Dennie and the latter's Tuesday Club (Thomas Payne Govan, *Nicholas Biddle, Nationalist and Public Banker, 1786–1844* [Chicago: University of Chicago Press, 1959], pp. 9–10). William introduced Nicholas to Dennie.

26. Jean F. Preston, curator of manuscripts, Princeton University Library, letter to the author, 24 June 1980. I am indebted to her and to Clark L. Beck, Jr., assistant curator, Special Collections Department, Archibald Stevens Alexander Library, Rutgers University, for furnishing me with photocopies of Elias E. Boudinot's manuscript signature. This volume is held by the Sterling Library, Yale University.

27. See George Adams Boyd, *Elias Boudinot, Patriot and Statesman, 1740–1821* (Princeton: Princeton University Press, 1952), p. 3.

28. This volume held by the Maryland Historical Society Library; I am indebted to J. W. Athey, library assistant, for having furnished a photocopy of the title page bearing Parris's signature, which plainly matches the reproduction thereof in *The National Cyclopaedia of American Biography (NCAB),* 6: 306. For Parris's biography, see *NCAB; Dictionary of American Biography,* 14: 254; and Ronald F. Banks, *Maine Becomes a State, The Movement to Separate Maine from Massachusetts, 1785–1820* (Middletown, Conn.: Wesleyan University Press, 1970), pp. 69–70, 383n.12. Banks gives the date of Parris's graduation from Dartmouth as 1807, which would have made him Ticknor's classmate.

29. Henry Knox Baker, *Old Times—How We Lived* (Hallowell [?]: n.p., n.d.), and H[enry]. K[nox]. Baker, *My Story—Part II* (Hallowell [?], n.p., n.d.). It is the opinion of Katherine H. Snell, librarian of the Hubbard Free Library, that the printed sheets of which she kindly furnished me photocopies are galley proofs of articles that did appear in a local newspaper (unidentified), but never in a volume (letter to the author, 18 May 1980). Judge Baker himself states that "These reminiscences have been prepared for my family and not for the public" (*My Story—Part II,* [p. 1]). My thanks to Mrs. Snell for furnishing me with a great deal of valuable information about Baker.

30. Mrs. William D. Rounds, letter to the author, Falmouth, Maine, 25 April 1980. I am grateful to Diane M. Gutscher, Special Collections, Bowdoin

College Library, for contacting Mrs. Rounds for me, and to Mrs. Rounds and her sister-in-law, Mrs. Sydney P. Snow, initially for identifying Judge Baker for me and, subsequently, for providing me with the means to learn more about him.

31. This volume held by the Houghton Library, Harvard University. I am grateful to Francis M. Rogers, Nancy Clark Smith Professor (emeritus) of the Language and Literature of Portugal, and to Jaime H. da Silva for their information about the Houghton's imprints.

32. See Linda K. Kerber and Walter John Morris, "Politics and Literature: The Adams Family and the *Port Folio*," *William and Mary Quarterly*, 3d ser. 23 (July 1966).

33. This volume is held by the Library of Congress. Slash before abbreviated date appears in original. I thank Leonard N. Beck, subject collections specialist at the Library of Congress, for his generous help.

34. Donna Burns, manuscripts librarian, Maryland Historical Society, letter to the author, 20 June 1980. I greatly appreciate Ms. Burns's efforts to find a signature for comparison, as well as her identification of Mary E. Porter Hicks as a possible owner.

35. *Re* Lord Strangford's "Romantic" Camões, see Letzring, "Strangford's *Poems*," p. 331 and passim.

36. This volume is held by the Beinecke Rare Book and Manuscript Library, Yale University. I am grateful to Patricia M. Howell, library services supervisor at the Beinecke, and to Patricia Bodak Stark, reference archivist, and Mary Ellen Bass, reference librarian, both of the Sterling Library, for their help.

37. *The Monthly Anthology and Boston Review* 6 (April 1809): 287, reviewed this imprint. Clearly, it was published in the year of E. E. Boudinot's graduation, and well in advance thereof: not until 1844 did Princetonians graduate in June. Prior to that year, they did so in September, *after* the harvests in the Garden State.

38. This volume is held by the Library Company of Philadelphia. A front endpaper bears the inscription "This little book which/belonged to my Aunt Myra/Montgomery sixty years ago/is presented to her namesake/Mrs. Myra Greely/by/Isabella Gaines/Cambridge, May 22, *1871*" [emphasis mine].

39. The Library Company of Philadelphia acquired Cox's collection in 1834.

40. This volume is held by the American Antiquarian Society. Either date is possible, but 182*1* seems the more likely. A. Cutter *may* prove to be the very literate grandfather of Charles Ammi Cutter, the librarian and founder of "The Cutter system" of cataloguing. I thank Francis Miksa, Graduate School of Library Science, Louisiana State University, and the Hon. R. Ammi Cutter, the librarian's grandson, for their help.

41. E.g., Col. Mercer Slaughter, C.S.A., who owned one of the University of Virginia's copies of Kid & Thomas. He was born in Orange County, Virginia, in 1844, and died in Richmond in 1897. His signature and "Orange

C[ourt] H[ouse], Virginia" are legible on an endpaper. His stepmother, Julia Bradford, also owned it, and affixed her bookplate to it. Julia was the second wife of the colonel's father, Dr. Thomas Towles Slaughter, by whom she had a daughter, Jane Chapman Slaughter (1860–1950). (See Louise Pecquet du Bellet, *Some Prominent Virginia Families* [Baltimore: Genealogical Publishing Co., 1976], 4 vols. in 2, 2 [old vol. 4]: 406–7. [Work first published in Lynchburg, 1907].) In the "front pages" appears the following inscription: "Janie C. Slaughter / (From Mommie)" (David T. Haberly, letter to author, Charlottesville, 25 May 1980).

42. Of the twenty-two owners I have cited by name, only Augustus James Pleasonton appears in W. Stewart Wallace's very useful *Dictionary of North American Authors Deceased Before 1950* (Toronto: The Ryerson Press, 1951), and that would seem to be by accident: General Pleasonton's publications all result directly from his military, business, and scientific activities (*NUCP-561*, 461, 494). Seven other members of my control group will be found to have— or to seem to have—publications to their names, but careful investigation reveals that they are either professionally related, like Pleasonton's, or altogether inconsequential, when they can be verified. Several members of the group do stand out as legitimate specialists in their own fields, e.g., Beverly R. Wellford as a physician and Albion K. Parrish as a politician. Such specializations, patently, have no relationship either with each other or with literary endeavor.

Os Lusíadas e Os Maias: um Binómio Português?

Alberto de Lacerda

A Maria da Graça Amado da Cunha

PERCORRE o poema épico de Camões uma curva muito larga e muito complexa desde a primeira estância do primeiro canto em que se propõe celebrar os "assinalados" lusíadas até chegar às palavras terríveis e amargas daquela estância do canto final em que se confessa com a lira destemperada e a voz enrouquecida por ter estado a cantar uma gente surda, rude, metida numa tristeza vil.

A curva percorrida por *Os Maias* de Eça de Queiroz é menos larga mas não menos complexa. Reportando-nos aos dados imediatos do livro, diríamos que vai dos fins do sec. XVII aos fins do sec. XIX. Mas a *durée* do livro vai beber as suas origens a um tempo histórico muito mais recuado aonde encontra a outra face: o tempo mítico. Atentai nesta descrição de Afonso da Maia, ao começo da obra:

> Afonso era um pouco baixo, maciço, de ombros quadrados e fortes : e com a sua face larga de nariz aquilino, a pele corada, quase vermelha, o cabelo branco todo cortado à escovinha, e a barba de neve aguda e longa—lembrava, como dizia Carlos, um varão esforçado das idades heróicas, um D. Duarte de Meneses ou um Afonso de Albuquerque. E isto fazia sorrir o velho, recordar ao neto, gracejando, quanto as aparências iludem![1]

Estamos perante uma daquelas figuras poderosas, fulminantes, sereníssimas, históricas e intemporais, retratadas por Nuno Gonçalves nos painéis de S. Vicente.

No parágrafo seguinte, e algures nesse mesmo primeiro capítulo do romance, Eça, sem qualquer ironia—pelo contrário, com ternura

219

inusitada—refere-se a Afonso da Maia como "o antepassado", naturalmente, como quem diz "o avô" ou "o tio".

É bem estranho o termo antepassado quando nos lembramos que
Afonso vive e se mantém elemento crucial até quase ao fim do volumoso romance. Eu diria que há uma figura crucial n*Os Maias:* e essa
figura são duas—Afonso da Maia e Carlos da Maia. A personagem
heróica—o avô, e a sua sombra irónica, degradada, decadente—o
neto. E contudo, a certos relances, e a determinadas perspectivas,
Carlos poderia vir a ser, na arquitectura temporal do romance, a
crítica do que Afonso, na sua juventude, prometeu—e não cumpriu.
Menos heróico do que o próprio Eça nos leva a crer. Repito a citação:
"lembrava, como dizia Carlos, um varão esforçado das idades heróicas, um Dom Duarte de Meneses ou um Afonso de Albuquerque. E
isto fazia sorrir o velho, recordar ao neto, gracejando, quanto as aparências iludem!" O pai de Afonso tinha-o expulso de casa devido à sua
simpatia pelos ideais da Revolução Francesa. E Eça elucida com uma
frieza sarcástica que nos deixa gelados:

> E todavia, o furor revolucionário do pobre moço consistia
> em ler Rousseau, Volney, Helvécio e a "Enciclopédia"; em
> atirar foguetes de lágrimas à Constituição; e ir, de chapéu à
> liberal e alta gravata azul, recitando pelas lojas maçónicas
> odes abomináveis ao Supremo Arquitecto do Universo.[2]

Eu disse que esta frieza sarcástica nos deixa gelados, mas só a uma
segunda ou terceira leitura: julgávamos Afonso—é essa a opinião predominante—uma ramalhal figura quase perfeita. E descobrimos que
a sua juventude prefigura o fracasso do neto: o mesmo diletantismo e
ineficácia.

Alexander Coleman no seu notável *Eça de Queiroz and European
Realism* chama também a atenção para o aspecto negativo de Afonso
de Maia:

> Afonso is a paradigm because he *seems* to be a patriarch, he
> *seems* to be the genealogical apex from which all succeeding
> generations decline. But this is not true, and Eça takes pains
> to point out how hollow a figure Afonso really is. He is more
> echo than substance, more a reflection of the past than the
> incarnation of lost or displaced values.[3]

Não creio que Eça se "empenha fortemente" ("takes great pains") em
frizar o que há de "oco" em Afonso. Nem o patriarca nos surge como

oco, nem é esse, jamais, o enfoque do autor. As contradições do personagem são-nos apresentadas, mas cedo o leitor as esquece, e Eça *pretende* esse esquecimento quase total dado o desvelo singular, o nimbo de ternura quase mística com que a figura é tratada. Em mais de um lanço do livro, o *ponto de vista* de Afonso é o *ponto de vista* do autor (exemplo: a superioridade da educação inglesa). Toda a leitura do romance é palimpsesto mental. Eça revela e quer esconder ao mesmo tempo. Poeticamente ele joga com os resíduos que a leitura deixa na memória e com a obliteração, pelo menos momentânea, desses resíduos. Por algum motivo a crítica nunca atentou devidamente nos aspectos menos admiráveis de Afonso. Mas não nos iludamos: Eça quere-o, e quere-lhe, como figura *exemplar,* com um cheiro de bondade não muito longe de um personagem de um Julio Diniz mais complexo e sofisticado.

Desde o início do livro, mesmo na criação de uma das figuras mais positivas e exaltantes, Eça de Queiroz chama a atenção, com dedos de veludo, para o que nesse personagem há de fundamentalmente negativo. Afonso e Carlos—avô e neto—são duas imagens do mesmo rosto, até certo ponto reversíveis. O que dá a Afonso da Maia uma dimensão mais profunda, mais nobre, é a unidade de personalidade, a inteireza de carácter, o ter-se encontrado ainda novo. Afonso da Maia sabe quem é; o mesmo não é verdade de Carlos da Maia.

Passado o fogacho revolucionário da primeira juventude, Afonso, *sem remorso,* volta a ser o que foram os Maias desde muitas gerações: fidalgos ricos para quem ser um *gentleman* é uma *realização* cabal. Não há remorso, porque não houve traição, aos seus olhos dele, pois nem sequer passa pela cabeça de tal gente considerar um crime não contribuir para a transformação de uma sociedade injusta. Afonso é, aliás, um anacronismo: pertence inteiramente ao *ancien régime;* nada tem a ver com as várias fases do sec. XIX. Isso permite ao autor dar uma luz muito mais contrastada, muito mais pungente, e até uma ironia misteriosa, às relações entre o avô e o neto. Permite ao autor manipular a arma que está na base do seu impulso criador: a crítica. Digo aqui crítica não confinada ao que a geração de Eça de Queiroz entendia pela palavra, mas crítica no sentido valéryano de outro lado do espelho, de análise implacável contígua à criação, crítica no sentido em que Baudelaire dizia que todo o grande poeta continha em si um crítico. E Eça de Queiroz, um pouco *malgré lui,* é um poeta. *Os Maias* é um grande romance sobretudo pela carga de poesia secreta que dele se solta como um perfume.

Carlos não se conhece, não sabe exactamente quem é; desorientação é a palavra que melhor lhe cabe. Há ansiedade nessa desorientação. Filho de uma idade que desde o Romantismo, e sobretudo desde Baudelaire vive obcecada com a introspecção, Carlos mira-se, e, tanto quanto pode ver nele próprio, vislumbra um vazio fundamental a que o livro chama por vezes, e pela boca de vários personagens, diletantismo.

Não é bem diletantismo—é um vazio, é uma ausência. Essa ausência, essa morte em vida, é pessoal e colectiva. É a ausência sonambúlica de um país decadente obcecado com as glórias do sec. XVI. Se a ausencia fosse absoluta—isto é, sem o orgulho impertinente do passado—talvez possibilitasse reconstruir a partir de zero. Mas não, o fantasma que é Carlos—sem vontade, sem vocação, inteligente mas destituído de profundeza e gravidade—é um fantasma opulento: árbitro de elegâncias, rico, viajado, belo, sedutor. Impossível partir de zero quando, o que noutro país seria um ornamento banal dos círculos mundanos, em Lisboa toma foros de um semi-deus.

A irradiação de Carlos na alta roda de Lisboa é a irradiação de um fenómeno, de um génio que se manifestará de um momento para o outro. Esse momento nunca chega a surgir. Não deixa de haver em Carlos alguma coisa do Conselheiro Acácio e do Pacheco das Cartas de Fradique. Dirão: mas por que não haveria de ser o jovem um ente feliz, satifeito com o que tem? Não, nunca, por pertencer à época que aspira a uma transformação profunda da sociedade, porque ele próprio, porta-voz que é até certo ponto do autor, aspira, com mais ou menos sinceridade, a essa transformação. Tem-se criticado a falta de incisão romanesca, de vida própria, na criação de Carlos da Maia. Em tempos também assim pensei. Mas inclino-me a crer que dentro da estrutura complexa e rigorosa da vasta máquina dos *Maias*—máquina foi termo utilizado pelo próprio Eça a propósito do livro—o elemento de vazio, de ausência no herói do romance é um elemento profundamente perturbador que só o enriquece. É um vazio baço, incómodo. É o vazio de um país esgotado, inerte, narcisista; é o vazio terrível de quem tem consciência que está vazio. É um vazio que obriga o leitor português a interrogar-se gravemente.

Carlos é infeliz—a infelicidade do Tédio, do vazio do Tédio, personagem gigante do livro—porque é um ser dividido, filho de uma época em que a análise ou conduz à lucidez e à acção, ou à desorientação estéril, à angústia ou, mais langorosamente, ao *spleen*. Carlos é um *blasé*, um exilado em relação à época, um príncipe mimado e ocioso que estaria perfeitamente à vontade—ausente qualquer farpa interna de sentimento de culpa—no sec. XVIII ou na Renascença. Vejo-o facilmente na pele de William Beckford, amoral, dissoluto e excêntrico, multi-milionário, que a Inglaterra expulsou e o sec. XVIII português recebeu de braços abertos com adolescentes acessíveis e uma cozinha incomparável e abundantíssima que nessa altura se praticava nos conventos. Típico de um personagem frívolo da alta sociedade do tempo, o grande desgosto do fim da vida de Beckford foi nunca ter conseguido ser apresentado na corte portuguesa: não estamos longe dos cómicos melindres e aspirações de ordem mundana, sofridos por vezes até à agonia, de alguns dos personagens d*Os Maias.*

Afonso da Maia não conhece o tédio, não é um ser dividido, não sofre de ansiedade. Porquê? É um homem que pertence inteiramente ao seu meio—o meio aristocrático—e à sua época, um sec. XVIII que ele arrasta, sem dar por isso, pelo sec. XIX. É tão naturalmente *grand-seigneur* de uma outra época, com uma tal simplicidade e ausência de snobismo, que essa nota, por assim dizer exótica, constitui um dos grandes factores da sua poderosa sedução. Inseguro, Carlos da Maia é desdenhoso e snob (o snobismo é sempre uma insegurança), e não resiste a uma certa ostentação. Não tem a bondade do avô, que apesar do seu sentido inato da hierarquia, o faz tratar da mesma maneira o marquês de Souselas, o Vilaça, e o gato Bonifácio.

Temos, pois, *Os Maias* como o tratado falhado da educação de um príncipe e da regeneração de um país. Um príncipe e um país sobre o qual pesa, esmagadoramente, o passado. A metáfora de velha casa como carga do tempo acumulado até limites imemoriais é um dos triunfos do livro. Sobre o tempo neste romance—tempo interior, tempo personagem, tempo proustiano—escreveu João Gaspar Simões passagens memoráveis no seu livro indispensável sobre Eça de Queiroz.[4] Aliás, devo possivelmente a Gaspar Simões a inspiração para este ensaio quando há anos li, sem concordar mas com uma espécie de sobressalto, esta frase acerca d*Os Maias:* "a mais perfeita obra de arte literária que ainda se escrevera em Portugal depois de *Os Lusíadas.*"[5]

O Ramalhete é uma das grandes criações poéticas da literatura portuguesa. O Ramalhete é Portugal—país muito antigo, oprimido por um pessimismo profundo, por um derrotismo doentio. Não foi sempre assim; essa apagada e vil tristeza, como lhe chamou Camões, data, se bem interpreto uma passagem de Gil Vicente no *Triunfo do Inverno,* sobretudo do reinado de D. João III. O nó da identidade portuguesa deslocou-se, depois da tão rica, mas não difusa, experiência medieval—para o prodígio esgotante das Descobertas. O cansaço e a decadência sobrevieram tão rapidamente que quase obscurecem o apogeu. Assentou arraiais o mito—que é a própria realidade brutal—de um país pequeno esmagado por uma empresa gigantesca (as descobertas e um vastíssimo império) superior às suas forças.

Os Lusíadas—tratado da educação de um príncipe? Porque não?

Numa tapeçaria dramática (ao mesmo tempo pictural e sonora) o cortesão-poeta desdobra perante o adolescente histérico que era D. Sebastião a história exemplar de Portugal, um modelo não muito diverso das vidas edificantes de Plutarco. O poema assumiria—e assume—proporções didáticas e moralistas. A ironia é que o virtual, virtualíssimo, pedagogo do príncipe—Camões, um dos maiores poetas do mundo—possivelmente nunca pôs os pés na corte nem enxergou as feições jesuíticas e fanáticas, com uma certa beleza perversa, do jovem rei demente. Embora não seja o herói, a sombra de D. Sebastião atravessa quase todo o poema. Paira por sobre a narrativa um pouco como Afonso da Maia no romance queirosiano, três séculos mais tarde.

A presença do jovem rei n*Os Lusíadas* é das mais complexas; ao nível imediato há o aspecto menos nobre da dedicatória do poeta à caça de umas coroas, aspecto aliás banalíssimo na época; mesmo assim consegue evitar a quase abjecção de Shakespeare nas dedicatórias ao Conde de Southampton. Há o aspecto mais importante de uma figura de carne e osso que é, em vida, o símbolo, a responsibilidade, embora não tenha provado ainda ser a garantia, do momento mais alto de um povo, momento que apesar de relativamente recente começa a ser engolido pela expressão fatídica "passado glorioso". Há o terceiro aspecto, miasmático e mais difícil de definir, que dá a D. Sebastião não sei que halo sinistro desde aquela estância sexta do primeiro canto:

E vós, ó bem nascida segurança
Da Lusitana antiga liberdade,
E não menos certíssima esperança
De aumento da pequena Cristandade;
Vós, ó novo temor da Maura lança,
Maravilha fatal da nossa idade,
Dada ao mundo por Deus, que todo o mande,
Para do mundo a Deus dar parte grande;[6]

"Lusitana antiga liberdade" rima estranhamente com "maravilha fatal da nossa idade". Eu sei que "fatal" tem conotações semânticas diferentes da carga maléfica que hoje em dia damos à palavra, mas já Faria e Sousa deu uma interpretação surpreendente ao verso, o que mostra a ambiguidade incómoda do seu sortilégio verbal. Lembra-me o "emblema fatal" de que fala Mallarmé no celebrado poema à memória de Théophile Gautier; "Ô de notre bonheur, toi, le fatal emblème!"

A maravilha fatal da nossa idade, o Adónis virgem da Companhia de Jesus que se irá sacrificar como num rito pagão, em Alcácer Quibir, é ele semi-deus, semi-Cristo na superstição popular—que nos vai fazer perder a "Lusitana antiga liberdade" em 1580, exactamente há quatrocentos anos. Este suicídio colectivo perpetrado obstinadamente pelo monarca tem uma origem: um homem que recusa enfrentar a realidade, que se recusa a ver "claramente visto", um homem que revolve "na mente pressurosa", como diria Camões, as figuras reais e imaginárias da Idade Média. Não é um imperador da Renascença, consolidando, fincando os novos horizontes territoriais e culturais que inauguraram realmente a Idade Moderna. Não: D. Sebastião é um demoníaco senhor feudal apostado numa cruzada totalmente egotista e anacrónica. Trata-se de um suicida que perpetra um crime colectivo. O país vai freudianamente expiar o seu fanatismo narcisista, a sua repressao sexual.

D. Sebastião representa o contrário trágico e grotesco da lição realista de Camões. Portugal do sec. XIX, sobretudo o destrambelho igualmente trágico e grotesco do último decénio, é o contrário do ideário realista de Eça de Queiroz. Expressões como ver "claramente visto" e "saber de experiências feito" poderiam ter sido escritas pelo Eça.

Parece-me, quanto mais releio o poema, que a figura de D. Sebastião lhe é muito mais central do que se imagina. Quando Camões termina a sua obra—três quartos de século volveram já sobre a descoberta da Índia. O jovem monarca constitui uma esperança e o poeta é porta-voz angustiado dessa esperança de que consiga manter em bases sólidas as descobertas e as conquistas dos seus antepassados imediatos. "Tomai as rédeas vós do Reino vosso": diz ele ao rei no primeiro canto num tom que não deixa de ser estranho. Mas o pessimismo entranhado do autor—que partilha com Eça de Queiroz—surge abruptamente no final do primeiro canto, como um dos motivos do poema:

Oh! Grandes e gravíssimos perigos,
Oh! Caminho da vida nunca certo,
Que, aonde a gente põe sua esperança,
Tenha a vida tão pouca segurança!

No mar, tanta tormenta e tanto dano,
Tantas vezes a morte apercebida;
Na terra, tanta guerra, tanto engano,
Tanta necessidade avorrecida!
Onde pode acolher-se um fraco humano,

Onde terá segura a curta vida,
Que não se arme e se indigne o Céu sereno
Contra um bicho da terra tão pequeno?[7]

Essa antinomia é quase chocante pois o leitor ainda guarda muito
vivas as cores do pórtico do poema, hipérbole patriótica levada às
fronteiras do paroxismo.

Os Lusíadas é uma celebração e ao mesmo tempo a crítica dessa
celebração. Nada de mais estranho num poema épico. Lado a lado
com a adulação ao monarca reinante, Camões, descaradamente, denuncia a *entourage* perniciosa e corrupta de que D. Sebastião se deixa
rodear:

Nem creiais, Ninfas, não, que fama desse
A quem ao bem comum e do seu Rei
Antepuser seu próprio interesse,
Imigo da divina e humana Lei.
Nenhum ambicioso, que quisesse
Subir a grandes cargos, cantarei,
Só por poder com torpes exercícios
Usar mais largamente de seus vícios;

Nenhum que use de seu poder bastante
Pera servir a seu desejo feio,
E que, por comprazer ao vulgo errante,
Se muda em mais figuras que Proteio.
Nem, Camenas, também cuideis que cante
Quem, com hábito honesto e grave, veio,
Por contentar o Rei, no ofício novo,
A despir e roubar o pobre povo!

Nem quem acha que é justo e que é direito
Guardar-se a lei do Rei severamente,
E não acha que é justo e bom respeito
Que se pague o suor da servil gente;
Nem quem sempre, com pouco experto peito,
Razões aprende, e cuida que é prudente,
Pera taxar, com mão rapace e escassa,
Os trabalhos alheios que não passa.[8]

E não critica apenas a *entourage* do Rei; critica o próprio rei, quase
directamente, na sua neurótica paixão pela caça, e o seu desinteresse

por mulheres, o que porá em mortal perigo o próprio país não lhe dando um legítimo sucessor lusitano:

Já sobre os Idálios montes pende,
Onde o filho frecheiro estava então,
Ajuntando outros muitos, que pretende
Fazer hũa famosa expedição
Contra o mundo revelde, por que emende
Erros grandes que há dias nele estão,
Amando cousas que nos foram dadas
Não pera ser amadas, mas usadas.

Via Actéon na caça tão austero,
De cego na alegria bruta, insana,
Que, por seguir um feio animal fero,
Foge da gente e bela forma humana;
E por castigo quer, doce e severo,
Mostrar-lhe a fermosura de Diana.
(E guarde-se não seja inda comido
Desses cães que agora ama, e consumido).

E vê do mundo todo os principais
Que nenhum no bem púbrico imagina;
Vê neles que não tem amor a mais
Que a si somente, e a quem Filáucia insina;
Vê que esses que frequentam os reais
Paços, por verdadeira e sã doctrina
Vendem adulação, que mal consente
Mondar-se o novo trigo florecente.

Vê que aqueles que devem à pobreza
Amor divino, e ao povo, caridade,
Amam somente mandos e riqueza,
Simulando justiça e integridade.
Da feia tirania e da aspereza
Fazem direito e vã severidade.
Leis em favor do Rei se estabelecem;
As em favor do povo só perecem.[9]

Poema épico: celebração de heróis, alçados a semi-deuses, e não meditação amarga sobre as fraquezas demasiado mortais de tais heróis ou semi-deuses. Tanto mais inusitada e eminentemente moderna a juxtaposição de endeusamento e de crítica quanto Camões nos quer convencer—na sua exaltação poética—que o desinteressante Vasco da Gama é parecidíssimo com os heróis de Virgílio e Homero e que não pode cantar Sebastião porque, sublime rei como o poeta lhe chama, não se atreve a tanto. Ouçamos parte da estrofe:

> E, enquanto eu estes canto, e a vós não posso,
> Sublime Rei, que não me atrevo a tanto,
> Tomai as rédeas vós do Reino vosso:
> Dareis matéria a nunca ouvido canto.[10]

O poema acaba com uma série de conselhos cheios de apreensão, conselhos dirigidos ao Rei, mas que mais parecem os conselhos de um pai lúcido, afectuoso, perfeitamente cônscio das fraquezas terríveis do filho. Permitam-me ouvir nestas últimas estâncias do poema como que a voz interior, torturada, de Afonso da Maia tentando dirigir-se ao irresponsável neto Carlos da Maia.

Os Lusíadas assentam sobre uma obsessiva mitificação da história e do povo português. Há no poema de Camões, alternadamente, e por vezes abruptamente, um êxtase, uma exaltação mítica, e logo a seguir uma queda, ou elegíaca, ou acusatória, ou simplesmente lamentosa, ou uma combinação das três, como na singularíssima fala do Velho do Restelo, um dos mais enigmáticos trechos da literatura portuguesa. É que tudo quanto o Velho diz é uma destruição sistemática e irrespondível da base heróica do poema. Camões, dialecticamente e baudelairianamente, é o crítico mais feroz do seu entusiasmo épico.

Os Maias—Os Lusíadas. Ouçamos o romancista falando do seu livro a Luís de Magalhães: "Eu continuo com *Os Maias*, essa vasta *machine*, com proporções enfadonhamente monumentais de pintura *a fresco*, toda trabalhada em tons pardos, pomposa e vã e que me há de talvez valer o nome de Miguel Ângelo da sensaboria."[11] Convenhamos que são termos um tanto ou quanto épicos com que Eça de Queiroz descreve *Os Maias*. Mas os dados da sua tapeçaria dramática são outros. Em vez da paixão patriótica de Camões—de proporções wagnerianas—há no Eça d*Os Maias* uma esperança renovadora bem vaga simbolizada pela geração de Carlos da Maia e João da Ega—transposição irónica da geração de 70—e não é preciso recordar como no romance acaba essa esperança. É uma curva em última análise elegíaca que ao fim de centenas de páginas termina com os dois amigos falhados—Carlos e João—interrompendo um diálogo de desalento extremo, a correrem, como se fosse uma resposta ao enigma da vida, para um transporte público.

Sim, duas obras profundamente pessimistas sobre essa coisa exquisita, essa sensação intransmissível e incómoda que é ser português. E no entanto—aparte os méritos literários diversos de uma e outra obra, *Os Lusíadas* e *Os Maias*—à medida que as tenho relido, uma outra dimensão se tem erguido: são dois livros obcecados com a identidade de Portugal e da criatura portuguesa. Duas obras pessimistas? Sim e não. A curva d*Os Maias* é menos dramática que a d*Os Lusíadas*— além da razão óbvia que Camões é um génio superior a Eça—porque parte de uma esperança e acaba numa desistência irónica e elegante, ao passo que *Os Lusíadas* vai de um triunfo majestoso a uma série de meditações amargas disseminadas pelo poema, a começar logo no primeiro canto. As duas obras têm eminentemente a ver com o passado, com a ambiguidade terrível do tempo revolvido, perdido ou não, dependendo dos temperamentos, dependendo dos países. Afonso da Maia *é* o passado, é aí que vive; o anacronismo é-lhe perdoado devido à sua bondade quase mítica. A bondade é tema tão raro na literatura universal, que a crítica, perante essa formidável, enternecedora criação romanesca, não deu por isto: Afonso é um anacronismo, um *gentleman* do sec. XVIII, dir-se-ia de antes da Revolução Americana e da Revolução Francesa—quase não faz sentido dizer que traiu os ideais libertários professados na juventude. Carlos da Maia—pseudomoderno, pseudo-revolucionário—acaba por cair nas ratoeiras todas de um nome e de uma fortuna passivamente herdados. D. Sebastião, Afonso e Carlos da Maia, se me é permitida a metáfora delirante, são um pouco como Orfeu; não resistem a olhar para trás, e com esse olhar retrógrado, passadista, cobarde, fatídico, fazem regressar Eurídice-Portugal à escuridade dos infernos, e são eles próprios esquartejados, ou em Alcácer Quibir, ou na ignomínia, na abjecção, ou na esterilidade.

Mas os mitos são cíclicos: é assim que sobrevivem. Portugal-Eurídice ainda há pouco ressurgiu mais uma vez à luz do sol não numa manhã de nevoeiro mas numa madrugada da Primavera de 1974.

Escrutando em *Os Lusíadas* e em *Os Maias* as duas constantes portuguesas do ímpeto fogoso e do pessimismo mórbido, desistente, será possível concluir que essas duas obras-primas se situam porventura além de uma visão pessimista ou optimista. O efeito último, a lição profunda que os dois livros nos deixam é que é, sim, imprescindível absorver o passado, não há crime nenhum em amá-lo, mas que essa absorpção e esse amor só se justificam como alicerces para o edifício que todos os homens e todas as mulheres têm a obrigação de construir: o presente.

Notas

1. Eça de Queiroz, *Os Maias*, 26a ed. (Lisboa: Livros do Brasil, s.d.), p. 12.

2. Ibid., p. 13.

3. Alexander Coleman, *Eça de Queiroz and European Realism* (New York: New York University Press, 1980), p. 202.

4. João Gaspar Simões, *Vida e Obra de Eça de Queirós* (Lisboa: Livraria Bertrand, 1973). Não menos notável é a versão resumida deste longo volume, intitulada *Eça de Queirós* (Lisboa: Editora Arcádia, 1961).

5. João Gaspar Simoes, *Vida e Obra de Eça de Queirós*, p. 574.

6. Luís de Camões, *Os Lusíadas*, ed. Emanuel Paulo Ramos (Porto: Porto Editora, s.d.), I,6.

7. Ibid., I, 105–6.

8. Ibid., VII, 84–86. Como todos nós, devo muito ao que nos abriu os olhos nesta matéria o precioso *Camões Panfletário* de António Sérgio inserto no IV vol. dos seus *Ensaios*.

9. Ibid., IX, 25–28.

10. Ibid., I, 15.

11. Citado por João Medina, *Eça de Queiroz e o seu Tempo* (Lisboa: Livros Horizonte, 1972), pp. 201–2.

Contributors

Norwood Andrews, Jr., is professor of Spanish and Portuguese at Texas Tech University and the author of several studies on Portuguese and Brazilian literature.

René Concepción is assistant professor of Spanish and Portuguese at Queens College, CUNY. His study of the hagiological elements in Eça de Queiroz is forthcoming.

Graça Silva Dias is a researcher at the Instituto Nacional de Investigação Científica in Lisbon. She is coauthor of *Os Primórdios da Maçonaria em Portugal* (4 vols.) and has also published *António Aleixo: Problemas de uma Cultura Popular* and *De Gil Vicente a Camões: Culturas e Mentalidades*.

José Sebastião da Silva Dias is professor of the history of ideas at the Universidade Nova de Lisboa. He has published *Correntes de Sentimento Religioso em Portugal* (2 vols.), *A Política Cultural da Época de D. João III* (2 vols.), *Portugal e a Cultura Europeia*, and *Os Descobrimentos e a Problemática Cultural do Século XVI*.

Peter Fothergill-Payne is associate professor of Romance studies at the University of Calgary. He has written a number of studies on the interplay of politics and literature in sixteenth- and seventeenth-century Portugal. The two most recent are to be found in the *Actas* of the IV Reunião Internacional de Camonistas (Ponta Delgada) and the Congresso Internacional sobre os Descobrimentos Portugueses e a Europa do Renascimento (Lisbon).

The late Frederick C. H. Garcia died in October 1984. He had been professor of Portuguese at the U.S. Military Academy at West Point since 1959. His last publications were *Aquilino Ribeiro: um Almocreve*

231

na Estrada de Santiago (Lisbon, 1981) and (with Edward F. Stanton) *The Uruguay: The Richard F. Burton Translation of Basílio de Gama's "O Uraguai."*

Alfred Hower is professor emeritus of Portuguese and Spanish at the University of Florida. He has published articles and reviews on Luso-Brazilian and Spanish subjects and co-translated (with John Saunders) António Olavo Pereira's novel, *Marcoré*. He has coedited (with Richard A. Preto-Rodas) *Crônicas Brasileiras: A Portuguese Reader* and *Quarenta Historinhas e Cinco Poemas* by Carlos Drummond de Andrade.

Alberto de Lacerda teaches comparative literature in the University Professors Program at Boston University. He has published five books of poetry in Portuguese, two of them translated into English, and essays on literary matters. The Imprensa Nacional in Lisbon is publishing his collected poems in several volumes under the title of *Oferenda*.

Harold V. Livermore is professor emeritus of Portuguese and Spanish and head of the Department of Hispanic Studies at the University of British Columbia. His *History of Portugal* was awarded the Camões Prize in 1947. His works also include *Portugal and Brazil: An Introduction* (1953), *History of Spain* (1958), and *Origins of Spain and Portugal* (1971), and he has just completed *Camões, from the Lyrics to the Lusiads*.

A. H. de Oliveira Marques is professor of history at the Universidade Nova de Lisboa. He is the author of *History of Portugal* (1976) and of numerous other books and articles on Portuguese history, especially on the medieval and twentieth-century periods. He has taught at several American universities, including the University of Florida (1966–69).

William Melczer is professor of comparative literature at Syracuse University. His scholarly work is divided between the history of ideas of the Renaissance and the history of art of the Middle Ages. His publications concern, among many others, Petrarch, Michelangelo, Leo Hebraeus, Vico, and Palladio. His book on the Bronze Door of Barisano of Trani in Ravello is in press.

Joseph C. Miller, professor of history at the University of Virginia, is engaged in studies of the history of Angola before 1800 and the comparative history of slavery and the slave trade. His publications include *Kings and Kinsmen: Early Mbundu States in Angola* (1976) and nearly forty other studies.

Gerald M. Moser is professor emeritus of Spanish and Portuguese at the Pennsylvania State University. He is on the advisory boards of the *Luso-Brazilian Review* and the executive council of the African Literature Association. He has published studies on Portuguese themes and was guest editor of the fall 1982 issue of *Research in African Literature*, a special issue on the Lusophone literatures.

Richard A. Preto-Rodas is professor of Spanish and Portuguese and director of the Division of Language at the University of South Florida. He is the author of *Rodrigues Lobo: Dialogue and Courtly Love in Renaissance Portugal* and *Negritude as a Theme in the Poetry of the Portuguese-Speaking World*. He has published several articles on Luso-Brazilian and Baroque Spanish themes and coedited (with Alfred Hower) *Crônicas Brasileiras: A Portuguese Reader* and *Quarenta Historinhas e Cinco Poemas* by Carlos Drummond de Andrade. He is also a contributing editor for the *Handbook of Latin American Studies*.

José Honório Rodrigues is a member of the Academia Brasileira de Letras, the Instituto Histórico Brasileiro, and other historical institutions. He is the author of over sixty books and pamphlets, including *Teoria da História do Brasil* (5th ed.); *A Pesquisa Histórica no Brasil* (4th ed.); *História da História do Brasil; Independência: Revolução e Contra-Revolução* (5 vols.); and the revisionist *Conciliaçaõ e Reforma no Brasil: um Desafio Histórico-Político* (2d ed.). His *Aspirações Nacionais: Interpretação Histórica* was translated by Ralph E. Dimmick as *The Brazilians: Their Character and Aspirations*.

Irwin Stern is lecturer in Portuguese and Brazilian literatures at Columbia University. He is the author of *Júlio Dinis e o Romance Português (1860–1870)* and many other studies of contemporary Portuguese fiction and coeditor of the forthcoming *Modern Iberian Literature: A Library of Literary Criticism*.

Fred Gillette Sturm is professor and chairman of philosophy at the University of New Mexico. He is past president of the Society for Iberian and Latin American Thought, on the board of directors of the Hispanic Enlightenment Society, and an honorary member of the Instituto Brasileiro de Filosofia. He has held Gulbenkian, Fulbright, and Social Science Research Council fellowships for research in Portugal, Brazil, and Mexico. His publications are concerned with Ibero-American philosophy and intellectual history.

Jack E. Tomlins is visiting professor of Portuguese at the University of Maryland, College Park. He has translated works by Mário de Andrade, Wilson Martins, and Jorge de Sena and has published articles on modern Brazilian poetry and continental Portuguese prose.

George D. Winius is professor of history at Leiden University, a board member of the International Seminar on Indo-Portuguese History, and co-editor of *Itinerario*. He is the author of *Fatal History of Portuguese Ceylon* and of *Diogo do Couto and the Portuguese Black Legend* and (with B. W. Diffie) coauthor of *Foundations of the Portuguese Empire, 1415–1580*.

www.ingramcontent.com/pod-product-compliance
Lightning Source LLC
Chambersburg PA
CBHW021356090426
42742CB00009B/881